LEGACY OF HOPE

Hidden Heroes from Generation to Generation

by Avi Mizrachi

with Kathi Macias

WESTBOW PRESS®
A DIVISION OF THOMAS NELSON & ZONDERVAN

WestBow Press books may be ordered through booksellers or by contacting:

WestBow Press
A Division of Thomas Nelson & Zondervan
1663 Liberty Drive
Bloomington, IN 47403
www.westbowpress.com
844-714-3454

Interior Graphics/Art Credit: Grayson Stallings

ISBN: 979-8-3850-0258-0 (sc)
ISBN: 979-8-3850-0264-1 (hc)
ISBN: 979-8-3850-0303-7 (e)

Library of Congress Control Number: 2023913817

Print information available on the last page.

WestBow Press rev. date: 12/05/2023

ADONAI foils the purpose of the nations.
He thwarts the plans of the peoples.
The plan of *ADONAI* stands forever,
the purposes of His heart from generation to generation.
Blessed is the nation whose God is *ADONAI*,
the people He chose for His own inheritance.
ADONAI looks down from heaven.
He observes all humanity.
From His dwelling place He gazes
on all the inhabitants of the earth—
He who fashions the hearts of all,
who discerns all their deeds.
No king is saved by his great army,
no warrior is delivered by great strength.
A horse is a false hope for victory,
nor can its great strength save.
Behold, the eyes of *ADONAI* are on those who fear Him,
  waiting for His love,
to deliver their souls from death,
  and to keep them alive in famine.
Our soul waits for *ADONAI*—
He is our help and our shield.
Our heart rejoices in Him,
because we trusted in His holy Name.
Let Your lovingkindness, *ADONAI*,
be upon us, as we have waited for You.

(Psalm 33:10-22, TLV)

ENDORSEMENTS

Oh that this book were in every library of the world! The book carefully and precisely adds otherwise unknown information about the horrors of the Holocaust years in Europe, but also honors the often hidden heroes of that era. Two of those heroes were the chief rabbi of Bulgaria and the Metropolitan bishop of Bulgaria. Together, the rabbi and the bishop successfully encouraged the King not to deliver their 48,000 Bulgarian Jews to the Nazis for extermination. The memory of the rabbi is indelibly etched in the hearts of those families who were later able to find safety in Israel.

Another less known part of the history that needs to be told is that this honored rabbi created quite a dilemma as he began to let people know that he had come to believe that Jesus is indeed the promised Messiah of Israel. Though the rabbi was deeply loved and honored, the rabbinic councils of Israel did not know what to do with him.

This amazing man of God looms large in Avi Mizrachi's own family, as well as others who came to faith in Jesus because of the rabbi's life and teaching. Even though the rabbi's life was not easy, made even more challenging because of his belief in Jesus, the Bulgarian Jewish population was adamant in seeing that at his death he was given a well-deserved state burial.

I strongly recommend this book. You will not be disappointed. You will be freshly encouraged in your own faith walk. Get this, read it, pass it to others, and buy a copy for your local library.

Don Finto,
Pastor Emeritus, Belmont Church, Nashville, TN
Founder, Caleb Global

* * *

Legacy of Hope by Avi Mizrachi is a milestone book. This story of Rabbi Daniel Zion is heartwarming and such a wonderful story to show the authenticity of Messianic Jewish faith through the life of this amazing man. His pastoral love and service was an exemplary model. I wholeheartedly urge you to read this book.

Dr. Daniel Juster
Author and Founding Director of the Tikkun International

* * *

Legacy of Hope is a moving story of God's faithfulness to the Jewish people. It highlights the amazing journey of Rabbi Daniel Zion, the Chief Rabbi of Bulgaria, who was instrumental in saving Bulgarian Jews from the Nazis in World War II. Rabbi Zion later immigrated to Israel and became a dedicated follower of Yeshua (Jesus) the Messiah. He paid a price for his faith, but his influence has had ripple effects from generation to generation, especially seen in the Mizrachi family and their special story of Yeshua's love and grace. This is not only an important historical account, but a moving testimony of God's goodness through obedient servants who simply said "yes" to Yeshua.

Wayne Wilks, PhD
Executive Pastor, Church and Jewish Relations
Gateway Church, Southlake, TX

* * *

Legacy of Hope is an important historical account that weaves together the unique history of the nation of Bulgaria in its relation to the Jewish Bulgarian population during the time of the Holocaust, as connected to the story of the chief rabbi of Sofia, Rabbi Daniel Zion. Rabbi Zion was the main hero who was instrumental in saving the Bulgarian Jewish population from destruction. *Legacy of Hope* connects this history to the Mizrachi family, both during the time of the Second World War when they lived in Bulgaria and afterwards, during the time they made their *aliyah* at the hour of the birth of the modern State of Israel. The book is not only an important document as concerns the most unique history of Bulgaria and of the rebirth of the nation of Israel in the Land of Israel, but it is a wonderful account of the intervention of God in the life of Rabbi Daniel and of the Mizrachi family. Rabbi Daniel is deeply motivated by his faith in the God of Israel and His Messiah, Yeshua, both as he risks his life to the utmost to save his people from the death camps of Eastern Europe and, when once in Israel, to testify boldly and courageously at all costs of the biblical legitimacy of his faith in the promised Messiah of Israel whom his people had rejected. Despite Rabbi Zion's own personal rejection by his religious contemporaries, he clings in love to God and to His Messiah, to Israel his beloved people, and to his own Jewishness, though he is defrocked by the Rabbinate. As the narrative of the rabbi's life develops, it becomes increasingly intertwined with the story of the Mizrachi family whose members will be counted among the early followers of the Messiah in the newly born State of Israel. The generational grace of salvation upon the Mizrachi family becomes a picture and a sign, not only of the rebirth of Israel as a nation but of the rebirth of the Messianic Community in Israel.

Reuvan Berger
Pastor, *Kehilat ha'Seh al Har Zion*
(The Congregation of the Lamb on Mt. Zion)

* * *

Legacy of Hope is a fascinating story of adventure and intrigue. The prophet Daniel declared that "the people that know their God shall be strong, and do exploits" (11:32). Another Daniel arose in the 20th century who did remarkable exploits—from rescuing fellow Jews from the ovens of the Holocaust to leading Israelis to their Redeemer. Rabbi Daniel Zion caused a ripple effect that is still being felt today. Read his story and be inspired.

Pastor Wayne Hilsden
President of FIRM: Fellowship of Israel Related Ministries
Co-founder & former lead pastor of King of Kings, Jerusalem

* * *

For years we have heard the name of Rabbi Daniel Zion and some of the stories about his faith and heroism. Avi Mizrachi, who knew Daniel, has done an invaluable service for the body of Messiah in Israel, as well as for Jews and Christians around the world. He has diligently documented the extraordinary events surrounding the man who was the chief rabbi of Bulgaria during WWII, and yet was a humble follower of Yeshua. It is an amazing story of faith in God and what He can do through courageous people. This book will be an encouragement for all believers, especially for those who find themselves in challenging times.

Carol and David Pileggi
Christ Church Jerusalem

* * *

Legacy of Hope is the inspiring story of the relationship between the chief rabbi of Bulgaria, Daniel Zion, and Metropolitan Stefan of Bulgaria. These two men worked together to prevent the deportment of Bulgarian Jews to the concentrations camps during World War II; this story highlights the eternal benefits of the collaboration of these two courageous men throughout history. The rescue of almost 50,000 Jewish souls from the ovens of Poland to the salvation, both physically and spiritually, of the Mizrachi family makes this story an exciting, inspirational one that brings hope to the heart during these darkening days in the world. Avi Mizrachi and his family have provided us a beneficial story of what G-d can do when people surrender to the love of G-d provided through Yeshua the Messiah.

Marty and Marleen Waldman
Toward Jerusalem Council II

ACKNOWLEDGEMENTS
... with Gratitude

Many people helped shape this book, and for that I am forever grateful. First, I want to thank my wife, Chaya, for inspiring me and encouraging me to write this story. I also thank our four daughters—Suzanne, D'vora, Sara, and OrEl—for their continued love and appreciation. I thank my sister, Simcha, and my brother, Immanuel, for their help and support for this project. I am grateful for all my cousins, especially Avraham Kedem, and other family members who have helped piece this story together.

And my thanks to those who assisted in various ways throughout the crafting of this project. Kathi Macias, thank you for your assistance in writing this book. We wouldn't be here without you. Thank you for your care and wisdom, as well as your creativity and experiences in writing. Terri Gillespie, thank you for all your encouragement, direction, and input into this project.

A special thank you to Lonnie Lane for all your help and input as well. Thank you to Nikolai Boyadjiev for your information and suggestions regarding Bulgaria and Rabbi Daniel Zion. My deep appreciation to Joseph Shulam and Dr. David and Martha Stern for your invaluable contributions and persevering help. Thank you to Boaz Michael and First Fruits of Zion for your input and support. Thank you to all who have read the manuscript and given suggestions throughout the writing of this book: Don Finto, Dr. Kerry Teplinsky, Wayne Hilsden, Dr. Dan Juster, David and Carol Pileggi, Reuven and Benjamin Berger, Dr. Wayne Wilks, Marty and Marleen Waldman, Jeff Henderson, Susan and Fred Rowe, Amanda Harris, Karen Gower, Adam Ben-Joseph, Dr. Golan Broshi, Sasha and Lilian Granovsky, Eitan Shishkoff, Danielah Castellini, Martin and Norma Sarvis, Avner Boskey, Noam and Joan Hendren, Dr. Yohanan Stanfield, and Dr. Erez Soref. A thank you to Jerry Gramckow and Mona Pelled, our copy editors, and to our translators, Rivka Nessim, Yonatan Alon, and Miriam Givoni, for your excellent work. A special thank you to Michael Hilsden for all the filming of the interviews, input, and persevering help during this project. With gratitude we want to thank Grayson Stallings for the graphic design of this book and your input to this project.

Thank you to my daughter D'vora, who did excellent research and oversaw this project, and thank you to my son-in-law Nathaniel Silverman, who helped so much in the writing and gave direction throughout the whole project. A special thank you to Dugit staff, especially Laura York, Leslie Cross, and Evan Santoro, for your wise counsel and work on this project in so many ways. And, of course, to Rabbi Daniel Zion's grandchildren, whom I had the honor of meeting and interviewing while writing this book: Pirchiya Cohen, Rachel Amir Zion, Shlomo Zion, and David Zion. Also, to David Cohen, former Israeli ambassador to Bulgaria, Doctor Moshe Mossek, Jacky Comforty, Peleg Levy, retired Colonel Professor Dimitar Nedialkov, and Doctor Daniel Vatchkov for their time and explanations.

A special thank you to Yad Mordechai Holocaust Museum for their cooperation and heartfelt assistance.

We our honored and appreciate very much to have been able to meet and interview Simeon Borisov von Saxe-Coburg-Gotha, better known as King Simeon II of Bulgaria.

TABLE OF CONTENTS

GLOSSARY OF HEBREW TERMS

- **Ahava, Emet, Emuna:** three Hebrew words beginning with the letter alef, meaning: love, truth, faith
- **Achuzat Bayit:** the name of the society that established Tel Aviv, the first modern city of Israel, Hebrew for "homestead"
- **Aliyah:** Jewish immigration to Israel, Hebrew for "ascent"
- **Am Yisrael Chai:** The people of Israel live!
- **Ani Yeshua:** I am Yeshua [Jesus].
- **Ar'vit (also known as Ma'ariv):** one of three Jewish daily prayers, the evening prayer
- **Av Beit Din:** head of a rabbinical court, literally a "father of a court of law"
- **Avraham:** Abraham
- **Avodat Shorashim**: family-history project for school; literally "roots project"
- **Bar Mitzvah/Bat Mitzvah:** Son of the Commandment/Daughter of the Commandment; a ceremony marking an important milestone often celebrated in the synagogue, including reading the weekly Torah portion, and parties with family and friends
- **Beit El:** a name of a school in the city of Haifa, Hebrew for "house of God"
- **Bonim ve'Lochamim:** Hebrew for "builders and warriors"
- **Brit Milah:** covenant of circumcision, performed on the 8th day of a baby boy's life
- **Cantor:** one who sings and leads liturgical prayer in Jewish religious services
- **Chagim:** Holidays/festivals
- **Chanukiah:** a special menorah/candelabra used during the holiday of Chanukkah, the Festival of Lights/Feast of Dedication

- **Chanukkah:** an eight-day Jewish festival commemorating the recovery of Jerusalem and subsequent rededication of the Second Temple at the beginning of the Maccabean revolt against the Seleucid (Greek) Empire in the 2nd century BCE; also known as the Festival of Lights and the Feast of Dedication
- **Diaspora:** dispersion of the Jewish people after being exiled from the Land of Israel, also used to refer to Jewish communities outside of Israel
- **Emeq Habacha:** The Valley of Tears
- **Gaon:** Hebrew for "a brilliant person or genius person"; the formal title for heads of Jewish religious academies
- **Gemara:** the component of the Talmud comprising rabbinical analysis and commentary on the *Mishnah*, the first written collection of Jewish oral traditions
- **Habrit Hachadasha:** New Covenant/New Testament
- **Haganah:** the Jewish paramilitary organization founded during the British mandate period and later became the Israel Defense Forces (IDF); Hebrew for "defense"
- **Halacha:** the collective body of Jewish religious laws that have developed since biblical times and govern daily life and conduct of religious Jews
- **Haredi:** an ultra-Orthodox Jew
- **Har Habayit Be'yadeinu:** "The Temple Mount is in our hands"
- **Hashem:** Literally "the name," a way religious Jews refer to God outside prayers or scripture reading so as to avoid taking His name in vain
- **Hashamayim:** sky, heaven
- **Hashomer Hatzair:** a Zionist youth movement founded in 1913, literally "the young guard"
- **Hatikvah:** Hebrew for "the hope," a 19th-century Jewish poem that later became Israel's national anthem
- **Cherem:** censure in the Jewish community, complete exclusion from communal life

- **Hey be'Iyar Tashach:** the 5th of the month of Iyar, the date on the Jewish calendar for Israel's Declaration of Independence (May 14, 1948)
- **(The) Holocaust:** the genocide of six million Jews during World War II (between 1939-1945); Jewish men, women, and children and other people were systematically exterminated by Nazi Germany and its collaborators
- **Hora:** a circle dance that originated in the Balkans
- **Jaffa (Joppa):** one of the oldest port cities in the Land of Israel, today part of the Tel Aviv municipality
- **Kibbutz:** communal settlement in Israel, traditionally based on agriculture or industry
- **Kosher:** satisfying the requirements of Jewish Law; a term used to describe food that is allowed to be eaten according to the dietary standards of Jewish Law
- **Kotel:** the Western Wall, a remnant of the Second Temple destroyed in 70 CE, the most sacred place for the Jewish people
- **Ladino:** a Judeo-Spanish language spoken by descendants of Jews expelled from Spain and Portugal during the Inquisition
- **Ma'apilim:** illegal Jewish immigrants who immigrated to the Land of Israel during the British Mandate (when the British made restrictions of Jewish immigration beginning in 1934) until the Declaration of Independence on May 14, 1948
- **Magen David:** a Jewish symbol called the "Star of David," but literally the "shield of David"
- **Mahal:** an acronym for **M**itnadvei **H**utz **L**aAretz, "volunteers from abroad" who fought alongside Israeli forces during the War of Independence
- **Matan Beseter:** a name of a Bulgarian charitable organization assisting the poor and needy; literally "giving in secret"
- **Menorah:** a lampstand, a sacred candelabrum with seven branches used in the Temple in Jerusalem, originally placed in the sanctuary of the Tabernacle; one of the oldest symbols of the Jewish faith

- **Minhelet HaAm:** the temporary legislative body founded on April 12, 1948, and became Israel's provisional government after its Declaration of Independence on May 14, 1948, literally "the people's administration"
- **Mishna:** the foundational text of the Oral Torah (Law), an authoritative collection of oral rabbinic teachings codified in the beginning of the 3rd century CE
- **Mitzvot:** Hebrew for "commandments," also used to refer to good deeds in Jewish tradition
- **Mohel:** a Jewish person trained in the ritual of circumcision, *Brit Milah*
- **Moshava:** a town; a term used in the Ottoman period for a rural Jewish settlement
- **Mossad:** Israel's national intelligence agency, founded in 1951
- **(The) Palmach:** an elite fighting force of the Haganah during the British Mandate period
- **Sha'arey Hashamayim:** The Gates of Heaven
- **Shabbat:** Sabbath, a day of rest and worship from Friday evening until Saturday evening, based on God's commandments in the Torah
- **Shacharit:** one of three Jewish daily prayers, the morning prayer
- **Shamash:** head caretaker (of a synagogue)
- **Shehecheyanu:** a prayer thanking God for sustaining the lives of the people so they could experience a historical moment
- **Shiva:** a week-long mourning period in Judaism for close relatives or immediate family
- **Shomer Shabbat:** One who observes commandments regarding Shabbat; literally, "keeper of Shabbat"
- **Sukkah:** a temporary dwelling or booth connected to the holiday of Sukkot
- **Sukkot:** the Feast of Booths or Feast of Tabernacles
- **Talmud:** the central text of Rabbinic Judaism and primary source of Jewish religious law and Jewish theology

- **Tanach:** an acronym for the three sections of the Hebrew Bible (Old Covenant/Old Testament): Torah (the Law of Moses), Nevi'im (the Prophets), and Ketuvim (the Writings)
- **Tel Aviv:** the name of Israel's first modern city: Tel (ancient archeological mound/hill, which represents the old), Aviv (spring, which represents the new)
- **Torah:** the first five books of the Hebrew Bible (Genesis, Exodus, Leviticus, Numbers, Deuteronomy); the Law of Moses; in Judaism can refer to traditional Jewish law
- **Torah student:** a student dedicated to the study of the Hebrew Bible and all Jewish religious texts
- **Tsabar/Tsabarit/Tsabarim:** literally, a prickly but sweet cactus fruit; a term used to denote a native-born Israeli
- **Tsena:** the period of austerity in Israel between the years 1949-1959
- **Yaakov:** Jacob
- **Yeshua HaMashiach:** Jesus the Messiah, the Anointed One
- **Yiddish:** a Judeo-German language, spoken by Jewish communities, which originated in Europe
- **Yitzhak:** Isaac
- **Yishuv:** the community of Jewish people living in the Land of Israel prior to the Declaration of Independence; today, a town or a settlement
- **Yeshua:** Jesus, Hebrew for "salvation"
- **Yom Kippur:** the Day of Atonement, the holiest day of the year in Judaism, traditionally observed by fasting and praying

DEDICATION

For my darling wife, Chaya.
You are the spark and powerhouse of my life in every way.
Were it not for your wisdom, love, and encouragement,
I never would have been inspired to write such a story.
Generations to come will owe it to your dynamic vision,
which you carry in your beautiful Israeli heart.

FOREWORD

Near the end of summer 2015, my father, Avi Mizrachi, announced with great excitement, "We are going on a family trip to Bulgaria to explore and discover more about our vague heritage."

He caught me off guard with his news, as I was right in the middle of finishing my final projects for my master's degree. After he left, my mind wandered from the books of study at hand to all the incredible memories I had of my grandparents and of the stories they occasionally—and tactfully—shared with my sisters and me.

Their sporadic narratives often left us girls wondering if there was more to our heritage than they remembered or intended to share with us. Despite my looming deadline for my M.A., I felt the growing excitement and irresistible urge to take this family heritage trip. I cleared my calendar, and within a couple of weeks I found myself in Sofia, Bulgaria.

Once there, I was in awe at seeing the very places my grandfather had described in his stories. I still have many good memories from that trip, but two stand out as especially important.

The first was when we located my grandfather's childhood home. I was ecstatic to identify the watering well outside the house, exactly as he described in his stories. I looked at the now dilapidated house and pondered many questions:

- How was it to live here during World War II as a Jewish family?
- Where did my grandfather play in the open courtyard?
- What did the Jewish holidays and festivals look like in this place during that time?
- How were the Jewish people treated by the Bulgarians?
- Did my family suffer under the Nazi Regime?

Though the answers were nowhere to be found, I continued taking pictures of the courtyard, surrounding houses, and watering well, as questions called to me from every corner.

My second meaningful memory was of visiting the Great Sephardic Synagogue of Sofia with my family. As we entered the synagogue, we were greeted by the *shamash* (head caretaker), who had a very austere demeanor about him. However, his demeanor changed dramatically when we told him who our grandparents were and that we were from Israel.

At that point, he excitedly showed us the books of records dating back to the opening of the synagogue in the Jewish quarter of the city. He also searched the records for the names of my grandfather and great-grandfather. When he found them, he eagerly showed us and told us he would take us to where my great-grandfather was buried.

After a quick taxi ride with the caretaker, we arrived at an old cemetery on the edge of town. We walked through groves of overgrown trees and rows of worn, crumbling gravestones before arriving at my great-grandfather's grave. There, I stood in silence, considering how much of my family heritage I had yet to discover. As I scanned the many gravesites in the cemetery, I knew there were stories buried within them. What started in that cemetery as my hope soon became my passion, which was not to leave our family's heritage buried there.

During our remaining time in Bulgaria, my sisters and I explored the city of my grandfather, discussing the many stories our grandparents had told us. I realized then that the more we talked and reminisced, the more stories we heard for the first time, since apparently our grandparents hadn't told us all the same stories. As a result, I asked many questions as I tried to piece together all the information we had absorbed and retained over the years. It was as if each sister held a piece of an ever-growing puzzle, a puzzle that grew with each memory shared.

The last evening in Sofia, I mulled over those many memories, one of which stood out from the others. It was something that happened ten years earlier, when I had participated in a delegation to Poland from my Israeli high school. The purpose of the trip was to learn more of the Jewish history during War World II. While there, we visited the Auschwitz concentration camp, the Warsaw ghetto, and the "Majdanek" concentration camp, all of which impressed me significantly.

My mind then wandered to the question of how it was possible that 50,000 Jewish Bulgarian souls were saved, while so many other European Jews were murdered by the Nazis, their communities destroyed forever. How is it that my grandparents never saw the inside of a Nazi death camp? What really happened here in Bulgaria? What is the whole, true story? And I recalled how my grandparents had told us of Rabbi Daniel Zion and his heroic deeds and acts of bravery, which helped prevent the deportation of his Jewish Bulgarian brothers and sisters.

With many pieces of the puzzle still missing, I decided I would try to find some of those missing pieces and start putting the puzzle together. Though this decision launched my personal journey of research into history and heritage, I realized that the things I discovered over the next seven years constituted the core of this book. My discoveries from that time span the years prior to the Holocaust all the way through to the establishment of the state of Israel, including each of the major wars Israel has fought. My hope is that you, the reader, will experience these historical events as if you were a part of our Jewish family in Bulgaria and later in Israel.

I never forgot something I heard when I was on that trip to Poland: "The past lives on in the present and in the future; otherwise, it has no meaning." May you be inspired by this family journey, from generation to generation, to continue to stand for what is true, right, and just.

*****D'vora M.B, daughter of Avi Mizrachi**

PREFACE

Prior to and throughout the time of World War II, Rabbi Daniel Zion was the head of the supreme rabbinical court of Bulgaria, with the prerogatives of Chief Rabbi of the Jewish people of Bulgaria. At the same time, Stefan of Sofia, known as Metropolitan (Chief Bishop of the Church) Stefan, was a priest and a prominent figure in the Orthodox Church in Bulgaria. In the years leading up to World War II, neither of these men could have imagined the bond they would form or the heroic part they would play in rescuing nearly 50,000 Bulgarian Jews from Nazi annihilation. Rabbi Daniel and Metropolitan Stefan faced many dangers, including the very real possibility of deportation and death. And yet they faced those dangers head-on and carried out their perilous plans, sustained by courage and faith, as they effectively saved not only the Bulgarian Jews of their generation but of many generations to come.

Theirs is a story worth telling, and I, Avi Mizrachi, have humbly set out to do so, ever mindful of the miracles that enabled these two men to perform such valiant deeds. I am, in fact, a walking testimony to those miracles, as both my parents lived in Bulgaria prior to World War II. My mother's family managed to flee to Turkey at the beginning of the war, but my father's family remained in Bulgaria, miraculously surviving the horrors of the Holocaust. That my family and I now live in the reborn State of Israel is yet another miracle, celebrated by so many Jewish descendants of that dark time. For many of us living out this miracle today, we owe our lives to the relatively unknown heroes of that era, particularly Rabbi Daniel Zion and Metropolitan Stefan, who were instrumental in rescuing not only the Bulgarian Jews at the beginning of and throughout the war, but also the generations that followed.

As one born in the generation following the Holocaust, I am honored to have the opportunity to share this incredible story and heritage with all who read it. And yet, had it not been for my daughters' *Avodat Shorashim* (a school project requiring research of their family's roots) near the time of their Bat Mitzvah, this story might never have been unearthed and told. Each time one of my daughters gathered materials for this project and asked their grandparents (my parents) questions, I was amazed by what I heard. As a result, I learned more and more about God's faithfulness to my family and the miracles He performed for them.

As the years went by, I knew this remarkable story had to be told. Yet, after my parents passed away, I felt I needed to learn more to fill in the gaps. It was then I decided to start writing this book, the story of my family's journey. As a native-born *tsabar* (Jewish-Israeli), I wanted to be sure to preserve this story for generations to come.

I am ever grateful to a God of miracles and perfect timing who brought this all about and allowed me to be a part of it.

PART I

The Rabbi, Bulgaria, the War

CHAPTER 1
A Friendship with Far-Reaching Effects

I will never forget the look of love and respect on my parents' faces each time they told me of the beloved rabbi who risked his own life to save the Jewish people of Bulgaria. Throughout the years, my parents told me many stories of World War II, as well as the time preceding and immediately following. They praised many, particularly those Bulgarians who shared in saving the nearly 50,000 Bulgarian Jews who lived among them. Yet it was especially when my beloved mother and father spoke of Rabbi Daniel Zion that their eyes sparkled and their faces shone. In addition to all those who worked to protect the Bulgarian Jews during that time, it is Rabbi Daniel Zion and the Metropolitan Stefan that have a special place in my heart.

My parents lived in Sofia, Bulgaria's capital city. The city sits at the foot of Mount Vitosha in the western part of the country at the center of the Balkans, midway between the Black Sea and the Adriatic Sea. The climate is humid with cold, snowy winters and generally mild summers. Occasional heat waves in July and August push temperatures into the mid to upper 30 degrees Celsius (90s Fahrenheit). Sofia is a relatively safe capital city, enjoyed by residents and tourists alike. Leading up to and during World War II, even while Bulgaria was an ally of Nazi Germany, Sofia was one of the safest places for Jews to live in all of Europe. This was due to the loyalty and bravery of Bulgaria's citizens, including and especially two religious leaders of that city—Rabbi Daniel Zion and Metropolitan Stefan.

Rabbi Daniel Zion's Early Years

Rabbi Daniel Zion has long been an important and respected figure among the Jewish community of Bulgaria. He was an educator, considered a moral and gracious man, courageous and humble, as well as an outspoken though gentle individual (see photo #3).

Born in the Greek city of Saloniki (also known as Thessalonica and Thessaloniki) on August 3, 1883, Daniel was raised in an exemplary Jewish home, distinguished by both piety and education. His father, Rabbi Solomon Zion, was head of the rabbinical school *Beit Yosef* (House of Joseph) in Saloniki. In addition to the family being strict observers of the commandments, Rabbi Solomon was highly intelligent, a *Torah scholar* (literally, a "student of the sages"), and a philosopher. He acquired extensive knowledge in science and philosophy, was a naturalist who loved the mountains and the sea, and spent his free time enjoying the outdoors.

Rabbi Solomon was a scribe by profession who, in his youth, became well known for his clear and beautiful script. One time, simply to amuse himself, he wrote two chapters of the Song of Solomon on an eggshell. While still young, he dedicated himself to the study of the *Torah* (the first five books of the Bible; the Jewish Law), the *Talmud* (the central text of Rabbinic Judaism and the primary source of Jewish religious law and Jewish theology), and *Gemara* (the component of the Talmud comprising rabbinical analysis of and commentary on the *Mishnah*, or the first written collection of the Jewish oral traditions).

Daniel's mother, Flora, was a gentle, loving woman, given to gracious hospitality to any and all in need. Though Solomon and Flora were not wealthy by any means, they never turned anyone away but rather gladly and openly shared whatever they had, even if they themselves were short on supplies. Daniel's family was known and respected in the community for regularly feeding the poor, as well as for hosting emissaries from the Land of Israel, both during the week and on the *Shabbat* (Sabbath/Saturday) and Holy Days. Flora warmly welcomed and cooked for visitors, regardless of their station or what she had on hand at the moment (see photo #5).

Daniel's father loved the Torah and prayed regularly. His mother was kind, gentle, and charitable. His parents' examples had a major impact on the impressionable young boy who deeply desired to love God and love people. Growing up in such a setting, Daniel spent much of his childhood in prayer, often from morning until night, quickly learning the Jewish prayers and blessings (many taken directly from the Scriptures) and meticulously observing the commandments.

Even as a toddler, Daniel was attracted to the prayers that became a part of his life at home and in the synagogue. He was a quick learner, who memorized them easily because he listened to his father every time he taught or prayed. The child spent a lot of time in the synagogue and loved being there. From his earliest days, Daniel and his six siblings were trained to observe the commandments relating to God and to one's neighbor.

As Daniel grew up under the positive influence of his father as both a rabbi and a strict Orthodox Jew, the boy desired to one day raise his own children with the same faith and mindset. Rabbi Solomon did not have to train or discipline Daniel to spend time in prayer, as is the case with some children. On the contrary, the boy was drawn to it with delight. A loose translation of the Hebrew document titled "A Passage of Second Act and Criticism" from The Central Archives for the History of the Jewish People, so aptly describe the young boy: "Because his soul greatly desired the blessings, and he clung to the prayers with all his heart."[1]

Their home became a center for the learned men who met there to discuss *Halacha* (the collective body of Jewish religious laws that have developed since biblical times and govern daily life and conduct of religious Jews). The study and practice of Halacha was extremely important to Daniel's family, and as he listened to these many discussions of the Law, his passion for it grew until it became a priority in his own life, as well as in his family's. Because the same passion for the Jewish Law reigned in their household, Daniel naturally desired to know it himself and to turn that knowledge into action.

Continuing His Studies

When Daniel completed *Talmud Torah*, the elementary-age children's and junior-high-age youth school, he continued his studies in rabbinical

1 | The Central Archives for the History of the Jewish People (CAHJP), file BU-456 at the Hebrew University of Jerusalem. The Edmond J. Safra Campus Givat Ram.

school where his father was quite possibly one of the teachers. Throughout his studies, Daniel meticulously adhered to the Law, particularly the commandment to honor one's father and mother. He was careful of his tongue, lest he speak evil of others, and was known in the *Haredi* (Jewish Ultra-Orthodox) community of Saloniki as a man who loved and feared God, a faithful advocate for the Jewish Law and faith.

From the age of twenty, Daniel dedicated himself to work in the Jewish community, and served as a *cantor* (one who sings and leads liturgical prayer in Jewish religious services). To this day, his grandchildren and great-grandchildren remember the aged rabbi when he was ninety-seven years old and bedridden, singing to the Lord at the top of his voice. When my father, Nissim, went to the synagogue, he often remembered hearing the rabbi's voice, which he said was strong and beautiful.

Rabbi Daniel was widely educated in more than just religious matters. He spoke several languages: Bulgarian, French, Greek, Hebrew, Turkish, Spanish, English, and Ladino, the Spanish-Hebrew language handed down from the time Sephardic Jews lived in Spain. He loved reading books and studied the great philosophers and scientists, including Aristotle, Plato, Newton, as well as others. Daniel was also well versed in the precepts of philosophy and logic and was known to have had a phenomenal memory (see photo #6).

Starting a Family

At the beginning of the twentieth century, Daniel completed a theological degree at the Israelite Higher Institute in Saloniki. Not long after, he married a lovely young woman named Rachel. Although it was an arranged marriage, which was quite common in those days and usually arranged by the rabbis, those who knew them said they were very close and had a deep love for one another, even at the early stages of their relationship.

Daniel and Rachel soon started a family of their own, eventually having five children. When they married, Daniel received a ring from his parents. Engraved inside were the letters *Alef-Alef-Alef*, which in Hebrew represent love, truth, and faith (*ahava*, *emet*, *emuna*). Those words were indelibly rooted in Daniel's heart and often showed up in his sermons and in his actions throughout his life.

With the encouragement of his father, in early 1915 Rabbi Daniel Zion, then thirty-two years old, was sent by Rabbi Yaakov Meir, the chief rabbi of Saloniki, to serve as cantor in the synagogue in Sofia, Bulgaria. Daniel and Rachel had two children at the time, and the little family of four soon settled in Sofia's Jewish neighborhood.

Daniel's extensive knowledge of Torah and Halacha, his ability to speak several languages, and his dedication to God and to the Jewish people quickly became evident to the Jewish community of Sofia, among whom he became highly respected and loved. Scarcely a year after arriving in Sofia, Daniel was appointed rabbi of the Youchbounar Synagogue.

Serving His People

Through the ensuing years, Rabbi Daniel worked tirelessly with the Jewish community, even establishing a charitable organization known as *Matan Beseter* (Giving in Secret). The purpose of the organization was to feed and care for the poorest members of the community. Rabbi Daniel placed a lot of emphasis on aiding the poor and helpless. He also opposed the dowry. The need to provide a dowry so a daughter could marry placed a heavy burden on families and caused marriage itself to become a matter of status, something the rabbi could not condone.

Later, at the age of forty, he was asked to serve as chairman on the rabbinical court of Sofia. Years later, in 1931, as a result of all his study and hard work, he was officially made *Av Bet Din*, the head of the supreme rabbinical court of Bulgaria. This great honor, which few rabbis received, gave Daniel enormous authority as well as the status of Chief Rabbi of Bulgarian Jewry.[2] With his wife and, by then, five children—Yaakov, Yaffa,

---

2 | Richard Simantov, The Central Archives for the History of the Jewish People (CAHJP), file BU-456 at the Hebrew University of Jerusalem, the Edmond J. Safra Campus Givat Ram.

Michael, Herzl, and Nissim—Rabbi Daniel gave himself to the study of Torah and service to his people, as well as to writing books and poems.

Metropolitan Stefan

Metropolitan Stefan was born in 1878 as Stoyan Popgeorgiev Shokov in Shiroka Laka, which lies in the central Rhodope Mountains in southern Bulgaria.[3] After completing four years of seminary studies in Kiev, rather than joining the priesthood, he attended an army officer military academy and graduated with the rank of Lieutenant.

In 1910, when Stoyan was thirty-two years old, he joined the Bulgarian Orthodox church, was anointed as a priest, and given the name of Stefan. Following this, he pursued doctoral studies at the University of Geneva before returning to Sofia. He was known as an intellectually brilliant, well-read, and independent person. He was also known for his booming voice and his pleasant sense of humor.[4] It wasn't long before this man with the salt-and-pepper beard rose to the head of the church in Sofia and became one of her greatest figures, being elected Metropolitan of Sofia in 1922 (see photo #9). "He was profoundly religious and believed that the presence of God in the world was important and tangible."[5] Stefan was a respected leader of the church, admired by his peers, and most remembered for actively contributing to the rescue of the Bulgarian Jews in World War II.

"Stefan lost no opportunity to express his criticism in articles that were frequently censured and led to alarming threats on the part of Fascists and Nazis. Arguing with a censor, he said: 'It's not true that I am anti German. I greatly admire numerous Germans, such as Stefan Zweig, Thomas Mann and Albert Wasserman,' deliberately selecting the names of illustrious German Jews. In September 1942 he infuriated Fascist and Nazi circles by openly preaching against anti-Semitism. He publicly declared

3 | Michael Bar-Zohar, *Beyond Hitler's Grasp: The Heroic Rescue of Bulgaria's Jews* (Holbrook, Massachusetts, 1998), p. 165.

4 | "People Recognized As Righteous; Metropolitan Stefan," *Gariwo: Garden of the the Righteous WorldWide*, <https://en.gariwo.net/righteous/the-righteous-biographies/Holocaust/people-recognized-as-righteous/metropolitan-Stefan-7661.html> [accessed June 7th, 2021].

5 | Ibid.

that the Bulgarians should consider the Jews as their brothers. In 1943, as German anti-Semitism took hold all over Europe, Stefan worked to engage the whole Bulgarian Church in his opposition to Nazi policies and effectively gained the compact backing of both the Church hierarchy and the believers, who supported him wholeheartedly."[6]

As a result of his heroic efforts, he received numerous awards and decorations, including the Order of the White Eagle, a high award given by the Polish government to honor its citizens,[7] and also the title of "Righteous among the Nations" from grateful Israeli Jews.

Putting Faith into Action

Stefan was highly religious and considered the presence of God and His law to be not only significant but also a solid reality. Upon the outbreak of World War II and despite the danger in doing so, Stefan openly condemned Bulgaria's pact with the Nazis, seeing Hitler as unstable. He went on to labor ceaselessly to defend the Bulgarian Jews from the Nazi ideology, and he paid a heavy price for his courage. The pro-government radio and press attacked and slandered him relentlessly, while the government-backed propaganda went so far as to print leaflets full of threats against him, distributing them throughout the country.

Metropolitan Stefan was one of the protesters against The Bill for the Defense of the Nation (see chapter 3 for more details). In January 1941, along with the Holy Synod, he sent a letter to the Prime Minister and to the Minister of Foreign Affairs, which stated, "... The principle of racialism which is the basic idea on which the above mentioned law is founded, has no justification from the point of view of the teachings of Jesus... The principle of racialism which encourages persecution and denies the rights of people, merely because of their race, in this case the Jewish race, has no justification, and therefore one cannot base the 'Law for the Protection of the Nation' [The Law for the Defense of the Nation] on the principle of

6 | Ibid.

7 | The Order of the White Eagle - Polish Military Medals & Orders - Poland (identifymedals.com).

racialism. One cannot turn the 'Law for the Protection of the Nation' into a means of oppression and persecution of the Jewish minority in the land."[8]

In addition to being one of the strongest opponents of The Bill for the Defense of the Nation, in February 1941 Stefan went to the police authorities and complained that the Brannik Fascist Organization (a Bulgarian pro-fascist youth group active during WW II) was harassing, persecuting, and beating Jewish people in the streets.[9] Stefan also provoked the fury of pro-Fascist elements in the government when, in September 1942, he preached that no one had the right to persecute the Jewish people, and the Bulgarian people must look upon them as their brothers.[10] It was no surprise, then, that Stefan was horrified in March 1943 when the Jewish population of Macedonia and Thrace were deported into the hands of the Nazis. When he witnessed the transport trains, loaded with terrified people heading to almost certain death, he tried to alert Boris, the tsar/king (terms used interchangeably for Bulgaria's sovereign leader), to put an end to such cruelty.

Sadly, Metropolitan Stefan was unsuccessful in convincing the Bulgarian tsar to intervene and stop the deportation of the Jewish people from Macedonia and Thrace (areas under the Bulgarian administration). The exact details of Tsar Boris's decision are problematic, but basically his decision had to do with the fact that when Germany gave Macedonia and Thrace to Bulgaria, only non-Jews immediately became Bulgarian citizens.[11] Because the Jewish people from those areas were not considered Bulgarian citizens and the areas where they lived were still under German control, it is argued that the tsar did not have the right or the ability to stop their deportation to the East. In addition, any decisions the tsar might make regarding those areas still had to be approved by the Germans.

---

8 | Johan M. Snoek, *The Grey Book: A collection of Protests Against Anti-Semitism and the Persecution of Jews Issued by Non-Roman Catholic Churches and Church Leaders During Hitler's Rule* (Van Gorcum & Comp. Assen, 1969), p. 183.

9 | Bar-Zohar, *Hitler's Grasp*, p. 168.

10 | Ibid.

11 | Nir Baruch, "The Jews in Bulgaria – 1941-1944 Chronological Development of Events", *The Bulgarian Jews*, http://www.thebulgarianjews.org.il/Uploads/dbsAttachedFiles/TheJewsNirBaruch.pdf, p. 8.

As Jewish people, we believe the tsar could have stopped the deportations of the Macedonia and Thrace Jews. He would have paid a price, but the Jewish people of Macedonia and Thrace could have been saved. The Bulgarians believe the tsar could not have stopped the deportations, and if he had tried to do so, the Jewish people of Bulgaria would ultimately have been lost. I personally believe that much more could have been done to stop the deportations of Macedonia and Thrace Jews, but we will probably never know what really would have happened to the Bulgarian, Macedonia, and Thrace Jews if the tsar had intervened. My heart is broken for the loss of the Macedonia and Trace Jews.

Increased Pressure ... and Danger

At about the same time, the first attempt was made to expel the Jewish citizens of Bulgaria. Stefan immediately acted, through writing letters and calling meetings, to unify all the leaders of the Bulgarian church against the repressive measures enacted against the Jewish population. Though anti-Semitic organizations called for Stefan's death, he pressed on in his labor on behalf of the Bulgarian Jews. It was partially because of Stefan's work that the order to expel them was rescinded on March 9, 1943.

Soon after, on April 2, 1943, the Holy Synod of the Bulgarian Church held a special plenary session. The topic of discussion was the government policy toward the Jews of Bulgaria, in light of the attempted deportation. In this meeting, Metropolitan Kiril of Plovdiv described the dramatic events that had happened in his city on March 10, when the police rounded up the Jewish population in preparation for deportation. The plan was to gather the Bulgarian Jews between March 9 and 10, then load them onto the trains and begin deporting them on the tenth. When Metropolitan Kiril heard of it, he immediately became involved in trying to stop the deportation. Because he and Metropolitan Stefan and Rabbi Zion and others were successful in stopping the deportations and having the Jewish people released back to their homes, the event is still known as the "March 9 Miracle."

At that time, Metropolitan Stefan warned the Bulgarian government that although he had always been a loyal citizen, he was now compelled to disobey the orders of the government and to act at his own discretion, as his conscience required of him. One after the other, the heads of the Bulgarian church joined him in speaking out against the measures taken against their Jewish population. Metropolitan Stefan declared that the Jews of Bulgaria knew full well that no one would offer them more stable and earnest support than the Bulgarian church, and that if the church acted more vigorously, the government would hear its voice.

"Unfortunately," he explained during a meeting with church leaders, "the Law for the Defense of the Nation is being implemented by a man [Belev] who, I am told, is not fully in equilibrium [agreement] on these questions. And if our Church doesn't intervene to defend these wretched people, we should expect even worse outrages and acts of cruelty, for which one day our goodhearted people is going to feel shame, and perhaps other misfortunes."[12] He concluded with these words: "When we ask the State authorities what the Jews of our country are guilty of, they have nothing to say. They took everything away from the Jews, but when they reached to take away their life, the Jews asked for the defense of the Church. We cannot refuse it. They are subjected to inhuman suffering."[13] Ultimately, the church decided it could not turn away its Jewish population; rather, as a whole, it needed to help and support them in such a treacherous time. The acting chairman then moved that the synod compose a letter to the government, clarifying its position with regard to the "Jewish Question."

The term "Jewish Question" or "Jewish problem" refers to the European discussions that took place from the eighteenth through the twentieth centuries regarding status, rights, and treatment of the Jewish people, either within a nation or in society in general. These terms were discussed because the Jewish people were a minority group in Europe, for centuries despised and looked upon negatively. However, Adolf Hitler and Nazi Germany looked upon the Jewish Question as a problem that needed to

12 | Bar-Zohar, *Hitler's Grasp*, pp. 170-171.

13 | Ibid, p. 172.

be resolved—once and for all. This led to the "Final Solution to the Jewish Question," the genocide of the Jewish people. As early as September 16, 1919, regarding the Jewish Question, Hitler declared that the "ultimate goal must definitely be the removal of the Jews altogether."[14] On January 30, 1939, during Hitler's speech at the Reichstag, he said that the outbreak of the war would mean the "annihilation of the Jewish race in Europe."[15]

The Orthodox Church of Bulgaria did not agree with Hitler's declarations, so the letter was written and sent to the tsar and to Prime Minister Filov, including the following paragraphs.

"The Law for the Protection of the Nation [Law for the Defense of the Nation] was created with the express purpose of limiting the Jewish minority; the main concept of the law is based on racialism. At that time the Holy Synod informed the Government, that the principle of racialism cannot be justified from the point of view of the Christian doctrine... The principle of racialism, according to which certain members of the community can be persecuted, restricted and deprived of their rights only because they belong to a certain race, in this case the Jewish race, cannot be justified from the standpoint of Christian ethics. Therefore the Church emphatically demands that the Law for the Protection of the Nation shall not be based mainly on the principles of racialism, but on those of spiritual wholeness and the protection of our people, so that it may safeguard them from those disintegrating influences which affect spiritual and religious values, and also from economic financial exploitation. They did not listen to the voice of our Holy Synod. We now see, that the Law for the Protection of the Nation, nearly two years after its promulgation, instead of meeting its great task of safeguarding the Nation from damaging and disintegrating influences, and uniting its creative, healthy, spiritual and economic powers into a spiritual and moral unity, has turned into a means of restricting and persecuting the Jewish minority in our country...

14 | Adolf Hitler Issues Comment on the "Jewish Question," *United States Holocaust Memorial Museum,* https://www.ushmm.org/learn/timeline-of-events/before-1933/adolf-hitler-issues-comment-on-the-jewish-question.

15 | Reichstag Speech, *United States Holocaust Memorial Museum,* https://www.ushmm.org/learn/timeline-of-events/1939-1941/hitler-speech-to-german-parliament

"… restrictions are increasing daily. It has gone so far that these citizens of our country are deprived of the most elementary rights, and the Department for Jewish Affairs is free to do with them as it wishes; sending them to camps and deporting them from the country. Our people, with soul and conscience, mind and conviction, cannot tolerate injustice, cruelty and violence against anybody. It cannot accept what is being done now to the Jewish minority. Its human and Christian conscience is perplexed. The Holy Synod of the Bulgarian Church cannot ignore its divine command and its holy duty. It must, according to the teaching of the Gospel concerning love of one's neighbor, raise a compassionate and defending voice in aid of the suffering and wronged people; it must beg, guide and convince, so that the measures in general against the Jews may cease or at least be eased. God's law, which transcends all human laws, definitely obliges us not to be indifferent in the face of the sufferings of innocent people, of whatever race. The majority of our people also place their relationship with the suffering Jewish minority on this biblical and humane foundation. … Until now, a historical line of justice and integrity has been the sure means for the protection of our people and our State. On these eternal foundations we also base our national and righteous demands, side along our hopes…

"The Bulgarian Orthodox Church fears that, if we destroy the eternal foundation—the right to live as free men and the divine commandment to be just—there no longer will be left to us, as a small people, any other strong support for our existence. The Bulgarian State must, therefore, abide by these truths, and apply them to all its subjects, who are guiltless…

"The Holy Synod, meeting in the special session of April 2, of this year [1943], has decided—after considering its deep concern for the honour and future of the Bulgarian people, and its responsibility before God—to inform you that the Bulgarian Orthodox Church, as a national and divine institution, cannot agree to principles such as racialism, in which it is possible to foment hatred and to indulge in violence and cruelty. It cannot accept the principle that any race be deprived of the human right to live, since this right is in accordance with the fundamental principles of Christian religion and morality. The Bulgarian Orthodox Church is of the opinion that she cannot deny help and protection to the persecuted and oppressed. If she were to refuse such help, she would be unfaithful to herself. In this case our Holy Church was asked for help, by the Jews as well as by Christian Bulgarians, in order to improve the fate of the Jews in general. The Church does not deny and even especially stresses the duty and the right of the honourable Government to take the necessary steps to protect the people and the State from all dangers. However, she must stress the duty of the State to abide by the principles of justice and the Christian Gospel."[16]

Another source of this letter states, "The Pravoslav [Orthodox] Bulgarian Church ... cannot accept ideas like the racist idea, by which people can be inspired with hatred, and acts of oppression and cruelty may be committed... Our Holy Church has been asked by the Jews for help, while Bulgarian Christians have asked us to act for the improvement of the fate of the Jews... the Saint [Holy] Synod decided to ask... not to deprive Christians of Jewish origin and the Jews in general [meaning any Jews who did not become Christians] of their elementary rights as human beings and citizens, and not to deprive them of the right to live in our country and to work here to assure a fair human living. [We ask] to ease the restrictions that have been imposed on the Jews and not to implement them firmly and cruelly... The Church cannot avoid reminding [you of] God's word: '... with the measure you use, it will be measured back to you' (Matthew 7:2, NKJV)."[17]

Standing Firm

This letter was delivered to Tsar Boris III shortly after his return from Germany. He was furious and insulted on reading it and summoned both Prime Minister Filov and the heads of the Holy Synod to come before him. They did so on April 15, 1943, with both the tsar and Filov being very agitated at the start of the meeting. The tsar proceeded to deliver a

16 | Snoek, *The Grey Book*, pp. 185-187.

17 | Bar-Zohar, *Hitler's Grasp*, pp. 172-173.

hard anti-Semitic speech against the Bulgarian Jews, though he withheld the information that he had fallen out with Joachim von Ribbentrop, the Foreign Minister of Nazi Germany, when he rejected Ribbentrop's demands to deport the Bulgarian Jews.

The prelates responded politely but did not change their stance regarding Bulgaria's Jews. Stefan (the last to speak for the Church) addressed the tsar and Filov with these words: "... I strongly intercede with the Supreme state authority to listen to the voice and the request of the Church and give instructions for the easing of the Law for the Defense of the Nation, and for its implementation with good will, humanity and justice."[18] In response, a furious Filov declared, "... the Parliament is against the Jews, and that the full powers that it had given the government [on the Jewish Question] have been given specially with the directive to aggravate the Jewish situation."[19]

In the months following, the Holy Synod continually criticized the anti-Semitic measures and wrote letters and warnings to Filov, which irked him terribly. In the space of two and a half months (from April through the first half of June 1943), the Holy Synod convened eight times, sent five letters to the heads of state, and met twice with Filov and once with the tsar himself. According to an article written by Paul Stefanov, "The bishops never wavered in their determination to rescue the Jews."[20]

The introduction of The Bill for the Defense of the Nation in 1940 became the tipping point for many in Bulgaria, not only the Jewish people but also the Christians. If passed, the bill would have severely harmed the Jewish people of Bulgaria, to the point of their being deported straight into the hands of the Nazis. At a time when many had to make a choice as to where they would stand on this bill and indeed on the entire Jewish Question, the Orthodox Church, among others, took a courageous position and worked hard to stop it.

At the forefront of the fight were several metropolitans (chief bishops of the Church), including Kiril of Plovdiv, Paisiy of Vratsa, Sophroniy of

18 | Ibid, p. 176.

19 | Ibid, p. 177.

20 | Paul Stefanov, "The Bulgarian Orthodox Church and the Holocaust: Addressing Common Misconceptions," *Religion in Eastern Europe* XXVI, 2 (2006), p. 15.

Turnovo, Neophit of Vidin, and, of course, Stefan of Sofia. They submitted memos, held meetings, and presented religious and moral arguments against this law. Stefan was especially active and courageous in this struggle, orchestrating the defense of the Bulgarian Jews and meeting with the Prime Minister and other government officials to argue against deporting Bulgaria's Jewish population into Nazi hands. The church's struggle against the government on behalf of Bulgaria's Jewish citizens is an indication of the good relations that existed between the Christians and the Jewish people at that time.

The Forging of a Friendship

Because of the close relationship between the Christians and Jews of Bulgaria, it was not at all unusual that a priest and a rabbi would become friends. Though the exact details of the first meeting between Metropolitan Stefan and Rabbi Daniel are unknown, it is clear their relationship grew during theological discussions and joint projects to help the needy in Sofia, particularly their work with the Bulgarian Jews.

As I mentioned earlier, my parents told me many stories about Bulgaria's Jewish population and World War II, none of which brought a glow to their faces more than when they spoke of Rabbi Daniel. I specifically remember my mother telling me about the relationship between the rabbi and the priest. Though she did not tell me how these two men first met, she did confirm they knew one another and often spent time together discussing theology. I don't know the exact dates or years, but I assume it was in the beginning of the 1930s.

My mother once related to me how, one day, Stefan gave Daniel a New Covenant (New Testament). The rabbi, believing this to be a forbidden book, tore out pages and threw them on the floor as Stefan watched. Though Stefan had presented the book as a gift and Daniel had seemingly rejected it, they continued with their theological discussion. As they talked, the rabbi realized he had not shown respect to Stefan, so he bent over and picked up the scattered pages. Then he took the damaged book home and placed it on a shelf in his study, where it collected dust for several years.

A Life-Changing Vision

Around the year 1934, a most amazing event took place. While in prayer, Rabbi Daniel had a vision of a glowing man. When the vision faded, he first went for advice to his fellow rabbis and Jewish friends, but they were unable to explain it. After some thought, he decided to go to Metropolitan Stefan. Rabbi Daniel told him about the vision; Stefan smiled and told him that if it happened again to say to the man, "Here I am."

The rabbi agreed and returned to his regular prayers. It was not long until he had a second vision. This time, when the glowing man appeared, Daniel said, "Here I am. Who are you?"

"*Ani Yeshua*," the glowing man replied, meaning, "I am Jesus."

As soon as the vision cleared, the rabbi retrieved his dusty, torn New Covenant from his study shelf and began to read. As he turned the pages, his heart swelled with joy and with the knowledge that Yeshua was indeed the long-awaited Messiah. With his New Covenant in hand, Rabbi Daniel once again went to visit his friend Metropolitan Stefan, this time to tell him what had happened and to ask what he should do with this newfound dilemma.

"Don't convert," Stefan advised him. "You can remain a Jew and still believe in [Yeshua] Jesus."

After much discussion, the two men agreed that Daniel should indeed remain a rabbi and head of the *Bet Din* (supreme rabbinical court) of Bulgaria. He could believe Yeshua was the Son of David, the Messiah of his people Israel, but at the same time continue to observe the Law and the Commandments, preserving his Jewish identity in full.

In addition to the rabbi coming to believe in Yeshua as the Jewish Messiah in 1934, another happy event took place that same year. Rabbi Daniel's elder daughter, Yaffa, was married to Avraham (Albert) Ben

Bassat. According to Rabbi Daniel's grandson, Shlomo Zion, it was Rabbi Zion himself who performed the wedding. The following year, Yaffa and Avraham had a baby girl they called Lydda. Then, in 1939, a second daughter was born to Yaffa and Avraham and named Flora (see photo #10). Later, in Israel, Flora's name was changed to Pirchiya, whom I had the honor of meeting in Israel while writing this book.

CHAPTER 2

The Bulgarian Jews

Before continuing with the story of Rabbi Daniel Zion and Metropolitan Stefan, I would like to give you some historical background about the Jewish people of Bulgaria.

The majority of Bulgarian Jews were descended from the Sephardic Jews (a minority were Ashkenazi Jews) who had been exiled from Spain in 1492. Some of the exiles had migrated to Hungary, others to Greece, but most to the Balkans, especially Bulgaria. The Sephardic Jews spoke *Ladino* (a Spanish-Hebrew language) rather than the *Yiddish* of the Ashkenazi Jews, who primarily lived in Eastern (Poland and Russia), Northern, and Western Europe.

The Jewish people often held positions in trade and commerce, while very few became involved in politics or farming, which is why most Jewish people lived in the city rather than in the country. This was the case in Bulgaria, as well as in the other European countries.

"The Fox" Rises to Power

In order to understand the tenuous fate of the Bulgarian Jews during the rise of Nazi Germany, it is essential to understand the rise of Tsar Boris III. In World War I, Bulgaria allied herself with the Central Powers—Austro-Hungary, Germany, and the Ottoman Empire—and was defeated along with them, leaving Bulgaria economically devastated. On November 27, 1919, Bulgaria was forced to sign an armistice agreement, called the Neuilly Treaty, with its victors. This treaty stipulated, among other things, the return of territory Bulgaria had conquered during the war, including Macedonia, as well as the payment of 2,260 million gold francs in financial reparation. In the ignominy of defeat, the tsar of Bulgaria, Ferdinand of Saxe-Coburg and Gotha, was forced to abdicate and relinquish the throne to his eldest son, Boris III, also known as Tsar (or King) Boris, who was twenty-four years old at the time.

Tsar Boris was born in Bulgaria and was known for his exceptional charm and complex personality. Educated by Bulgarian and German scholars, he was smart and did well in anything he studied, excelling in languages. A graduate of the military school in Sofia, Boris enjoyed hunting, hiking, and driving cars and locomotives.[1] He served in the Bulgarian army and was respected by many, including army officials, for being mature beyond his years and for gaining the people's admiration.

Cunning and shrewd, Boris was often called "the Fox" due to the way he dealt and negotiated with other rulers and countries. Foreign leaders and even Bulgarian citizens, particularly the Jews, admired this man as a leader. Many, however, wondered if he would ultimately spare the Jewish people, or if he would yield to Germany's pressure and hand them over to the Nazis. That question would be answered by the time he died in 1943, but much would come to pass before that.

In the beginning of his rule, Boris was faced with much political unrest and even escaped two assassinations attempts in the 1920s. As the years passed, he was able to establish himself as a strong ruler and leader of the country, assuming control from the military and establishing his long-desired regime in 1935. By 1938, members of parliament were elected only on the basis of their support and loyalty to the king. In order to be re-elected, they were obliged to prove themselves obedient and submissive.

A Delicate Balance

Toward the end of the 1930s, as World War II drew near, Tsar Boris supported the League of Nations and endeavored to ensure Bulgaria's neutrality, a policy forged to spare his people the bloodshed and financial destruction often brought on by war. He knew the Bulgarian people would not fight against the Russians because the Russian army had delivered them from Ottoman rule some sixty-two years earlier. Also, he feared Bulgaria

---

1 | Bar-Zohar, *Hitler's Grasp*, pp. 11-14.

might be destroyed if he entered the war with the Great Powers—in his words, "when the horses start kicking each other in the stable, the donkeys get hurt."[2] On the other hand, the tsar also knew he could benefit from a treaty with Hitler; most specifically, Bulgaria would recover the territory taken from them in 1919 as a result of the Neuilly Treaty. Boris understood that neither Britain nor the Soviet Union could satisfy his territorial demands; it was Hitler who held the key to the dream of a greater Bulgaria (the areas of Thrace, Macedonia, and Southern Dobrudja).[3]

In addition, the small country of Bulgaria was located between the Soviet Union and Nazi Germany, symbolic of the dangerous position the Bulgarians were in when it came to choosing loyalties. Even today, Bulgaria's Parliament Building stands prominently on the main square in Sofia. Directly behind it is the Alexander Nevsky Cathedral, which was the main church prior to and during World War II. On the corner across from the Parliament is the Austrian Embassy, which during the war served as the German Embassy, with its Nazi flags flying prominently for all to see.

At the same time, the Russian Church, officially known as the Church of St. Nicholas the Miracle-Maker, was across the way from the Alexander Nevsky Cathedral. Next door to the Russian Church was the Soviet Embassy. If you walked along that location in Sofia during World War II, you would encounter the Orthodox Church, Parliament, the German Embassy with the Nazi flag flying, and the Soviet Union's Embassy with the Communist flag.

Though the Bulgarians felt some loyalty toward Russia for having liberated them from 500 years of Ottoman rule in 1878, pre-World War II Bulgaria was not sure it could trust Stalin. As a result, upon the outbreak of World War II, Bulgaria's head of state declared a position of neutrality.

During the war, however, this neutrality began to sway toward Nazi Germany. Despite the tsar's efforts to retain neutrality, Bulgaria was drawn into Germany's sphere of influence, mainly through the economy.[4]

---

2 | Ibid, p. 19.
3 | Ibid, p. 21.
4 | Ibid, pp. 20-22.

Germany provided Bulgaria with the largest percentage of import and export compared to other countries. And so, the alliance between Germany and Bulgaria was forged, though reluctantly on the tsar's part, by what he believed was economic necessity.

Also, all of Europe was subdued at that time (Europe was in flames, Great Britain stood alone, and England was on the other side of Europe, far from Bulgaria), making this decision for the tsar inevitable. It was nearly impossible for Bulgaria to maintain neutrality when Germany wanted to go through their lands in order to invade Greece. The decision came down to a choice of joining Hitler or seeing Bulgaria destroyed.

Zionism

In the midst of the buildup to World War II, the Jewish community of Bulgaria was unique in its wholehearted adoption of the vision of Zionism, a movement that sought the re-establishment (and later the development and protection) of a Jewish nation in what is now Israel. Since the founding of the Zionist movement in Bulgaria at the end of the 19th century, the social life of the Jews of Bulgaria had developed mainly under the influence of Zionism, so much so that the first Zionist organization established in Bulgaria was founded in 1864 in Ruse, Bulgaria.[5] The religious establishments in Bulgaria chose to support Zionist efforts and were sympathetic and enthusiastic about it. Motivated by a sincere desire to return to the Land of their fathers, a full 90 percent of this Jewish community immigrated to Israel after the establishment of the State in 1948.[6] (Pre-war, the Jewish population of Bulgaria was 48,000; after the war, it was about 50,000.)

In the period preceding World War II, the Zionist aspirations of the Jewish community in Bulgaria were clear. By 1927, 80 percent of the Jewish children were being taught Hebrew, Bible, and the History of the Jewish

5 | Vicki Tamir, *Bulgaria and Her Jews: The History of a Dubious Symbiosis* (New York: Sepher-Hermon Press for Yeshiva University Press, 1979), pp. 135-136.

6 | Bar-Zohar, *Hitler's Grasp*, p. vii.

people in thirty-eight Zionist schools throughout Bulgaria.[7] In addition, youth groups, such as the *Hashomer HaTsa'ir* (The Young Guard), were established in 1923.

My father, Nissim, went to meetings of the Shomer HaTsa'ir twice a week from the time he was a young boy in the early 1930s until 1941, when newly passed legislation prevented him from attending any longer.[8] Though he had heard at the synagogue and from his parents the biblical prophecies that the Jewish people would one day return to Israel, the Land of our forefathers—*Avraham* (Abraham), *Yitzhak* (Isaac), and *Yaakov* (Jacob)—this amazing concept was reinforced at the youth group. My father became so excited about Zionism and the very real possibility that he might see biblical prophecy fulfilled in his lifetime that his already dedicated pursuit of Torah and prayer grew even more passionate.

Nissim read and reread the Bible stories and other materials about when the Jewish people were taken from their land as slaves after the destruction of the first and second temple and then dispersed among the nations (referred to as the *Diaspora*, places throughout the world where the Jewish people had been dispersed after losing their Land). Could it be that one day he might see with his own eyes the Land of Israel, the Promised Land? He was indeed awed to think that prophecy might come to pass in his lifetime.

When my father told me all this, his eyes were full of joy and excitement. He explained that he had been born into a world where the State of Israel was just a hope, a dream and not a reality, unlike the world into which I myself was born a generation later.

My father also told me of the many good friends he had made at the Shomer HaTsa'ir. He explained how the youth group leaders taught the Hebrew language and educated the youth in the Zionist dream and love

---

7 | Guy H. Haskell, *From Sofia to Jaffa; The Jews of Bulgaria and Israel* (Detroit: Wayne State University Press, 1994) pp.94-97.

8 | The Shomer HaTsa'ir was a youth movement with Zionist and socialist views. In this youth group, though most of its members were secular, they emphasized Jewish history and Jewish Heritage (teaching Hebrew and Bible stories) as well as socialistic principles. The Shomer Hatzair's goal was to promote Aliyah, immigration to Israel.

of the homeland. In turn, even prior to WW II, the Jewish community in the Land of Israel sent educators to teach the Jewish children of Bulgaria, and a close relationship developed between the settlement in Israel and the Bulgarian Jews.

Rabbi Daniel was involved in the Zionist movement almost from the time he arrived in Sofia. In the 1920s and 1930s, when Daniel was in his forties, he began to preach about the idea of awakening the new spirit of Zionism. He believed the exile of the Jewish people from their ancestral homeland had wounded the Jewish soul. He also believed those wounds would not be healed until the people returned to the Land of their forefathers. During that time, he established the movement known as "*Shomer Shabbat*" (Keepers of the Shabbat) in order to raise awareness about the Jewish law and commandments. It was important to Daniel that his Jewish friends understood how deeply he loved and respected the Torah, and he saw Shomer Shabbat as a means to do so, as well as to pass that love and respect to others.[9]

My Family on the Eve of WW II

As the approach of World War II began to look inevitable, my parents and their families were deeply affected. My mother, Rivka (Rebecca), was born in Plovdiv, Bulgaria, on July 18, 1932. Her parents were Yehuda (Judah) and Rachel Bahat, and her maiden name was Taregno. Rachel had two brothers and a sister: Yossi (short for Joseph), Yacov (Jacob), and Sollena, while Yehuda had three sisters and two brothers. Yehuda and Rachel had four children, including my mother: Robert, Suzanne, Sarah (Sali), and Rivka.

My mother was a very intelligent woman, hardworking and enterprising, who knew several languages, including Ladino, Bulgarian, Arabic, Turkish, Hebrew, and French. When she saw something that needed to be done, nothing would stop her until the issue was resolved. A strong, active, independent woman, she bluntly spoke her mind.

---

9 | Isaac Avraamov, "Daniel Zion (1883-1976)," *Yearbook*, Issue 22 (1987), p.330.

At the same time, she had a gentle, caring side and would fight for those who were weak. She loved books and had a passion to learn new things and to obtain as much education as possible. She was seven years old when the war broke out in Europe, and the family moved from Bulgaria to Istanbul, having decided it was safer in Turkey. As a child in Turkey, where girls seldom attended school or got a formal education, she convinced her parents to allow her to do so. Because of her tenacity, she learned to read and write Turkish and was at the top of her class.

My mother's father was a rabbi who taught at a rabbinical school in Turkey, so it is not surprising that her family strictly observed the Jewish traditions. Even in her old age, my mother was still feisty and strong and would often help other elderly people, some of them older than she.

My father's family, however, lived in Sofia, where my father was born on February 18, 1928, the fourth in a family of six sons: Mordechai, Eliezer, David, Nissim, Samuel (Sami), and Yitzhak (often called Zako). Avraham Mizrachi, my grandfather, was a welder who owned a metal shop. He built metal boxes and *Chanukiyot* (Chanukkah menorahs). My father would often tell me how he loved visiting my grandfather at the tin shop. He would drop by each day after school before returning home, sometimes staying until his father closed the shop. My father, Nissim, said he was fascinated to see how his father was so good at building metal objects with his hands. Nissim sometimes dropped by just to say hello and ended up staying for hours.

Nissim was very good with jobs using his hands—a true handyman—especially with gardening. He was a practical person, one of the qualities my mother loved about him. I imagine his love for working with his hands started when he saw his own father working at the tin shop. His love for gardening has been passed on to me. In fact, some of my best teachings come to me when I am tending the garden. When I am doing so, I remember my father and how we have that love of gardening in common.

My grandmother Sofie was known as an accomplished seamstress and a wonderful cook, so much so that she was asked many times to cook for the Jewish schools and their families. Sofie, in fact, was known for being able to cook delicious meals with very few ingredients. My father watched her do so many times, even learning her gift and practicing it through the years. Many years later, while in a detention camp in Cyprus, he was walking by the kitchen when the smell of food drew him in. He asked if he could help, and the cooks welcomed him warmly. It was not long before Nissim's gift, inherited from his mother, elevated him to being one of the top cooks in the camp.

Everybody loved Grandmother Sofie. My cousins and I remember her as an amazing and remarkable woman. She was a very hard worker, always ready to help others. And yet, she was illiterate, never having learned to read or write. But she dearly loved her family, raising her sons and helping to raise and care for all the grandchildren (see photo # 11).

During an interview with my cousin Avraham Kedem in Tel Aviv on January 23, 2017, he reminded me of how Grandmother Sofie cleaned the homes of her daughters-in-law. Each day, she cleaned a different apartment or house. One day, while cleaning Avraham's and his family's apartment in Jaffa, Grandmother Sofie found a rat. Horrified, she chased the rat all over the apartment until she managed to catch it by its tail. Then she promptly took it outside, never to be seen in their apartment again.

During this same interview, Avraham mentioned how their grandmother didn't just help clean their houses, but she helped care for the grandchildren as well. She dearly loved all of them and was so blessed to know they were being raised in the Land of Israel.

One of the duties she helped with was making sure all the grandchildren got their baths. Avraham and I chuckled at the memory of how Sofie would fill the basin or laundry tub with water. Then she lined up the grandchildren and bathed each one, from the oldest to the youngest, in this large basin. Since the water was cold, if the sun was shining, she would fill the basin outside and allow the sun to warm the water. As a result, because I was one of the youngest grandchildren, I usually got the warmest baths, though it's questionable how clean the water was when it got to me.

My grandparents' family in Bulgaria was poor, as were most of the Jews of Bulgaria at that time. They worked hard, lived modestly, and were loyal citizens. On the Holy Days, the family assembled in the synagogue in Sofia. Because they were descended from the Sephardic Jews who were expelled from Spain in 1492, they attended a Sephardic synagogue.

My parents were wonderful storytellers, and I was fascinated with the memories they shared with me and my siblings. One story that has stayed with me all these years took place at the very beginning of World War II, when the Germans were invading Poland. My father was eleven then, and he and his family would gather around the radio and listen to the news of these unnerving events. Rumors had circulated for years that trouble was afoot, but now it was becoming ominously clear that the situation in Europe was changing, and not for the better, at least not for the Jewish people.

I remember how my father recoiled at hearing the voice of Adolf Hitler and the Nazi propaganda over the radio. He could not understand how so much persecution, hatred, and painful words could be spoken against the Jews, against him; nor could he understand how this man and the Nazi party could hate him so much, a boy living in a different nation then theirs. As a Jewish boy, he saw Nazi Germany as a Christian nation as well as a modern, western nation. He struggled to understand how such a nation could cheer and encourage anti-Semitism, especially since the Jews and Christians of Bulgaria lived together in harmony. By the time he was eleven, Nissim found himself fearful of a world that had seemingly turned upside down, being fueled by rising hatred and bigotry. Though he could not explain why, just hearing Hitler speak sent chills down his spine.

A few weeks later, a radio announcement proclaimed that Bulgaria would be having new elections. The Jewish community's concern increased, and for good reason. Things were not going well for the Jewish people in Poland and other places. With political change looming, could the Jews of Bulgaria fare any better?

Anti-Semitism Grows

It was in 1939, about a month after Germany invaded Poland, that the Bulgarian Prime Minister, Georgi Kyoseivanov, resigned, and new elections were held. After the elections, as the Bulgarian government felt increasing pressure to abandon their position of neutrality, Tsar Boris realized the extremely dangerous and precarious position they were in. He knew he had to make a choice of where his loyalties would lie, and he needed to do so quickly, as Bulgaria's very survival could be at stake.

Though not wholeheartedly, the tsar chose to place new people in power, people who were pro-German. One of them was Bodgan Filov, whom he nominated to be Prime Minister. Filov was a professor, a renowned archaeologist and president of the Bulgarian Academy of Science. Before becoming Prime Minister, he served as Minister of Education.

Filov's nomination caused a certain paradox because, on one hand, his loyalty was to Germany; on the other, he was dependent upon the tsar, who could depose him at any moment. In the government established by Filov, Petŭr Gabrovski was appointed Minister of Interior. Gabrovski was a lawyer from Sofia, who with the help of other leaders had established one of Bulgaria's anti-Semitic movements called "Ratnik," an acronym meaning "Warriors for the Advancement of the Bulgarian National Spirit."

Besides Ratnik, two other anti-Semitic movements existed in Bulgaria during this time, the "Legionnaires" (The Union of the Bulgarian National Legions) and the Branick (anti-Semitic organization established for high-school students). Membership in all three of these organizations—Ratnik, Legionnaires, and Branick—amounted to about 60,000 Bulgarian youth and young adults, who were taught in the ways of Nazi Germany with anti-Semitic thought. These organizations were organized and received government support.[10]

On September 20, 1939, some days after the outbreak of the war, fascist groups perpetrated an anti-Semitic attack on the Jewish community of Bulgaria, smashing the windows of Jewish-owned businesses in the

10 | Baruch, "The Jews in Bulgaria," p. 3. http://www.thebulgarianjews.org.il/ Uploads/dbsAttachedFiles/TheJewsNirBaruch.pdf

main streets of Sofia, including my grandfather's tin shop. The initiative for the attack came from Bulgaria's two main anti-Semitic organizations: Ratnik and the Legionnaires.

Following the incident, the Chief Inspector of Police published an announcement on September 21, 1939, requesting the public of Sofia to maintain law and order, and announcing that any perpetrators of such incidents in the future would be dealt with in full accordance with the law. Unfortunately, according to Dr. Moshe Mossek (a Bulgarian Jew who made aliyah to Israel and an expert on this subject), the police did little to stop the anti-Semitic attack.[11] In fact, though the chief of police issued a request for law and order, the people responsible for the damages to the Jewish community were unharmed and even protected during and after the attack.

Prime Minister Bogdan Filov and the Minister of Interior, Petŭr Gabrovski, pushed for the signing of an agreement with Germany. They got their wish when, on June 19, 1940, an agreement of cultural collaboration was signed between Germany and Bulgaria. Then, on June 26, 1940, Filov visited Hitler in Berlin in order to strengthen ties between Germany and the Bulgarians, and ostensibly to discuss what was referred to as the "Jewish Question."

Later on, following Germany's intervention, an agreement was signed on September 7, 1940, in which Romania returned to Bulgaria all of Southern Dobrudja, which Bulgaria had lost following her defeat in World War I. Germany's influence in having this territory returned to Bulgaria brought the two countries closer together, and Bulgaria saw Germany as a key state that would enable her to retrieve all the territories she had previously lost.

Though I've heard stories from my family of what it was like for the nearly 50,000 Bulgarian Jews at that time, I can only imagine how grim the future appeared to them, as the frightening rumors of change seemed destined to become reality.

---

11 | On December 18, 2020, Dr. Moshe Mossek lectured on the Bulgarian Jews during the Holocaust, and I was honored to participate. Mossek was the former director of the Israel State Archives and the Gnazim Institute of the Hebrew Writer's Association of Israel.

CHAPTER 3

The Bill for the Defense of the Nation

After the anti-Semitic attack on the Jewish community of Bulgaria on September 20, 1939, resulting in the destruction of many Jewish businesses including my grandfather's tin shop, the community was determined to rebuild. But when The Bill for the Defense of the Nation—also known as the Bill for the Protection of the Nation—passed in January 1941, rebuilding was no longer an option, as the bill forbade Jewish Bulgarians from having certain jobs or retaining and using their money. Not only did the law prevent the Jewish community from working at most jobs or rebuilding their businesses, it also affected nearly every aspect of their personal lives, including the very real fear of the possibility of being deported into the clutches of the Nazis.

Effects on My Family

My father was no exception. Along with all the members of his family, Nissim was a devout Jew. As such, he greatly anticipated his Bar Mitzvah (literally, "son of the commandment"), which would take place when he turned thirteen in February 1941.[1] The Bar Mitzvah is undeniably the most important event in a Jewish boy's life, one he studies and prepares for throughout his younger years but particularly during the year preceding his thirteenth birthday.

Nissim had wholeheartedly prepared for this monumental event, studying with Rabbi Zion to learn the many Jewish prayers and blessings. That year leading up to the Bar Mitzvah is also the time when the young man invites his family and friends to come and celebrate this joyous day with him. How Nissim yearned for and anticipated this wonderful celebration!

1 | Bar Mitzvah: The coming-of-age ceremony for Jewish boys, age thirteen.

And then The Bill for the Defense of the Nation was announced in October 1940, just a few months before Nissim's Bar Mitzvah. As a result of the bill becoming law, not only was he unable to celebrate his long-awaited day, he could no longer attend his beloved youth group meetings, which were closed down as a result of the law. His heart was crushed as he walked to the synagogue with his father, Avraham, asking some hard questions along the way. How could so much have changed in so short a time? And how was he to know what else might change in the near future?

For the first time, Nissim found himself questioning his Jewishness, something he had previously considered a great honor. He wondered aloud why he had been born Jewish, even daring to consider how much better his life might have been if he were not Jewish. He pondered the many biblical stories he had read about how his ancestors had suffered, time and again, and he wondered why the Jewish people, if they were indeed chosen by God, were so hated and persecuted by others.

"Why is this law only for us Jews?" he asked his father. "Why, just because I'm Jewish, am I not able to do things or go places like my non-Jewish friends?"

Though my grandfather Avraham was not always able to give his son clear, direct answers, he did his best to encourage Nissim to hold tight to his faith. Sadly, less than a month later, in November 1940, my father and his family experienced another crushing blow when my grandfather, Avraham Mizrachi, died of a heart attack.

Avraham had been having chest pains for some time, no doubt at least in part stress-related as a result of wondering how he would support his family now that he might no longer run his business or get a job. Whatever little money they had was used for food, with nothing left over for doctor's visits. Then, on his way home one night, he was beaten by pro-Nazis from one of the anti-Semitic organizations, triggering the heart attack that killed him at the age of fifty-two.

And so, the head of their family was gone, leaving my grandmother widowed and the children fatherless, a story that would play out far too often in the lives of many other Jewish families of the time. Like so many other Jewish individuals in pre-World War II Europe, the approximately 50,000 Jewish people living in Bulgaria in 1940 just prior to the passing and enactment of The Law for the Defense of the Nation—a mere one percent of the total Bulgarian population—had no idea how bad things would get in the coming years.

Descent into Darkness

When speaking of the Bulgarians who persecuted the Jewish people during that dark era, three key names come to mind: Bogdan Filov, Petŭr Gabrovski, and Alexander Belev. As previously mentioned, Filov was an ally of Tsar Boris III and served as Prime Minister during World War II, while Gabrovski served as Bulgaria's Minister of Interior during that same time. Alexander Belev was appointed Bulgarian Commissar of Jewish Affairs. Filled with anti-Semitic hatred and a desire to see all Jews exterminated, Belev actively persecuted the Jews of Bulgaria.

In the summer of 1940, Minister of Interior Petŭr Gabrovski sent Alexander Belev to Germany. Belev, a well-known lawyer who worked under Gabrovski's protection, was head of the legal department of the Ministry of Interior as well as being in charge of the Department of Jewish Affairs. As legal advisor of the Ministry of Interior and one of the leaders of the anti-Semitic organization Ratnik, Belev, as described by one of his colleagues, was "dedicated to the annihilation of the Jews."[2] Of the three Bulgarian officials, Belev was, in fact, considered the "worst of the worst" when it came to his desire to obliterate the Jewish people.

Belev was so fervent in his hatred toward the Jews that he became the Bulgarian official responsible for executing the Nazi's "Final Solution to the Jewish Question" for the Jews of

Bulgaria. What began as widespread persecution and repression at the start of the war in Europe quickly escalated to mass murder. Whole towns of Jews—men, women, and children—were led to the outskirts of their villages where they were forced to dig their own graves, then line up and

2 | Bar Zohar, *Hitler's Grasp*, p. 52.

be shot. In some towns, Jews were locked in their community synagogues and burned alive.

As the war progressed, the bloodlust of the Nazis boiled over, and a plan was created for systematic annihilation of the Jewish people, the Final Solution. "The term 'Final Solution of the Jewish Question' was a euphemism used by Nazi Germany's leaders, referring to the mass murder of Europe's Jews. It brought an end to policies aimed at encouraging or forcing Jews to leave the German Reich and other parts of Europe. Those policies were replaced by systematic annihilation."[3]

The plan involved first moving Jews into overcrowded wall ghettos, which allowed the Nazis to easily monitor them. Food was scarce and disease ran rampant in these ghettos that existed in most major European cities under Nazi control. "During the Holocaust, the creation of ghettos was a key step in the Nazi process of brutally separating, persecuting, and ultimately destroying Europe's Jews. Jews were forced to move into ghettos, where living conditions were miserable. Ghettos were often enclosed districts that isolated Jews from the non-Jewish population and from other Jewish communities."[4] The ghettos, as terrible as they were, existed as a holding place before Jews were transported to death camps, such as Auschwitz and Treblinka. The lives of millions of Jews were cut short in the death camps by asphyxiation at the hand of the Nazis using Zyklon B gas. The completion of the Final Solution would have meant total eradication of the Jewish people from the earth. It did not matter where they lived or their gender or age; if at least one of their parents or grandparents was Jewish, they were destined to die, for no other reason than that they had Jewish blood.

Belev's primary role and mission during the war was the extermination of the entire

Jewish population of Bulgaria, though he also played a key role in the deportation of the 12,000 Jewish individuals from Macedonia and Thrace

3 | The Final Solution, *United States Holocaust Memorial Museum*, https://encyclopedia.ushmm.org/content/en/article/final-solution-overview.

4 | The Jewish Question, *United States Holocaust Memorial Museum*, https://encyclopedia.ushmm.org/content/en/article/ghettos

(territories under Bulgarian administration). All three men—Bogdan Filov, Petur Gabrovski, and Alexander Belev—were closely allied with and supportive of Nazi Germany; however, some have argued that Belev was the worst because of his overtly zealous persecution.

One of Gabrovski's purposes in sending Belev to Germany was to study the Nuremberg Laws (anti-Semitic, racist laws enacted in Germany on September 15, 1935, at a special meeting of the Reichstag during the annual Nuremberg Rally of the Nazi Party). On October 10, 1940, Gabrovski, strongly influenced by Nazi thinking, announced "The Bill for the [Defense] of the Nation," emphasizing that it was directed first and foremost at the Jewish population in Bulgaria.[5] In November 1940, the bill was presented for ratification by Parliament.

Point of Controversy

The bill was a point of controversy among members of the Bulgarian Parliament, where representatives of the parties of the people—the Democratic party, the Social Democratic party, and most of the members of the Communist party—opposed the proposed law. However, the bill was ratified by a majority of the members of Parliament. It was then signed on January 21, 1941, and endorsed by Tsar Boris III.

In this law, the Jewish people were depicted as the enemies of the Bulgarian people and a danger to the country's very existence. They were also described as acting against the interests of the state and preventing the Bulgarian people from creating or maintaining certain values.

The bill was composed of three main sections. The first referred to international and undercover organizations; the second, to people of Jewish descent; the third was a set of general instructions with the intent to limit, as far as possible, the freedom of the Bulgarian Jews. The first part of the bill affected the Zionist movement in Bulgaria. For example, HaShomer HaTsa'ir, the youth movement my father belonged to, was shut down.

The other two parts of the bill directly harmed the local Jewish

5 | Haim Kechales, *Korot Yehude Balgaryah, The Shoah* (Tkofat Ha'shoah, Tel Aviv, 1969), pp. 40-41.

population. For instance, according to the Bill, one was considered Jewish if he had at least one Jewish parent. All Jewish people were required to report to the authorities within one month to declare they were indeed Jewish and to specifically declare all their property. They were also required to deposit all their cash in closed bank accounts and were not able to withdraw funds without permission from the government.

In addition to the requirement that all Jews declare their ethnicity, they were not allowed to vote or be elected to public office, and those currently in office were obliged to resign. They were required to use their Hebrew names and were forbidden to use family names considered to be Bulgarian. Restrictions were placed on food items they were permitted to purchase, including where they could purchase them. The number of Jewish individuals permitted to study in schools of higher education was limited to their representation in the general population, meaning less than one percent.

All these prohibitions and others were included in The Law for the Defense of the Nation. In addition to the bill requiring all Jewish people to declare their ethnicity, they were also forbidden to marry or have sexual relations with a man or woman of Bulgarian extract. They were not permitted to own real estate such as land, apartments, or houses. They would not be allowed to live in Sofia in the future and were forbidden to change their domicile without police permission.

Bulgarian Jews were also not permitted to own shares in business or real estate, or to hold administrative positions. They were forbidden to work in the free professions of commerce or industry. The government was authorized to set limits on Jewish investment in certain industries, and they had to declare all their assets. They were forbidden to invest or participate in the cinema, the theater, in commercials, or in publishing firms. The Bulgarian Jews were not permitted to belong to administrative councils, to serve as legal advisors, managers, commercial representatives, or to own a pharmacy. The Law for the Defense of the Nation was intended to deprive the Bulgarian Jewish community of all rights and to weaken them financially.

Outcries of Support

The law caused a wave of public outcry from all levels of Bulgarian society, from the illiterate farmers to those in key social positions. The public objections revealed the way the nation truly felt when it came to their Jewish population.

Just days after The Bill for the Defense of the Nation was proposed in October 1940, the government offices in parliament were flooded with letters of protest from all corners of the state and all strata of society. This included writers, doctors, lawyers, professors, artists, heads of the church, ministers, and former heads of state, among others.

The Church's Efforts

As previously stated, the Orthodox Church in Bulgaria was actively involved in trying to prevent the bill from becoming law. Metropolitan Stefan of Sofia was at the forefront of this struggle, trying desperately to defend the country's Jewish population, many of whom were close friends and neighbors. There was little if any separation or conflict between the Bulgarian Jews and the Christians of Bulgaria at that time, as evidenced by the church's efforts to save their Jewish population.

On November 12, 1940, a special meeting was held of the Holy Synod, the most elite body of the Bulgarian Church.[6] The eight metropolitans, including Stefan, took part in the meeting and discussed The Law for the Defense of the Nation and the Jewish minority. Among other things, the metropolitans stated that the law sharply contradicted Christian principles and the values of the state they had known so far. They also stated that the Jews of Bulgaria had never harmed the state and had, in fact, fought on her behalf in previous wars, particularly World War I.

During the discussion, one metropolitan by the name of Michael of Dorostol and Cherven even noted that the Jewish people were the most

6 | "The Session of 12 November 1940 of the All-Member Meeting of the Holy Synod of the Bulgarian Orthodox Church," in *The Power of Civil Society in a Time of Genocide: Proceedings of the Holy Synod of the Bulgarian Orthodox Church on the Jews in Bulgaria 1940-1945*, ed. by Albena Taneva and Ivanka Gezenko (Sofia: Sofia University Press St. Kliment Ohridski, 2005), pp. 51-59.

generous people he knew. He went on to say it was the duty of the church to ensure fair and proper treatment of the Jewish population on the part of the governmental officials. Another metropolitan, Paisiy of Vratza, noted that if the Bulgarian government passed and enacted such legislation, there was a good chance the Jewish population would be forced to flee from Bulgaria. If that happened, the Church would lose one of its main missions, which was to bring the Jewish people to faith in Yeshua, to "provoke them to jealousy" over the salvation of the Gentiles, as stated in the Book of Romans.

The metropolitan went on to say that as shepherds of the church, their duty was to preach the gospel and to dedicate their lives to God, not to man. According to Paisiy, the persecution of the Jewish people strictly because they were Jewish contradicted justice and the Christian gospel; therefore, they—the church leaders—must raise their voices against the proposed bill. In addition, the meeting concluded that it was the responsibility of the metropolitans to be more like Peter, as written in Acts 5:29: "'We ought to obey God rather than men'" (NKJV). All eight metropolitans signed the protocol of the meeting, a courageous step of faith when you consider the political climate in Europe at the time.

After publication of the [proposed] Bill for the Defense of the Nation, another meeting of the Holy Synod was convened on November 15, 1940.[7] Present at this meeting were Stefan of Sofia, Kiril of Plovdiv, Paisiy of Vratza, and the metropolitans of Turnovo, Dorostol, and Cherven, Lovech, Varna, and Preslav. Together they published a joint declaration, which read: "...The Church considers it her duty, however, precisely for the benefit of the nation, to draw the attention of the competent authorities to several defects in the proposed law, which could have bad consequences, and which also touch the Church as a divine institution, whose duty it is to watch over all her spiritual children and cause the will of God to rule in the cause of righteousness and mercy among human beings and the nations."[8]

7 | Ibid, p. 66.

8 | Snoek, *The Grey Book*, pp. 181-183a.

The decision was unanimous and signed by all the leaders of the Bulgarian Church.

Metropolitan Stefan's Ongoing Support

On November 23, 1940, Metropolitan Stefan sent a letter to all the clergy in the district of Sofia, stressing the need to warmly receive the Jewish people into the Christian Church.[9] He explained that the Orthodox Church is forbidden to close its doors to the Jewish community, for perhaps in such a time God would reveal Himself to His people, Israel. Stefan said the time may have come when the Jew and the Gentile would be one in Christ, noting Isaiah 59:20, which says, "The Redeemer shall come to Zion, And to those who turn from transgression in Jacob" (NKJV).

Stefan then went on to quote from Romans 11: "God has not rejected His people whom He knew beforehand. …just as it is written, 'God gave them a spirit of stupor, eyes not to see and ears not to hear, until this very day. ...Now if their transgression leads to riches for the world, and their loss riches for the Gentiles, then how much more their fullness! … For if you were cut out of that which by nature is a wild olive tree, and grafted contrary to nature into a cultivated olive tree, how much more will these natural branches be grafted into their own olive tree? For I do not want you, brothers and sisters, to be ignorant of this mystery—lest you be wise in your own eyes—that a partial hardening has come upon Israel until the fullness of the Gentiles has come in; and in this way all Israel will be saved, as it is written, 'The Deliverer shall come out of Zion. He shall turn away ungodliness from Jacob'" (vv. 2, 8, 12, 24-26, TLV).

Stefan then wrote that perhaps the time had come for God to remove the veil from the hearts of the people of Israel (see 2 Corinthians 3:14-16). Stefan called on all the priests (pastors of the congregation) to set an

9 | "11/23/1940 of the Sofia Diocese on the Acceptance of the Jews in the Arms of the Orthodox Church," in *The Power of Civil Society in a Time of Genocide: Proceedings of the Holy Synod of the Bulgarian Orthodox Church on the Jews in Bulgaria 1940-1945*, ed. by Albena Taneva and Ivanka Gezenko (Sofia: Sofia University Press St. Kliment Ohridski, 2005), pp. 75-79.

example to the Jewish people in those evil days in order to show them the light of [Yeshua].

Finally, the Metropolitan wrote that they must do all things to the glory of God, and he quoted from the Epistle to the Colossians: "And whatever you do in word or deed, *do* all in the name of the Lord Jesus, giving thanks to God the Father through Him" (3:17, NKJV).

Stefan's passion for protecting and rescuing the Jewish people was profoundly evident throughout his letter, moving many who read it to tears. He also encouraged Christians to be a living example to the Jewish people, modeling the love of Yeshua to them. Stefan's words were a much-needed light shining in a very dark time.

Defending God's Chosen People

These strong examples of the Bulgarian Church's help and support for their Jewish population was in stark contrast to much of what happened in other European countries at that time. While the German Nazi army was taking over large swaths of Europe, the vast majority of Christian churches in those occupied countries registered hardly any opposition to the plans of Adolf Hitler regarding the Jewish Question or the Final Solution.[10] There were, of course, individual exceptions throughout Europe, Christians who risked their very lives to rescue Jewish people, but they were the minority.

The Bulgarian Orthodox Church was exceptional in its entirety because it openly and actively opposed the Nazi ideology during the Second World War. The Bulgarian Church also served as a practical example of good will toward the Jewish population throughout the history of Judeo-Christian relations, not only during World War II. In contrast to the history of cruel Christian persecution of the Jews, such as the Crusades, the Spanish Inquisition, pogroms, etc., the Bulgarian Church lived in peace and tranquility with their Jewish population. Anti-Semitism existed in

---

10 | This does not mean that there were not Christians who stood by the Jewish people. Some individuals and leaders supported and tried to help them, but they were in the minority. Among the heroic and courageous stories of Christians who risked their lives on behalf of the Jews was of Corrie Ten Boom's family in Holland and their sacrifice in order to save Jewish people.

Bulgaria, but it was a rare phenomenon, especially among the Christian clergy.

The Holy Scriptures teach that God chose the people of Israel 4,000 years earlier to keep His commandments and to be a light to the (Gentile) nations. Since then, the Jewish people have suffered through many anti-Semitic persecutions which, at times, brought them to despair. In my opinion, the Bulgarian Church held to a different approach than what was common in Europe. In return, the Jews of Bulgaria appreciated the Bulgarian Church for her moral stance and her good relations with them, particularly during the time preceding and throughout World War II.

For instance, during the war, the Bulgarian Church exemplified Christian, moral, and humane values. These Christians felt they needed to act on behalf of the Jewish people to prevent Bulgaria's good name from being tarnished. The Bulgarian Church, as a whole, acted on behalf of the Jews of Bulgaria throughout the war and thus played a key role in saving them from the hands of the Nazis. These Christians fought for the Jewish population and strove to defend and save them from mass destruction. It is stunning to think how the church went to such measures in order to safeguard their Jewish friends and neighbors, who were less than one percent of the entire Bulgarian population and not even part of their congregation. At the same time, there were some in the Jewish community who applied to the Church for baptism, despite the governmental prohibition against the Church baptizing known Jews.[11] It is possible they thought Christian baptism might save them from the death camps.

This phenomenon created a dilemma among the Christian clergy, but in the end, without exception, they decided to do all they could to save the Bulgarian Jews from deportation, even if it meant baptizing some who were not in the least interested in the Christian faith. The clergy felt they were acting in accordance with the highest value of all: the saving of lives. Furthermore, such Bulgarian Jews who had undergone baptism by decision

11 | Albena Taneva, "The Rescue of the Jews in Bulgaria: An Old Theme in a New Political SCIENCE Interpretation," in *The Power of Civil Society in a Time of Genocide: Proceedings of the Holy Synod of the Bulgarian Orthodox Church on the Jews in Bulgaria 1940-194*, ed. by Albena Taneva and Ivanka Gezenko (Sofia: Sofia University Press St. Kliment Ohridski, 2005), pp. 18-19; 26-29.

of the church were not obliged to celebrate Christian holidays, and the church encouraged them to preserve their Jewish identity. This was indeed rare treatment and behavior by Christians during that time.[12]

To summarize, the church was especially pro-active in protecting Bulgaria's Jews during the months of November and December of 1940:

- they held two meetings on this subject on November 12 and 15, composing a strong pronouncement of their stand at the second meeting;
- Stefan wrote his powerful letter of biblical defense of the Jewish people on November 23;
- the church leaders decided unanimously that because saving lives was their priority, they would do fake baptisms for those who requested it.

Additional Letters of Protest

Many more letters of protest were written and sent. For instance, one letter sent to Prime Minister Filov, with a copy to the chairman of the Parliament, was signed by twenty-one well-known Bulgarian writers. The letter read: "We the undersigned, Bulgarian writers, find it right to address his Honor with the following request: on the 8th of the month the words of the Minister of Interior were published, from which it is clear that the government has decided to present Parliament with a Bill for the [Defense] of the Nation. From the words of the minister it has become clear that by this Bill all civil rights will be taken away from one of the minorities in our country. We are very surprised and ashamed that the idea to legislate such a law could have arisen in Bulgaria at a time when there is no danger to our nation from any side. We are of the opinion that such a law will harm our people. The forces of law should not allow legislation of a law that will enslave a part of the Bulgarian people and write a black

12 | Albena Taneva and Ivanka Gezenko, "The Bulgarian Orthodox Church: 1200 Years of Unique History and Traditions," in *The Power of Civil Society in a Time of Genocide: Proceedings of the Holy Synod of the Bulgarian Orthodox Church on the Jews in Bulgaria 1940-1945*, ed. by Albena Taneva and Ivanka Gezenko (Sofia: Sofia University Press St. Kliment Ohridski, 2005), pp. 36-37.

page on our modern history. ...In the name of culture and for the good name of Bulgaria, we ask you to prevent legislation of a law whose results will darken the constitution of our state and will leave behind dark and heavy memories."[13]

An additional letter of protest was sent from the Union of Doctors to Minister of Interior Gabrovski: "Mr. Minister, the union of Bulgarian doctors, being an apolitical organization, cannot sit by passively and apathetically regarding the great issues that stand to be resolved before the people of Bulgaria. Such an issue is at this moment the proposed Bill for the [Defense] of the Nation, which is soon to be brought before Parliament for discussion ...the Union of Doctors asks to emphasize... that the people of Bulgaria are able to preserve their national character... and doesn't see any danger to the purity of our people...on the basis of the above and the accepted premise that the Jews of Bulgaria have always been loyal citizens in every sense, the union of Bulgarian doctors, as a professional organization alone, cannot remain apathetic regarding the fate of their friends—doctors of Jewish descent. In bringing this to your attention we request the honourable minister to do all that is possible to prevent the restrictions mentioned in the bill, a thing that would express the minister's sense of humanity and justice."[14]

A particularly strong letter came from the leader of the Social Democratic Party, Mr. Christo Ponev: "How will such 'leaders' as these manage with the new generation which is being educated in a spirit of hatred and injustice...the Anti-Jewish movement has developed only in the uncultured parts of our public. The Antisemitism that exists today in several cultured countries is simply a means to achieve economic and political goals. In view of this...is not now the time to ask ourselves: Who is this enemy, who are these traitors, who for their own personal interest bring such shame and confusion upon the lives of the people..."[15]

13 | Kechales, *The Shoah*, pp. 43-44.

14 | Ibid, p. 45.

15 | Ibid, pp. 48-49.

Ulterior Motives Finally Exposed

The Jews of Bulgaria now sensed the approaching days of terror and the knowledge that a time of suffering would soon be upon them. In the streets of the Jewish community, rumors ran rampant over the passing of The Law for the Defense of the Nation. The Jewish people, quite rightly, felt the purpose of the bill was to eradicate them physically, spiritually, and materially.

Finally, the *State Gazette*, Newspaper no. 16, owned by the Government of Bulgaria, published the bill on January 23, 1941, and it became law. The Jewish people saw the law as the first step of war against them, a step that would ultimately lead to their destruction. The immediate effect of the law was that thousands of Bulgarian Jews were cut off from economic life. Jewish workers had to leave the factories and workshops belonging to the "Aryan" race, just as Jewish doctors, lawyers, pharmacists, clerks, and others were forced to leave or terminate their employment.

As stated earlier, this included my grandfather Avraham who, because of the new bill, would have his tin shop taken from him. The deterioration of his health soon followed, leading to the stress that undoubtedly contributed to his fatal heart attack. Jewish people throughout Bulgaria now despaired over how they would support their families.

I remember my father telling me how he felt when he saw my grandmother lock the shop for the last time. My father remembered coming back from school, planning to stop by and say hello as he often did before going home, but he immediately realized something was wrong. My grandmother and older brothers had gathered their things and had them in their arms when, with a sad but brave face, my grandmother closed and locked the family's shop, never to see it again. My father told me how sad and helpless he felt at that moment, how unjust the world seemed to have become. He felt hopeless, knowing he could not stop this evil from overcoming his family. His parents, who were loyal citizens, were now deprived of their store for no reason other than being Jewish. When my father shared this memory with me, he did so with tears in his eyes, and then he became serious and immediately changed the subject.

As a Jewish man, my heart is pained when I consider the extent of evil purposed against my people at that dark point in history. It was indeed a sad time for the citizens of Bulgaria in general and for its Jewish population specifically. However, without providential help, it would have been much worse.

CHAPTER 4

Bulgaria as One of the Axis States

I have heard others question—and have even wondered myself—how anyone could possibly ally themselves with such an evil entity as Nazi Germany. And yet, there is always more to such a story than we might think. The tenuous relationship between Bulgaria and Germany is the perfect example.

Joining the Tripartite Axis

The governments of Germany and Bulgaria signed an agreement on August 23, 1940. As a result, Southern Dobruja was returned to Bulgaria. Then, on January 15, 1941, Germany announced it was prepared to ensure Bulgaria access to the White Sea, between the Struma and Maritza rivers, on condition that Bulgaria join the Tripartite Axis (a coalition of states/countries headed by Germany, Italy, and Japan, which opposed the Allied powers in World War II). On March 1, 1941, some months after ratification of the Law for the Defense of the Nation, the government of Bulgaria announced it had joined the Axis, giving up the neutrality it had declared at the beginning of World War II.

Prime Minister Filov also signed the Tripartite Pact, giving the German army permission to enter the territory of Bulgaria. Germany's army quickly crossed the border in order to prepare for the invasion of Greece and Russia. In return, Germany bestowed on Bulgaria the territories of Macedonia, part of conquered Yugoslavia, and Western Thrace, part of conquered Greece.

The significance of Bulgaria's inclusion in the Tripartite Axis was the acceptance of Nazi Germany's public and political ideology. German economics and political control also increased Germany's cultural influence on Bulgaria. Anti-Semitic organizations were encouraged and supported by the Nazi party and stepped up their activities in disseminating Nazi ideology among the Bulgarian people.

De Facto Labor Camps

The Bulgarian Government published an order on May 1, 1941, requiring all Jewish men between the ages of twenty and forty to report to government-run camps where they would work in special labor battalions. These *de facto* labor camps were not the death camps of Poland, and some were slightly better than others; however, they were far from pleasant.

The prominent theory for the establishment of such camps is that the king saw it as a way to keep the Nazis from insisting the Bulgarian government send them all their Jews, which would have been much worse than their enduring the hardships of Bulgaria's labor camps. Each time Germany pressured the king to deport the Bulgarian Jews—which happened time and again throughout the war—the king responded that he needed them to work on maintaining roads, buildings, and other infrastructures. The king and many others believed that "proving" to Nazi Germany that they needed the Jewish people for their own purposes was the only way to save them from deportation.

This was a difficult tightrope to walk for the small country of Bulgaria, being allies of Germany yet trying to keep their Jewish population in Bulgaria. Even as Germany pushed the king to hand them over, others within Bulgaria, including Rabbi Daniel and Metropolitan Stefan, urged him to do whatever was necessary to protect them. Though many believe the conditions of Bulgaria's work camps should have been better, they did seem to serve the purpose of keeping their Jewish population within Bulgarian boundaries. It is important to remember that these were forced labor camps, bestowed on the Jewish men just because they were Jewish.

Jewish Participation in Bulgaria's Military

When I interviewed retired Colonel Professor Dimitar Nedialkov (now a professor at the National Institute for Military History in Bulgaria) on September 27, 2020, he explained that the labor camps during the years 1940-1942 were run by the military. The men in these camps, which were not as harsh at that time as they were later in the war, were required to do physical civil duty (labor in lieu of military or other types of service). Until 1941, the Bulgarian army still included Jewish officers, noncommissioned officers, and soldiers, about 2,000 in all.

Nedialkov also explained that the first thing the Nazi Germany representatives noticed when Bulgaria joined the Axis pact was that Jewish soldiers, even soldiers in authority, existed within the Bulgarian army. The Germans were furious that the Bulgarian army leaders would let the "enemy" serve in their military.

The Bulgarian Minister of War tried to explain to the German representatives that the Jewish community had been a part of the military for years and were integrated into the system. In fact, the Jewish community was a big part of the army from the end of the 19th century until the beginning of the 20th century. For example, 7,300 Jewish soldiers fought in the Bulgarian army in World War I. During that time, about 40,000 Jewish people lived in Bulgaria. Allowing for the portion of that number who were women, children, and the elderly, that left a large percentage of the Jewish men who volunteered and enlisted in the army.

The professor told me many stories about how those heroic Jewish soldiers fought during the Balkan wars and World War I. The military leaders and soldiers never forgot the Jewish soldiers' sacrifices, and they appreciated them and looked upon them with honor and respect. Fighting together in the trenches during the wars brought about a special honor, love, respect, and dignity between the Jewish and non-Jewish soldier. This also brought about friendships and tolerance between the soldiers and their families. As a result, the entire Bulgarian population developed a respect for those valiant Jewish soldiers.

Despite the explanation by the Bulgarian Minister of War, the Nazi German representatives were not convinced, and they pressured the Bulgarian government and the army to let go all their soldiers of

Jewish descent. In the end, despite the resistance of many who valued the contributions of the Jewish soldiers, that is exactly what happened.

Creative Ways to Save Bulgarian Jews

The professor explained to me that as a result of this, the army generals were concerned about the Jewish population and gathered together to search for a solution. This was when they came up with the idea that they should have work-labor stations, like work camps, where they could use the Jewish men as labor power to build up the country in order to strengthen Bulgaria in time of war. They felt they needed to prove to Germany that Bulgaria needed its Jewish community—i.e., to "use or abuse" them—in order to keep them in Bulgaria. However, in 1943, these camps were turned over to the charge of the Commissariat for the Jewish Question in Bulgaria. At that point, the treatment of the Jewish laborers within these camps became brutal and harsh, about which there are countless stories.

Since the authority primarily went to the commissariat and Belev was the head of the commissariat, he saw these camps as a way to gather and collect the Jewish people at certain places in order to more easily turn them over to the Nazis. On the other hand, some army generals still saw these camps, however brutal, as the only way to save the Jewish population from the Nazi gas chambers.

During the interview, Professor Nedialkov told me of a colonel by the name of Tsvetan Mumdzhiev, who gave official papers (passes) to about 100 Jewish people, some of whom were from Thrace and Macedonia, as well as Bulgaria. These passes stated that these Jewish individuals could not be deported but could move freely in the Bulgarian state. The colonel distributed these papers in secret, though it presented a danger for him. Because of his respect and honor for the Jewish soldiers, however, he could not turn his back on them. As it turned out, these papers saved many lives.

As one of the overseers of the labor camps, Colonel Mumdzhiev also worked to improve conditions for the Jewish men. He considered them soldiers, though formally they were not. Mumdzhiev aimed for reasonable work shifts, giving them medical treatment and emergency leave to attend to urgent family matters. He viewed the Jews as neighbors and comrades, opposing the anti-Semitic officers who had beaten and extorted the Jewish men.[1]

Professor Nedialkov believed that this story, as well as the fact that numerous army officials looked for and found creative ways to save the Jewish Bulgarians from deportation, was an example of how the military can be used for saving lives and for contributing to the better overall good of the nation. In the professor's opinion, the Jews of Bulgaria were saved because of the collective efforts of the Bulgarian nation, including the king, the heads of the church, and many throughout the Bulgarian population and their military. Though their combined efforts saved less than one percent of the entire worldwide Jewish population, all involved believed it was a worthy effort.

Memories of a Trying Time

Ultimately, the Bulgarians believed that the labor camps were the only way to save the Bulgarian Jews from the gas chambers. And yet, in the end, the reason these men were forced to go to labor camps in the first place was for no reason other than being Jewish.

When the Jewish men were ordered to go to these camps and join the labor battalions, this included my grandparents' two oldest sons, my uncles Mordecai and Eliezer Mizrachi. Mordecai was the eldest son, a hard-working young man of caring and responsible character, and also the family's primary provider after the death of my grandfather, Avraham. My uncle Eliezer helped support the family as well, so to lose both of them at once was hard on the family financially. Also, during this time, my uncle Mordecai was married to my lovely and gentle aunt Roza. He had just recently become a father for the first time when my cousin Avraham Kedem was born. When Mordecai was ordered to go to these camps, my aunt Roza and cousin Avraham moved in with my father and grandmother

1 | Military Hero: Tale of Bulgarian Commander Tsvetan Mumdzhiev, *Gariwo*, https://en.gariwo.net/righteous/shoah-and-nazism/military-hero-7772.html.

Sofie. As a father myself, I can only imagine how difficult it was for my uncle to leave his wife and baby, not knowing what the future would bring or if they would ever see each other again.

Known for his "big brother" demeanor, Mordecai had always sought to care for his younger siblings. Eliezer, on the other hand, was the second son, known for being intelligent and reasonable. He was, by nature, more philosophical than his siblings, and he enjoyed reading and learning. Though the family was poor and could not afford much in the way of a formal education, Eliezer was still respected in the community as an intelligent young man.

All of this took place around the time my grandfather died, when my grandmother became a widow and a single mother with four boys to care for at home, including my father, Nissim. It was a very difficult time for her, and she was grateful when Rabbi Daniel and his wife, Rachel, reached out to her and helped whenever they could. My father specifically remembers Rabbi Daniel coming to the house and bringing some of his family's meager rations to share with our family, as he often did for other families in need. He also remembers the rabbi's many words of encouragement and faith, which were often difficult for Nissim, then thirteen, to understand or accept.

My father recalled one time in particular when Rabbi Daniel and his wife came over, and Nissim noticed the rabbi's ring, which his parents had given him. Rabbi Daniel explained to my father that the Hebrew letters engraved on the ring, *alef-alef-alef*, represented truth, faith, and love. My father said his heart was sad when he heard the rabbi's words because he immediately wondered, *How can truth, faith, and love exist in this dark time we're living through right now?*

The rabbi laid his hand on Nissim's shoulder and, as if in answer to the boy's unspoken question, said, "Even in my darkest times, these words give me comfort and hope."

Nissim still was not convinced, pondering how anyone could have faith or hope when the situation got worse by the day. How could anyone believe so strongly in God in such a dark hour? And yet, he stored the wise rabbi's words in his heart and later credited his visits and encouraging words for helping him hold on to his own shaky faith in the God of Avraham, Yitzhak, and Yaakov.

I remember my father telling me how the rabbi would say the blessings with great authority, honor, and love to God, King of the universe. It was an example my father would later emulate in future years. But until then, he had to wrestle with the Jewish community's growing horror and despondency over their situation, including the absence of Nissim's two older brothers, my uncles, when they were sent to the camps.

The Bulgarian labor camps were a type of work camp, where the Jewish men performed hard forced labor in difficult conditions. In each of the camps, the Jewish labor battalions were given backbreaking work, often beyond acceptable work hours, were treated badly by those in charge, and were, for the most part, deprived of any contact with their families. There was a shortage of food, and the men slept in uninsulated shacks and tents exposed to the elements. The sleeping quarters were infected with fleas and lice, the guards were vulgar and cruel, and the men were regularly beaten.

Dr. Shlomo Shealtiel, historian and expert on Bulgarian Jews in the 20th century, explains that the labor camps were in the forests, and the work was executed in malaria-infested grounds, which brought much damage to the men's health.[2] The regime in the working camps was severely strict and carried out brutal punishments, causing the Jewish men to feel they were deprived of their basic human rights. The labor included making roads through the mountains, maintaining train tracks, digging canals, clearing rock, and much more. Under the supervision of the Bulgarian army (both soldiers and officers), the men worked throughout the daylight hours. These Jewish men were recruited for slave labor during spring, summer, fall, and occasionally during part of the winter months.[3]

According to the October 5, 2001, testimony of Benjamin Hanne (now living in Netanya, Israel), who was kept in a work camp by the Bulgarian

---

2 | Shlomo Shealtiel, *Youthful Innocence and Passion for Achievement: Hashomer Hatzair Movement in Bulgaria 1923-2020* (Yad Yaari and Moreshet, Givat Haviva, 2021), p. 125.
3 | Ibid.

government from 1941 until 1944, "The concentration camp of Eny Kyoi near the town of Xanti was established on the 4th or 5th of September 1941. ... I was sent to the camp as soon as I completed my high school studies. The camp was fenced in with barbed wire and at every corner there was a watchtower guarded with armed guards. ... We were not allowed to receive food from outside the camp. The sick did not receive any medical care. Among the inmates there were some good doctors but the medication was nowhere near enough. ... Tropical fever and other diseases were our lot, and those who suffered the most were the older ones and those with chronic diseases. ... Lice and other noxious pests spread through the camp quickly... we were subjected to cruel beatings, as a result of which I lost an eye and have remained crippled until today." [4]

Bulgaria and the Final Solution

On June 25, 1941, by decree of the Minister of Interior, Petŭr Gabrovski, all Bulgarian Jews were forbidden to discuss political-public subjects and were forbidden to be on the street or in any public place between 9 P.M. and 6 A.M. Those who disobeyed the curfew were subject to arrest or exile from the borders of Bulgaria.

As mentioned earlier and noted in the Population Survey of 1940, Bulgaria had nearly 50,000 Jews, half of whom lived in the capital, Sofia. Following the annexation of Macedonia and Thrace to Bulgaria, some 12,000 Jewish individuals were added to Bulgarian territory, bringing to approximately 62,000 the total number of Jewish people under the Bulgarian government. However, the additional 12,000 Jewish people from Macedonia and Thrace were not given Bulgarian citizenship and were, therefore, still subject to Nazi rule.

Reinhard Heydrich, Head of Security and Defense of the Reich, convened the "Wannsee Conference" on January 20, 1942, in order "to find a solution to the problems associated with the Final Solution of the Jewish

4 | Nir Baruch, "Annihilation and Survival in United Bulgaria," by the non-profit organization for studies on Jewish communities in the Balkans, 2003, p.45.

Question…"[5] The intention was not only toward the Jews of Germany but also to all Jews in occupied lands and territories under German influence. The Wannsee Conference laid the foundation for the mass destruction of the Jews of Europe, putting into effect the Final Solution of the Jewish Question, a destruction that was already underway.[6]

That Final Solution was the plan to murder all Jews. The Wannsee Conference is where the Nazi German officials discussed and coordinated "the implementation of what they called the 'Final Solution of the Jewish Question.'"[7] The plan was to transfer all Jewish people to the eastern areas of Poland (and other countries), to extermination camps or concentration camps, which would bring about the physical annihilation of the Jewish people. This meant deporting Jewish people to killing centers, then murdering them by asphyxiation with poison gas or by shooting and other means. This plan would be used on all Jewish men, women, children, and babies.

Bulgaria was among the countries discussed at the conference regarding where the Final Solution must be put into place for its Jewish population. Clauses 5 and 6 of the Wannsee protocol read, "Declaration before the governments of Romania, Slovakia, Bulgaria and Hungary on their willingness to send the Jews resident in their countries to the Eastern territories."[8] Clause 6 goes on to say, "To pressure the governments of Bulgaria and Hungary to enact anti-Jewish legislation in their countries, according to the decisions of Nuremberg."[9] In other words, the Jews of Bulgaria, according to the Wannsee conference, were to be included in the Final Solution and annihilated.

On December 29, 1941, just before the Wannsee Conference, Minister of Interior Petŭr Grubovsky sent the Bulgarian lawyer Alexander Belev to Berlin. Belev, who worked in Bulgaria's legal department of the Ministry

5 | Kechales, *The Shoah*, p. 68.
6 | Bar-Zohar, *Hitler's Grasp*, pp. 52-53.
7 | Wannsee Conference and the "Final Solution", *United States Holocaust Memorial Museum*, https://encyclopedia.ushmm.org/content/en/article/wannsee-conference-and-the-final-solution
8 | Kechales, *The Shoah*, p. 68.
9 | Ibid.

of Interior and served as Bulgaria's Commissar of Jewish Affairs, was instructed by the *Gestapo* (secret police of Nazi Germany) in all the intricacies of anti-Semitic legislation.

During Belev's stay in Berlin, the most momentous decision about the Jewish Question had been reached; Belev's close friends in the Gestapo and the SS had informed him of the horrendous task the Reich had secretly decided to undertake.[10] When Belev left Berlin on February 4, 1942, and returned to Bulgaria, the eradication of the Jewish people and the Zionist movement began. New regulations were decreed that proved the Bulgarian government was preparing itself for implementing the Final Solution of the Jewish Question.

Two months after the Wannsee conference, Germany began to pressure Bulgaria to send her Jewish population to the death camps in occupied Poland. On June 5, 1942, the United Bulgarian Council of Ministers published Decree Number 31, which prepared the way for the deportation of the Jewish people of Macedonia, Thrace, and the city of Pirot. According to the decree, when the territories were given to Bulgaria by Germany, all Jewish individuals living in these areas were refused Bulgarian citizenship, even though all other inhabitants automatically received it.

On July 6, 1942, the Bulgarian government agreed to transport the approximately 12,000 Jewish individuals who lived in the recently annexed German occupation territories of Macedonia and Thrace to the East, toward Poland, effectively revoking Bulgaria's protection of them. This order released Bulgaria from any responsibility for these Jewish people and gave the green light for their deportation, one and a half years later, to their ultimate end in the death camps in Poland.

In the beginning, Germany thought it would be less controversial to deport Jews from Macedonia and Thrace than from Bulgaria proper.[11] However, it didn't take long until the government of Germany was not satisfied and continued to pressure Gabrovski and Belev to begin

10 | Bar-Zohar, *Hitler's Grasp*, p. 52.
11 | Frederick B. Chary, *The Bulgarian Jews and the Final Solution, 1940-1944* (University of Pittsburgh Press, 1972), pp.44, 83.

transporting the 50,000 Jewish individuals and families who lived within Bulgaria's borders to extermination camps in the East.

The Authorization Law and the Establishment of the Commissariat

On June 25, 1942, the government of Bulgaria submitted a bill to Parliament that would empower the government to take measures against the Jewish residents of their country. The government claimed the Law for the Defense of the Nation was insufficient and faulty; therefore, the government requested blank authorization from Parliament to take steps toward the Final Solution of the Jewish Question in Bulgaria.

Tsar Boris III ratified "The Law of Authorization" on July 4, 1942. According to this law, the United Bulgarian Cabinet was given authority to take any and all measures deemed necessary to "solve the Jewish Question," and this without any prior consent from the Parliament. In the spirit of this law, preparations were made for the deportation of the Bulgarian Jews to death camps. The law went into effect on July 9, 1942.

Despite the fact that this law authorized the Bulgarian government to deal with this Jewish issue on their own, they still felt it necessary to receive authorization from the Parliament to put into action the "instructions" received from Germany. Because there had been no clear supervision or discussion in Parliament regarding this issue, the government was wary of public opinion in Bulgaria, which might rise up against the government's decisions in this case. Thus, even while engaging Parliament in their discussions, the government pushed to receive sole authority with no possibility of public debate.

Suffering and Sacrificing for Others

Prior to the law being enacted, arguments on this topic raged between members of Parliament. Two members in particular expressed their opposition to the law: Nikola Moshanov, the leader of the Democratic Party, and Petko Stainov. Stainov announced that "...the struggle against the Jews in our country is not a matter of pleasing outsiders. In my opinion, the struggle against the Jews is, in any event, an act of diversion, and first and foremost a reaction that we have seen before and today, and sadly will see in the future."[12] Despite the opposition in the summer of 1942, Alexander Belev succeeded, with the support of Prime Minister Filov, to pass the new law that gave the government full authority to pass laws and take measures against the Bulgarian Jews without input from Parliament.

On August 12, 1942, on the basis of the Law for the Defense of the Nation, a new decree, Number 113, was passed, requiring every Jewish male from the age of eighteen (rather than twenty, as in the previous decree) to forty to serve in the labor brigades. All Jews summoned to these labor brigades needed to do so bearing a yellow ribbon on their right arm.[13] These brigades were deployed in twenty-five different areas throughout Bulgaria, and those held there were used to construct roads, bridges, and public installations in return for very little food. As a result of the arduous conditions, many fell sick with various diseases, such as malaria.[14]

In a December 9, 2015, interview with Joseph Shulam, who has written about Rabbi Daniel and whose family members were Holocaust survivors from Bulgaria, Shulam related how his mother and sister recalled that during the war, the Nazis would find Rabbi Daniel Zion every Friday after prayers and beat him terribly.[15] The rabbi, despite the blows he suffered from the Nazis, thought only of his people and how to work for a better future for them. The Bulgarian Jewry regarded Rabbi Daniel with high esteem for his knowledge of comparative theology and the way he actively tried to stop the persecution of his people.[16]

The despair and uncertainty of what the next day would bring never left the Jewish community, and it lay heavily on Rabbi Daniel's spirit. He was certain the repression of the people by the fascist oppressor Adolph Hitler would pass. At the same time, the despair he saw in his Jewish brothers and

12 | Kechales, *The Shoah*, p. 75.

13 | Nir Baruch, *The Bulgarian Jews*, http://www.thebulgarianjews.org.il/ Uploads/dbsAttachedFiles/TheJewsNirBaruch.pdf, p. 9.

14 | Nir Baruch, "Annihilation and Survival," pp. 21-22.

15 | Joseph Shulam, founding pastor of Netivya congregation, Jerusalem, Israel.

16 | Chary, *Bulgarian Jews*, p.147.

sisters convinced him not to wait for the storm, however devastating and destructive, to end. Rather, he resolved to be proactive and do all he could to immediately better the lot of his people. These acts strengthened his belief that "his first duty in these moments was to do anything possible, or even impossible, to ease the plight of his people. Seized by this inspiration, he was fully absorbed in searching for and finding ways to achieve that goal..."[17]

Rabbi Zion was prepared to sacrifice himself, his honor, and his livelihood in order to save his people. In the summer of 1942, he could not stop thinking of the fate of his poor brethren, and he did all he could to help them and deliver them from despair. For instance, he began an active campaign of advocacy. Every chance he had and in any place he was able, he preached to the Jewish people in an effort to calm and comfort them. Then, in the fall of 1942, Rabbi Daniel started to intercede for his people with dignitaries he knew in Sofia.[18] He believed God was giving him the words so he could speak on behalf of Bulgaria's Jewish community. He felt God was calling him to warn these dignitaries against persecuting the Jewish people. The rabbi believed it was his duty to turn to political parties for assistance because they could significantly relieve the burden on his beloved people, whether partially or fully.

"I first sought the help of one of the closest private advisers of the late King Boris," the rabbi once told his secretary. "My petition to this man was that he appear before the king to intercede for the partial or full cancellation of the anti-Jewish Law and the easing of anti-Jewish policy in the country. Regrettably, this intervention did not yield significant results. The king's adviser relayed to me 'the assurances of the king that this Law is set up only to meet the demands of our allies, the Germans, and that this Law will not be applied in its entirety,' a statement that time proved emphatically wrong, as the Law for the Defense of the Nation was applied not only fully but with cruelty and brutality.

---

17 | Daniel Zion, *Five Years under the Nazi Regime* (Sofia, Bulgaria, 1945), pp. 15-16.
18 | Chary, Bulgarian Jews, p. 147.

"Frustrated by this failure on the one hand, and on the other by the constantly deteriorating situation of Bulgarian Jewry, which, as already mentioned, had fallen into total despair in the face of the continuously multiplying restrictive regulations, I decided to again look for influential people close to the king. I settled on his secretary. I appeared before him and implored him to intercede before the king to receive me for a hearing. I was told that the king was not in the palace, but the secretary showed interest concerning the purpose of my meeting request. I explained that I wished to personally meet the king to discuss the political course of the government of Prime Minister Filov and Interior Minister Gabrovski regarding one part of the Bulgarian citizens—the Jews. I tried to explain that the king as a leader and as a man should not discriminate between his citizens as Bulgarians, Jews, or otherwise. They are all equal before the Constitution, and so he is obligated before the people and before the Constitution, on which he took an oath, to protect his citizens, their property, their lives, and their freedom. I also explained that just as the Almighty does not distinguish between whites and blacks, Christians and Jews, so also he should not divide his citizens into 'higher' and 'lower,' into 'friends' and 'enemies.' And so on. Finally, I said that if despite all this, he continues to tolerate such a clearly unconstitutional law, he would be responsible before God and the people."[19]

The secretary then asked the rabbi if The Law for the Defense of the Nation had personally affected him and if that was why he had come to the palace. The rabbi replied that the law did not affect him because he did not own property, but he had come to speak on principle of his infinite concerns for the fate of his people. In his words, "I emphasized that I hadn't come to the palace to seek personal mercy but to warn the king against throwing himself and the country under the wrath of the Almighty."[20]

19 | Ibid, pp. 16-17.
20 | Ibid, pp. 16-17.

"The Word of God"

The rabbi pleaded for an audience with the tsar, but if he could not see him, then at least for the secretary to pass his message on to him. He believed this audience was for the good of the Bulgarian nation. The king's secretary promised he would do what he could.

Two days after his visit to the palace, Rabbi Daniel Zion appealed to the Minister of Finance, Dovri Bozilov. At first, the minister did not wish to meet with him because he was busy with the bill for The Law of Authorization. However, the rabbi did not give in but rather waited patiently until Bozilov was free. When at long last the minister had time to meet, the rabbi told him the following: "I emphasized that persecuting the Jews was an anti-Christian deed, that it was unconstitutional, and that by the will of the Almighty, I was obliged to warn the Bulgarian government about the dangers that would ensue for the country should undeserved, anti-Jewish persecution set in."[21]

The Minister of Finance was displeased with these words and claimed he was unable to do anything about the situation, as everything was in the hands of Petur Garbovsky, the one in charge and the one to whom the rabbi should appeal. In response to the minister's suggestion, the rabbi continued: "I objected and replied that my coming to him was not by my own will but by the will of the Almighty and that His will was for me to hand my warning to him personally and not to Petur Garbovsky ...."[22] After these words, the minister promised to talk with Garbovsky about the Jewish Question.

Following this meeting with the Minister of Finance, the rabbi wrote a letter titled "The Word of God":

"As I left the ministry," he wrote, "an inspiration from on high seized me. An inner voice spoke to me:

- The Kingdom of God comes to Earth. It is coming, and it will destroy all those who take the crooked path. Life and wealth will be left to be enjoyed only be those who walk the straight path.

21 | Ibid, p. 17.
22 | Ibid, p. 17.

- The People and nations who live will be those who give life and freedom to others. There will be no more bondage. Each child of God has the right to live and grow freely.
- This is the will of God! Whoever opposes it will suffer and disappear. The divine love that embraces all creation and every creature will supplant hatred and disagreement. Brotherly love will replace disharmony.
- Whoever accepts [receives this] and practices [acts on it] will forever be provided for [live forever in security]. The nation that applies this word of God will succeed because all its political and economic affairs will turn in its favor. The converse is also true. Beware you [watch out] Nations! God is speaking! Whatever He says comes to pass!
- And my heart told me: 'Go and write down this word of God, and hand it to the King and the rulers. Let it shock all who walk the paths of darkness!'"[23]

Rabbi Daniel Zion sent this letter to the tsar, with copies sent to all the ministers in the government, including the minister of finance. The rabbi noted that when the minister of finance read the letter, his hands trembled. The rabbi also gave a copy to the head of police and other high-ranking officials.

Some hours after "The Word of God" was published and distributed, the president of the Jewish Council, Mr. Joseph Garon, confronted the rabbi to ask why he had visited the offices of the minister of police. The rabbi answered that he had delivered his letter to his bureau. Joseph Garon did not look kindly on this act, believing it would only serve to stir up more trouble for the Jewish community, but the rabbi answered that he was the servant of God and did what was right in God's eyes. He also stressed that he felt in his spirit that he had to act, that he could not sit by and watch how the Jewish people—his people—were suffering.

The following day, the Jewish Council summoned the rabbi to a special

23 | Ibid, pp. 18-19.

meeting to discuss his letter. According to the rabbi's testimony, all those present were extremely concerned. The atmosphere in the room was frigid. Joseph Garon asked him to explain the letter he had written and distributed in the palace and to the intelligentsia and those in government.

The rabbi answered, "This is a word written under the inspiration of God, given with a direct obligation to present it personally to all the major actors in the country...."[24]

Jewish Leaders Oppose Rabbi Zion

Garon then asked the rabbi why he was interfering with affairs of state, and he replied that he was acting against any action directed against the Jewish people. He added that the council should support his actions instead of accusing him and trying to hinder him. He rehearsed the story of Moses, how Moses appeared before Pharaoh to ask him to let his people go from slavery to liberty. He reminded them how the Bible goes on to relate that some of the people of Israel turned against Moses (for example, Korah and his followers; see Numbers 16) after Moses had led the people of Israel out of Egypt and delivered them from slavery into liberty. The rabbi went on to say, "The obstacles you are erecting against my campaign to alleviate the fate of the Bulgarian Jewry is your gratitude for all I do for our common good."[25]

In response to his words, one of the members of the Jewish Council of Bulgaria asked whether these actions could lead to a worsening in the situation of the Jews. The rabbi answered, "I have thought it all out. I have not caused trouble or distress to anyone, and least of all to the Jewish people. On the contrary, this fear that has gripped all of you will bring even greater evils and misfortunes to the Jews."[26] In other words, Rabbi Daniel Zion said that if they did not act, or at least support his actions, the Jews of Bulgaria would be fated to suffer even greater tragedies.

Finally, the rabbi said, "And if you are afraid that I, as a spiritual leader

24 | Ibid, p. 19.
25 | Ibid, pp. 19-20.
26 | Ibid, pp. 20-21.

of Bulgarian Jewry, could harm its interests with my actions, then I am prepared to resign."[27]

After this meeting between the council and Rabbi Daniel, the members of the council announced to the government of Bulgaria that the rabbi had acted on his own initiative, that he was not in his right mind, and that they as members of the council were not in agreement with his actions. This incident caused the rabbi some embarrassment because instead of supporting him as the spiritual leader of the Jewish people, they chose to thwart him and publicly question his sanity.

Following this, the subject of "The Word of God" was discussed among the Jews of Sofia. The President of the Jewish Council in Bulgaria again attempted to explain that the steps taken by the rabbi could be harmful. One of the community's counselors said, "In these times we are in, it would be better not to act thoughtlessly, lest we do something to worsen our situation."[28]

Rabbi Daniel responded, "Yes, I see that all your faces are haggard, that you have lost all peace of mind, and that you have lost faith in yourselves. I undertook this action because the power of the Almighty stands behind it. I am afraid of no one because the right hand of God guides me, as it is written, 'The right hand of God is mighty.'" The rabbi went on to explain that he was fulfilling the will of One only: "The cause I have dedicated myself to is not mine; I am only the executor of the one will—the Will of the Almighty to help an ill-fated nation."[29]

One of the members of the council responded by demanding to know why the rabbi had acted without the approbation of the council.

The rabbi replied that he had not even considered that in acting to relieve the situation the Jewish people were in, they would be opposed to his actions. He went on to say, "…given the impasse the Jews are in, I had hoped that my action would receive your full support and approval, and that I would be encouraged to continue the work I started, and that I would

27 | Ibid, pp. 20-21.
28 | Ibid, pp. 20-21.
29 | Ibid, pp. 20-21.

benefit from your advice. However, just like the Consistory members, you are consumed with fear, and you endure the blows that rain down on you as Jews. All day long, you whine while seeing the approaching storm but take no measures whatsoever. Not only do you do nothing, but you also hinder those who are brave and who seek to avert the blow that the enemies of the Jewish people are preparing. You should know, however, that I am not working in this direction alone. There are other people who, without your permission, have undertaken to act for the benefit of Bulgarian Jewry. Regarding the fact that I am chairman of the Jewish Spiritual Court [rabbinical court/beit din], and the Chief Rabbi in the Sofia Central Synagogue, if you consider it to be in the interest of all Bulgarian Jews, I'm ready to resign from these posts. I must declare that here on earth, I am subordinate to no one! I am a free man, and I only obey my God! I serve Him and Him alone!"[30] Further, the rabbi asserted there was no justifiable reason for him to resign from his duties.

Rabbi Daniel continued by saying, "If you and your colleagues in the Consistory do not feel strong enough to resist any attack directed against us, leave your posts. Other people braver than you will come, who are ready to sacrifice anything for the good of the Jewish people."[31] After seeing the Jewish Council's reaction to his actions, Rabbi Daniel was discouraged that the members of the Council didn't roll up their sleeves and work for the good of the Jewish people.

After publication and distribution of "The Word of God," the Jewish Council of Bulgaria turned on the rabbi because they feared the letter would lead to a worsening of their situation. They claimed the letter could cause harm, and it would be better not to do anything, as any action on their part could lead to a deterioration of their state. This way of thinking was widespread across Europe during World War II. The idea that it is better not to take any action at all until the situation passes arose, in part, because the Jewish community did not believe at this time that they were destined to be "sheep to the slaughter."

30 | Ibid, p. 21.
31 | Ibid, pp. 22-23.

Accused and Deposed from Service

The publication of "The Word of God" caused much distress to the Committee of the Jewish Community in Sofia. They felt the need to explain the letter and thus found themselves at odds with Rabbi Daniel. As a step of appeasement toward the government, the rabbi was formally deposed from his service, though in actual fact he continued to fulfill all his duties.

Rabbi Daniel replied to this accusation by saying he feared nothing because the right hand of God was leading him, as it is written, "*ADONAI*'s right hand is mighty! *ADONAI*'s right hand is lifted high! *ADONAI*'s right hand is mighty!" (Psalm 118:15-16, TLV). His actions were not of himself, but rather a result of his fulfilling the will of the Almighty God in order to help the people.

During this time, certain people began to spread rumors regarding the rabbi's religious inclinations, saying that eight years earlier, around the year 1934, the rabbi had converted to Christianity and become a Dunovist (a member of the Universal White Brotherhood, a mystical Christian sect formed by Peter Dunov in Bulgaria in the early twentieth century). In response to these rumors, the rabbi asserted that who he was and what he believed was well known by every Jew in Bulgaria, except for a few persons in the city council who wished to brand him in order to discredit him before the Bulgarian Jews.

"For thirty years, I have been working incessantly, honestly, and selflessly," he declared, "for the benefit of the Bulgarian Jewry. During this period, I did not cease to be and to feel Jewish for a moment. I love my people; I love the Bible as a young man loves life and commits to it with all his being. But even so, I do not forget that I am a man, and at that, one who seeks to be part of all humanity."[32]

Rabbi Daniel explained the reason he had contacted the representatives of other religious communities was that he wished to understand more deeply their spiritual-philosophical thought. For instance, he studied the writings of the Dunovists but did not join them or adopt their beliefs.

---

32 | Ibid, pp. 22-23.

Continuing to Intercede for His People

Joseph Shulam relates that he once asked Daniel if he had been a Dunovist, and the rabbi answered that no, he had never belonged to that sect, though he did have friends who were Dunovists. According to Rabbi Daniel, the fact that he looked into other religions did not make him cease to be Jewish. He went on to explain that visiting certain spiritual circles did not make him their disciple. Rabbi Zion stated he did meet with members of the "White Brotherhood" in order to alleviate the situation of the Jewish community in Bulgaria. In other words, he approached them to ask them to act for the welfare of the Bulgarian Jews.

For example, in November 1942, Rabbi Daniel went with a small group to meet with Colonel Lyubomir Lulchev, one of the king's personal secretaries and a member of the "White Brotherhood." He wanted to ask Lulchev's help in suspending the work labor camps during the winter, so the Jewish men could go home during the coldest months.[33]

Then, in March 1943, a document written by Metodi Konstantinov (a Bulgarian government official during World War II), states that Rabbi Daniel went to meet with Lulchev to convince him to save the Bulgarian Jews from deportation.

After Rabbi Daniel talked to the colonel, the two of them went to speak with Peter Dunov, the leader of the White Brotherhood, to ask him to give his support in saving the Jews of Bulgaria. Dunov immediately agreed to do so and sent the colonel with a message to the king, which said, "If you would send even one Jew to Poland, you and your reign will be destroyed." When the colonel found the king three days later, he delivered the message. It is argued that, as a result, the king decided to cancel the deportation order that was planned for March 9, 1943, one of the reasons this date is referred to as the March 9 Miracle.[34]

In explaining his reasons for going to members of the "White

---

33 | Nikolai Boyadjiev, "Foreword to the English Edition," *Rescued From the Reich: How a Rabbi, a Priest, and a King Evaded Hitler's Grasp,* (FAI Publishing, 2021), p.vi.

34 | Harri Salaman and Simona Mazliach Hanock, "Rabbi Daniel, the White Brotherhood and the saving of the Bulgarian Jews during the Holocaust," *Adam Olam*, March 23, 2020.

Brotherhood," Rabbi Daniel said, "I did this all out of love for my people. And if sometimes, in a desire to help my people, I failed to heed the 'advice' of one or another dignitary, I acted so only because it was clear to me that their ways were not in accordance with the people's wishes…."[35]

In an interview by the *Herut* newspaper, Rabbi Zion reiterated that he had never been and never would be a Dunovist. He declared he had never prayed to the sun with the "White Brotherhood" cult.[36] He noted that in the past he had gotten up early in the morning with the people of this cult in order to praise God, but he had never prayed to the sun. He had always and only ever prayed to the Lord God, the God of Avraham, Yitzhak, and Yaakov.

The rabbi also explained that when he left the last meeting with the Jewish Council, he did so with renewed vigor and courage to continue to act on behalf of the Jewish people. A special joy overtook him when he realized he was fulfilling a calling from God on his life. In his own words, "I can hardly describe the joy that came over me after these oppressive meetings. I left the last meeting with a new invigorating jet of energy and courage to continue my action, regardless of all obstacles. I felt a special joy that I was fulfilling a holy duty to my people who were so afflicted and at the brink of death. Nothing else in the world had as much worth or meaning to me as my desire to help my brethren. At this moment, I felt I was able to bear the biggest sacrifice; I was ready to resign from all my positions, just to be able to follow the bidding of the voice of God inside me, which continued to push me forward on the path I was already following… It was as if I had rid myself of a heavy burden that was weighing on my soul. I was in a state of spiritual bliss in the reflection of my spiritual ambitions and actions, such that I had never before come home with a heart so filled with joy as I did that day…."[37]

Despite his clear defense and explanation of his actions, the distribution of "The Word of God" to political parties did not sit well with the Council

35 | Zion, *Nazi Regime*, pp. 22-23.

36 | Yair Dekel, "Stiff Annex Missionaries: The `Rabbi` who believes the doctrine of Yeshu," *Herut* (April 21, 1960).

37 | Zion, *Nazi Regime*, p.23.

of Jews of Bulgaria. As a result of his actions, Rabbi Daniel was dismissed on August 2, 1942, from his position as President of the rabbinical court in Sofia. The decision was made by the administration in order to seal the punishment meted out to the rabbi. It was a political decision motivated by fear that if they failed to punish the rabbi, the government of Bulgaria would punish the Jewish population for the published letter.

Maintaining Rabbinical Authority

Some days following his meeting with the Jewish Council, Rabbi Daniel Zion came across one of the city council representatives in the street. The representative told the rabbi that the entire council had wept when they decided to dismiss him, for they knew he had risked himself for the good of the Jewish people. He went on to tell Rabbi Daniel that the steps taken against him were strictly political. Afterward, it was made known to the rabbi through a third party that the President of the Jewish Council, Mr. Yosef Garon, had said he had nothing against the pamphlets the rabbi had distributed; nevertheless, the council agreed the rabbi must be dismissed lest his actions harm the Jewish community. And yet, though he was officially dismissed, the Bulgarian Jews still considered him their chief rabbi.

As a result of the Bulgarian Jews' loyalty to Rabbi Zion, he maintained his rabbinical authority and did not cease his efforts on behalf of his people. He continued to visit and seek prominent political actors, pleading with them on behalf of his people. He also came a second time to the royal palace and warned the tsar against igniting "the wrath of God against him and his entire country."[38] He addressed the secretary of the palace and instructed him to tell the king he must not be influenced by the dark powers that would quickly be conquered, but that he should trust in God. Moreover, the tsar was to take what the rabbi had written, "The Word of God," seriously; otherwise, things would be bitter and evil for him and the entire country.

---

38 | Ibid, pp. 24-25.

Rabbi Daniel wrote in *Five Years under the Fascist Oppression*, "I appeared before the palace secretary and told him that I knew that the king had been influenced by the dark, reactionary forces that rule the world. 'Tell the king not to be influenced by these dark forces; they will fall very soon. Let him trust only in the one and eternal God!' Tell him also to take under most serious consequences which will come for him and for the country."[39] Then he handed the following letter, which he had written to the king, to the head of the Court Chancellery to pass on to Tsar Boris. Though he was assured the letter would reach the king, he also gave a copy of the letter to the king's private adviser/palace secretary.

> "To His Majesty Tsar Boris III, king of the Bulgarian people,
>
> Over the past two years the National Assembly has been enacting legislation against my people, and their implementation threatens all Jewry with ruin.
>
> I do not want to bother your Majesty with the impact of these laws, but they have led to a state of hopeless [loss of hope] misery for thousands of workers, peddlers, petty traders, and their families.
>
> I find this misery hopeless because the latest laws and orders deprive the Jewish parishes, the Synagogue boards, and charities of their incomes. It is well known that all these institutions are principally engaged in helping poor Jews. The implementation of these laws will lead to the closure of schools and synagogues, which on top of the material burden, will heap spiritual misery on my compatriots [my people].
>
> I beg your Majesty to put yourself in the position of those thousands of fathers, mothers, and children who have fallen into black misery and whose misfortune is a fortune to no one. Does the Gospel not say, 'With the measure you use, it will be measured to you'?

39 | Ibid, pp. 24-25.

> This current situation is not in accord with the laws of God, which are good, just, and rational.
>
> In the name of He who sits on High I must remind His Majesty of the letter '[The] Word of God,' that I had the honor to convey to you. Each one must comply with this word, especially His Majesty, as the head of the Bulgarian people for whose fate you are responsible before God.
>
> If these laws are not implemented, Bulgaria will become the conduit of the will of God, and the light of peace will shine on it for the good of all mankind. Amen."

Some days later, much to Rabbi Daniel's delight and joy, the head of the bureau informed him that the tsar had given his word that the Jewish community would not be deported from Bulgaria.

Afterward, the rabbi appeared before Metropolitan Stefan, who read "The Word of God" carefully and proclaimed it a true revelation from God. The metropolitan also said he would go to Minister of Finance Bozilov to warn him to cease his persecution of the Jewish population lest all that is written in "The Word of God" come to pass. Stefan told the rabbi he was opposed to all that was being done to the Jews in Bulgaria, and that he and the Holy Synod were working to stop the anti-Jewish trend. He agreed these actions were not humane and were in contradiction to the principles of Christianity.

On leaving, Stefan said to the rabbi, "The doors are always open for you. You can come whenever you want; you are always welcome."[40] As stated earlier, Metropolitan Stefan was one of the key figures responsible for saving the Jews of Bulgaria from annihilation. He and other leaders of the Bulgarian Orthodox Church actively opposed the anti-Semitic policies of the fascist Bulgarian government, thanks in part to the excellent relations between Metropolitan Stefan and Rabbi Daniel Zion.

---

40 | Zion, *Nazi Regime*, p. 25.

Taking a Stand for Rabbi Daniel

My mother told me that Rabbi Daniel was encouraged after this meeting with Metropolitan Stefan. He never forgot the friendship and relationship he had with him. During this dark time, Stefan was there to support and help by any means necessary. At that same time, Rabbi Daniel decided to continue praying and interceding on behalf of the fate of the Bulgarian Jews. He prayed that God would raise up more people to come against the plans of evil, including more non-Jewish individuals to stand in the gap for them.

Following this, the subject of Rabbi Daniel's "The Word of God" letter became a regular topic of discussion among the Jewish community of Sofia, mostly among themselves in their own homes. My family was no different as they heard these rumors about their rabbi. My father told me about a dinner that took place during this same time, an event that stayed with him as an especially fond memory. The family was sitting down in the living room, waiting for my grandmother Sofie to finish preparing dinner. When she called out for my uncle David, who was around sixteen at the time, to please go outside and get more water from the well, he grabbed the bucket and went to do as he was told.

Nissim, a couple years younger than David, went outside to help him. As they lowered the bucket to get the water, Nissim asked, "How will we survive now, without Father and our older brothers?" David, busy pulling up the bucket, did not answer him. My father then asked him, "Was Rabbi Daniel right to act? Should the Jewish leaders be more active, or should they wait for this storm to pass?"

David had more of a fighting spirit than his brothers. Though he was compassionate, he was always busy doing something to try to help. He simply could not sit around and do nothing. My father knew this, so he had an idea how David felt, but he wanted to hear it for himself. Even as David, still silent, brought the water inside the house, Nissim could see he had an opinion on the matter.

It was then that Sofie called the family to come to dinner, even though there was little food for them to share. My grandmother tried to prepare nutritious and tasty meals from the little they had, but it was no small task. She tried not to show her worries, but her children could sense her concern.

As they all sat down at the table, David took the bread and blessed it, saying, *"Baruch Ata Adonai Eloheinu Melech Ha'olam, Hamotzi Lechem min HaEretz"* ("Blessed are You, O Lord our God, King of the universe, who brings forth bread from the earth"), and everybody said "amen" in unison. Sofie passed around the bread and porridge, and they all began to eat. As they did so, my father decided to ask his question regarding Rabbi Daniel's letter again, this time to his younger brothers as well as David. When he did, the brothers began to wonder aloud what would be better—to do nothing and hope the trouble would pass, or to be more active and resist what were now rumors but could quickly become reality.

My grandmother listened without responding. David, however, finally decided to speak up. He said he felt that Rabbi Daniel was brave and courageous to stand up the way he did. My father answered that it might be so, but would it prove to be worth it if there were repercussions to his actions? My father was trying to build an opinion for himself because he did not know what to think, so he expressed something he had heard around town that perhaps the "rabbi's belief in this Messiah had made him lose his senses."

It was then that their mother stood up, breaking her silence. She fixed her eyes on her sons and said, "No matter what Rabbi Daniel believes, he has never for one second forsaken his Jewishness. He has always acted for the betterment of his people. Never thinking of himself, he always looks out and risks his own well-being for the sake of his congregation and what he feels is right for his people. Your father, Avraham, loved and respected him. He was a dear friend to your father; always remember that." Then, with a stern look, she said, "Don't believe the rumors that are said in the streets. As well as I know and your father knew him, Rabbi Daniel Zion sees himself as Jewish and has never for one second forsaken his Jewishness. He loves God, the Bible, and the Jewish traditions. Regardless of his personal beliefs, he has been a true and faithful rabbi to his community.

He trusts in God, and all that he does is out of love for his Jewish people. For us, the Mizrachi family, he will always be our beloved rabbi."

This was a memory that impacted and stayed with the boys because their mother was such a soft and kind spirit, who seldom raised her voice. This time, however, she felt she had to speak out about Rabbi Daniel on behalf of her late husband. It was an action that impressed upon my father the deep respect with which his parents held Rabbi Daniel Zion. He knew from that moment on, no matter what rumors he heard on the street, that he would give the beloved rabbi the same level of respect as that given by his parents.

Law Passed and Commissariat Established

On August 26, 1942, the Law of Authorization was passed, and it was published in the *Official Gazette*, number 192, on August 29. The law determined the establishment of a commissariat for dealing with the Jewish Question in Bulgaria. The budget for the commissariat was covered by the taxes taken from the frozen accounts of the Jewish people in various banks, and by the imposition of fees for permits and other documents they needed. In effect, the budget of the commissariat was financed by taxes placed on the Bulgarian Jews, blocked Jewish bank accounts, and appropriated Jewish property.

The Commissariat for Jewish Affairs was authorized to handle all matters relating to the Jewish people, with no need to apply for permission or aid of other governmental factors, including the ministry of finance, the ministry of interior, or the police. The commissariat and the Law of Authorization made it possible to conspire to plan deportations, arrests, and drastic measures in order to bring about the exile of the Jewish population from the lands of Bulgaria.

The government nominated Alexander Belev to head the commissariat. This was the first step in sending the Jews of Macedonia, Thrace, and Pirot to their deaths in the East. It was also meant to be the first step in deporting the Bulgarian Jews, including my father, Nissim, and his family.

More Restrictions and Regulations

The new regulations led to further restrictions on the Bulgarian Jews, including the requirement for every one of them above the age of ten to wear a yellow six-pointed star.[41] They were required to wear this star on the left side of their breast as a sign that would visibly separate them from the rest of Bulgaria's citizens. It was a small mark in comparison to the larger star worn in other European countries at the time, but the goal was the same: it was intended to isolate them.

In Hebrew, the symbol of the star represented the *Magen David*, the Shield of David, Israel's warrior king, who led their armies to defeat all their enemies. But this star was no shield, and it did not represent victory to the Jewish people. Instead, it was a badge of humiliation and impotency.

The imposition of wearing the yellow stars aroused the greatest consternation and humiliation within the Jewish community, beyond anything they had experienced thus far. To take the symbol that meant so much to them as Jewish people and make it an insignia of hateful rejection went to the core of who they were as God's chosen people. They felt so controlled… so despised… and so impotent to do anything to protect themselves. But what could they possibly have done? With their houses now identified as Jewish property, it was only a matter of time before their homes became targets for violence.

It was also required that the women of each household sew the stars on their own clothing as well as the clothes of their family members, an act regarded by the women as a mandatory participation with their enemies. The very thought that it was imposed upon the women to do that which would label their own loved ones as people worthy only of abuse and hatred was reprehensible to them.

My grandmother, though she despised having to sew those stars onto her family's clothing and shared the women's sense of injustice, advised others to do as told lest they bring greater trouble upon their families. The

41 | Kechales, *The Shoah*, p. 81.

Nazis' intention of isolating and shaming the Jewish people was indeed working.

Others, however, felt a great sense of rage for what they were being forced to do, not only for themselves but for their families. My father was one of them. He explained that the symbol was to mark those who were the lowest form of life. Being labeled as Jewish meant you were worthless, of no value. It also meant that those who were not Jewish were superior to you. The entire evil system was built upon the race into which they were born.

The anti-Semitic organization, which was now rising in power in Bulgaria, saw the Jewish race as not even deserving to live, as lower than rodents, deserving of dehumanization. In the eyes of the Nazis, being marked as Jewish by the yellow star meant you were worthless, that it would be better if you died and let the worthy races live. Marking yourself with the yellow star meant much more than just wearing a piece of cloth; it served to dehumanize the wearer.

However, despite his strong opinions on the matter, my father told me a story about his mother's feelings and how they influenced him. In the beginning, he was determined not to allow his mother to sew any stars onto his clothes. However, seeing her submission to the rule, in her words, "for the sake of the preservation of the family" and hearing her beg him not to rebel against the order, Nissim finally agreed. As he explained it, in the end, as he looked into her face, knowing she was a woman of integrity and courage, he capitulated and allowed her to sew the stars onto his coat.

Isolation and Shame

Nissim was greatly embarrassed each time he wore that coat, and he often found himself wishing he had not been born Jewish. It was difficult for him to disclose that part of his memory because,

later in life, his Jewish identity became very important to him, something he impressed upon me many times as I was growing up. The entire ordeal, however, left him with a cry for justice deep within his soul, something that remained a part of him his entire life.

My father not only remembered the humiliation of being forced to wear the yellow star, but he also remembered that the Jewish people were required to place special signs in their windows, marking their homes and businesses. Every Jewish home had a sign stating "Jewish Home," with a Magen David on the left corner of the sign. The same thing applied to Jewish factories, which had signs prominently declaring "Jewish Factory." Certain public places were likewise required to post signs saying, "No Jews allowed."[42]

My father also remembered feeling very ashamed the first time he left the house wearing the yellow star. He looked at his own house, now marked as Jewish as was he, and wondered if there was any escape from the Nazis. Now that he, his family, and his people were all marked, could they possibly escape the evil verdict of the Reich? As he walked down the street and saw signs saying "No Jews allowed," his feeling of being trapped grew. Those signs also added to the shame and loneliness he felt over simply being Jewish. Seeing himself banned from places he used to enjoy—such as restaurants and theaters—was a bitter pill to swallow.

All these signs aroused great consternation and embarrassment among the Jewish community. The Jews of Bulgaria were forbidden to own cars, radio sets, and telephones, and were also forbidden to walk on certain streets or to gather in groups. A curfew prohibited them from going outside after 9 P.M. Again, the intention of all these actions was to isolate and shame them and bring them to a state of helplessness.

The Jews of Bulgaria were greatly affected by these bans and regulations. "They were brought to despair in view of the uncertainty of what their lot would be the following day. In this mental state and influenced by rumors from outside the country of the tragic fate of the Jews of Germany, Austria, Poland and Romania—each one could imagine to himself the dark deeds in the countries that were controlled by the Germans who had murdered

42 | Nir Baruch, "Annihilation and Survival," pp.21-23.

hundreds of thousands of sisters and brothers, events that affected the lives of each of the Jews of Bulgaria…."[43]

Rabbi Daniel Zion and his family were likewise compelled to wear a yellow star, also considered a Jewish badge. The rabbi's grandchildren have pictures of Rabbi Daniel and his family during the Second World War, all wearing the Jewish badge. The picture was taken at Rabbi Daniel's son's wedding. (See photo # 12) According to a booklet written by the Zion family, the years of the war were difficult for the Zions and also the Ben Bassats (the family of the rabbi's eldest daughter's husband). Fear and anxiety that they would be sent to Poland's death camps took hold of them. The anti-Semitic organizations calling for "Death to the Jews," the regulation to wear the yellow star, and the limitations placed on them caused the Jews of Bulgaria to fear that their end had indeed come.

Men of Prayer and Action

Through it all, Rabbi Daniel Zion continued to stand firm, ready to sacrifice whatever necessary for what he believed. While he still served as the chief rabbi of the Jews of Bulgaria, Rabbi Zion stood in the gap in order to save his people from destruction. Even when most members of the community believed it was better to accept the decrees of the government quietly, Rabbi Daniel continued to do all he could to act for the good of the Bulgarian Jews.

Rabbi Daniel was willing to lay down his position, his title, and his life on behalf of his people. In my opinion, he was like a modern-day Esther in a time when the Jewish people were once again being threatened by evil. He was nearly sixty years old at the time, and because of his faith in the God of Israel, he willingly put himself on the line time and again. Even if, at the time, some did not believe he should make a stand, he knew in his heart that he could not sit down while evil prevailed.

My mother often told me that it was during his time of prayer and quiet time with God that Rabbi Daniel found the strength to do what he

43 | Eliezer Ansky, "The Introduction to Rabbi Daniel's book: Five Years Under the Nazi Regime" thebulgarianjews.org.il.

did. Once, as he was praying, he sensed the worst was not yet over, and the situation would continue to deteriorate. Because he could not allow evil to prevail, he asked God to use him for "such a time as this." (See Esther 4:14, NKJV.) Even if he perished in the process, he was willing to lay down his life for his people, even as the Messiah he knew and loved had done.

Rabbi Daniel Zion was a man who believed in prayer and action. When God called him to prayer, he prayed; when he felt God had called him to action, he acted. Rabbi Daniel, like Esther, was willing to go to the king of Bulgaria, though he was not summoned, to plead for his people, even if he perished in the process. He was a man of faith and courage in a dark age. He did whatever God led him to do, trusting God each step of the way. He was bold and courageous. Even when at times he felt alone, he did not let that stop him. He cared only about doing what God wanted him to do and doing all he could to save lives because he dearly loved his people and the God of Israel.

Despite the dubious partnership between Germany and Bulgaria, there are many reasons the Jews of Bulgaria were not sent to the death camps in Poland. I believe that one of the primary ones was the actions of Rabbi Daniel Zion, the courageous and selfless spiritual head of the Jews of Bulgaria, as well as the actions of Metropolitan Stefan, a prominent leader of the Bulgarian Orthodox Church. Many times these two heroic friends worked together, even risking their own lives to protect their beloved Bulgarian Jews. My family and I, as descendants of those Bulgarian Jews, owe a lot to those two men's acts of heroism.

CHAPTER 5

Initial Plans for Deportation

Countless times, my thoughts returned to the many courageous and tireless efforts of those who put their lives on the line to protect the Jews of Bulgaria. And yet, despite those efforts, the Nazis never ceased to pressure Tsar Boris to hand over the Bulgarian Jews. The Germans were determined to have them loaded into trains and sent to the death camps, where so many Jewish people from other European countries were ultimately exterminated. Had my own Jewish family lived in one of those European countries, we most likely would have ceased to exist, meaning that I would never have been born.

Plans Put into Place

On November 12, 1942, Prime Minister of Bulgaria Bogdan Filov spoke with the German Ambassador in Sofia, expressing his agreement to deport the Jewish people "eastward." Filov, however, requested that the ambassador send a special coordinator from Germany to assist with the work of deportation. Also, on the same day, the German delegation in Sofia received a written formal communication from the Bulgarian foreign ministry agreeing to the deportation of Bulgarian Jews.[1]

In accordance with Filov's request, an SS commander named Theodore Dannecker, the SS *HauptsturmFuhrer* (a mid-level commander in the Nazi army), was sent to Bulgaria. Because of Dannecker's previous experience of executing the Final Solution in France, Adolf Hitler and his close associate Adolf Eichmann nominated Dannecker to coordinate that same Final Solution in Bulgaria. With the cooperation of Commissar for Jewish

1 | Nir Baruch, "The Jews in Bulgaria," http://www.thebulgarianjews.org.il/ Uploads/dbsAttachedFiles/TheJewsNirBaruch.pdf, p. 10.

Affairs Alexander Belev, Dannecker officially stepped into his position on January 21, 1943. (After Dannecker failed in Sofia, Bulgaria, he was successful in executing the Final Solution in Northern Italy in 1943, and then in Hungry in 1944. Bulgaria was the only country in which he was not able to destroy its Jewry.)

During the months of January-March 1943, Dannecker and Belev began coordinating the work that needed to be done to accomplish the deportation of the Jewish people to the death camps. They established departure stations near the railroads, collected documents, held secret meetings, determined the place for the transit camps, and gathered the necessary equipment.

Then, on February 2, 1943, two Germans entered Alexander Belev's office: Theodore Dannecker and a Gestapo agent named Adolf Hoffman. Following this meeting, Belev asked his secretary, Liliana Feniza, to write a report to Minister of Interior Gabrovski.

This report, which was sent on February 4, detailed the plan to deport and exterminate thousands of Jewish people. It stated, "The Reich is ready to receive the Jewish populations of Thrace and Macedonia, as well as the undesired Jews from the old boundaries [of Bulgaria], in a number that will be indicated by the Commissariat... The deportation should start at the beginning of March; 10,000-20,000 people [Jews] can be deported each month, equivalent to 10-20 special deportation trains... The gathering of the Jews in concentration camps and their transport to the relevant train stations is under the responsibility of the Commissariat... Once the Jews are delivered to the German authorities, they lose their Bulgarian citizenship, if they are Bulgarian citizens...."[2] This meant that from the moment the Jewish people were deported from Bulgaria and arrived at the German concentration camps, they would be stripped of their Bulgarian citizenship and from the protection of the Bulgarian government. This gave the Nazis the authorization to do with the Jews as they saw fit—in other words, the green light to wipe out the Jewish population of the "United

2 | Bar-Zohar, *Hitler's Grasp*, p. 64.

Bulgaria" (thus, including the Jews from the areas of Macedonia, Thrace, and Pirot).

Belev stressed the importance of keeping the deportation secret, particularly since it would apply not only to the Jewish populations of Thrace and Macedonia but also to those within the Bulgarian borders.[3] According to Belev, the deportation of Jewish individuals from the annexed territories first would provide the precedent for deporting the Jewish citizens of Bulgaria as well.

Order Rescinded

The official agreement between Alexander Belev and Theodore Dannecker was signed on February 21, 1943, authorizing the handover of 20,000 Jewish people to the Germans. This agreement was the only official document signed between Germany and another nation regarding the delivery of Jews.

At first the agreement stated that only "Jews from the new Bulgarian lands of Thrace and Macedonia"[4] would be handed over to the Germans; however, while signing it, Belev took his pen and scratched out those words in the title and in the text. The significance of this act was that the deportation would not be limited to the Jewish population of the 1941-annexed territories of Thrace and Macedonia, where they had not been afforded citizenship, but would extend to all those within the Bulgarian borders prior to the annexation. Likewise, Bulgaria declared publicly that it would pay a monetary compensation fee to the Germans, based on the number of deported Bulgarian Jews, and also committed not to demand the return of any who had been deported.

Belev knew before the signing that the total number of Jewish people in Thrace, Macedonia, and the city of Pirot was only 12,000, so he

---

3 | The Balkan Peninsula of Southeast Europe has had a complicated history with its many different ethnic groups and ever-changing boundaries. When Germany invaded Yugoslavia and divided it among its allies, Bulgaria received Macedonia (south of Yugoslavia) and parts of Thrace (south of Bulgaria) with the goal of regaining its pre-World War I access to the Aegean Sea. These areas were considered under Bulgarian administration.

4 | Bar Zohar, Hitler's Grasp, p. 69.

purposely decided to raise the number of Jews whose deportation should be agreed upon to 20,000, since he was interested in deporting all the Jews from Bulgaria's old borders as well as the Jews from the new borders.[5] Following the signing of the agreement between SS Commander Theodore Dannecker and Belev, the government of Bulgaria began the necessary actions to bring about the deportation of 20,000 Jews.

The Commissariat was no doubt pleased with this agreement because it would now be very easy to insist on adding 8,000 from Bulgaria's old borders for deportation along with the existing 12,000 already scheduled to leave. Because Belev, as a Bulgarian representative, and Dannecker, the Nazi Germany representative, had both signed this despicable and immoral document, by which it was agreed upon and made official, they succeeded in granting the commissariat the authority to make this move regarding the 8,000 additional Jewish individuals. It is also believed that the king was well aware of this and actually supported it up until the time he was persuaded to cancel it, resulting in the March 9 Miracle (described in more detail later in this chapter).

Prior to the king's canceling of the deportation of the Jewish people from Old Bulgaria, however, the commissariat moved forward to come up with 8,000 more to fill the quota of deportees as specified in the agreement. There was no way of getting around it: 8,000 Jewish individuals of Bulgarian citizenship would have to be deported, along with the 12,000 from the annexed areas. Thus, the agreement between Belev and Dannecker provided the seal of approval and opened the door for the deportation of all the Jews of Bulgaria.

In February, the Bulgarian Representatives for the Jewish Question produced a list of 8,400 Jewish individuals from within Bulgaria's old borders for deportation, including some from Sofia, Plovdiv, and other cities in the country.[6] On March 5, 1943, the Commissariat of Jewish Affairs discussed in detail the plan for the deportations of these Jews,

---

5 | Ibid, p. 66.

6 | Esther Benbassa and Aron Rodrigue, *The Jews of the Balkans: The Judeo-Spanish Community, 15th to 20th Centuries* (The Zalman Shazar Center for the Jewish History: Jerusalem, 2001), pp. 180-181.

believing it was certain to happen.[7] Had it not been for the pressure from Rabbi Zion and Metropolitan Stefan and many others, who convinced the king to rescind the order to include those additional 8,400 Jews, they most certainly would have been sent to their deaths.

The Jewish Populations of Thrace, Macedonia, and Pirot

According to the agreement, the Jewish people of Thrace, Macedonia, and Pirot were, without question or recourse, sentenced to destruction. On the pre-dawn morning of March 4, 1943, the Bulgarian army and police force surrounded the Jewish quarters in Thrace. At 4:00 A.M., they began to raid the Jewish homes, shouting loudly to wake them from their sleep. Rudely awakened, they were terrified as they were immediately commanded to hand over all their money and valuables. They were given only a half-hour to pack a small suitcase, not more than forty kilos, or eighty-eight pounds, per adult and twenty kilos, or forty-four pounds, per child.[8] Both men and women were cruelly beaten with fists, batons, and whips.

Driven from their homes with nothing but a suitcase and the clothes on their backs, these Jews were then taken to warehouses, where they were deprived of heat, food, and medical attention, regardless of the freezing temperatures and snow on the ground. Some 4,058 Jewish people from Thrace were detained in these warehouses for two weeks. On March 18-19, they were transferred to the trains, together with 158 Jewish individuals from Pirot, currently a city in southeastern Serbia, and taken to northwest Bulgaria, where they were handed over to the Germans. Some days later, they were loaded onto four transport ships to Vienna. From there, they were taken by train in cattle cars to the death camp of Treblinka, where they were all murdered. Not one of them—man, woman, or child—survived.[9]

Scarcely a week after the Jewish population of Thrace was driven from their homes on March 11, 1943, the Bulgarian police did the same to the

---

7 | Nir Baruch, "The Jews in Bulgaria," http://www.thebulgarianjews.org.il/ Uploads/dbsAttachedFiles/TheJewsNirBaruch.pdf, p. 12.

8 | Bar-Zohar, *Hitler's Grasp*, p. 87.

9 | Esther Benbassa and Aron Rodrigue, *The Jews of the Balkans: The Judeo-Spanish Community, 15th to 20th Centuries* (The Zalman Shazar Center for the Jewish History: Jerusalem, 2001), pp. 180-181.

Jewish community of Macedonia. It is estimated that 7,300 Macedonian Jews were deported to a transit camp, set up in the tobacco warehouses in Skopje. They remained there until they were deported to Treblinka on March 22-25, where they were all murdered in the gas chambers.

While writing this book, I was able to hear several testimonies of Bulgarian Jews who remembered the cries of the Macedonian Jews as the train passed through Bulgaria on the way to Poland. After they were loaded onto the trains in sealed cars, they were not given food or water or any sort of basic sanitary needs. The Bulgarian Jews could hear their Macedonian brethren crying out in Ladino for bread and water. Many who told me of this incident did so in tears, remembering the trauma and fear in the weeping and groaning of men, women, and children. They, including some of my family members, told of how they ran to pass whatever food they had through the cracks of the cattle cars. Some even talked about the stench of urine and the bad conditions those Jews were in. They remembered the fear on their faces. At that moment, while watching the trains go farther and farther away, they feared the worst for their brethren—and rightfully so. They were indeed being sent to their death. It was easy to imagine that they could be next.

The loss of the Jews of Macedonia, Thrace, and Pirot causes me much grief, even to this day. My heart is to always remember those innocent victims (see photos #13 and #14).

The March 9 Miracle

The Bulgarian government, with the help of the Commissariat for Jewish Affairs, organized and planned the deportation of the Thrace, Macedonia, and Bulgarian Jews. Everything had been planned and set in motion; the only difference was that they succeeded in deporting the Thrace and Macedonian Jews but failed with the Bulgarian Jews. The first (failed) plan for the deportation of Bulgaria's Jews led to what is known as "The March 9 Miracle" (as referenced earlier).

It seems Liliana Panitza, an attractive woman in her twenties, who served as Belev's private secretary and also his secret lover, typed up the official confidential agreement between Dannecker and Belev and was present at its signing. She did not understand why Belev hated the Jewish people so much, and despite her relationship with him, she could not comprehend his anti-Semitism. As a result, she found herself in a deep internal conflict, torn between her love for Belev, and her conscience and moral principles.

In the end, Liliana decided she must at all costs help the Jewish people, even if it meant deep personal sacrifice on her part. She leaked the plans regarding the deportation of the Jewish population of Old Bulgaria to well-known Sofia lawyer Dr. Nissim (Buko) Levi, one of the most active leaders of the Bulgarian Jewish community. He was also the vice-president of the city's Jewish Consistory, the governing body of the Jewish congregations.

Because Panitza was a friend of the Levi family and knew of his standing among the Jewish people, she also knew that by warning him, she was warning the entire Jewish community. She informed Dr. Levi that Alexander Belev was intent on deporting the Jews of Bulgaria and that he was cooperating closely with the German police. She told him Belev had signed a secret agreement with Dannecker for the deportation of 20,000 Jewish people, 12,000 from Macedonia, Thrace, and Pirot, and the rest from within Bulgarian borders, thus opening the door to further deportation of Bulgaria's Jewish population. This brave young woman gave Levi the details of the planned deportation down to the very dates that had been set, despite the risks involved in her speaking out.

Panitza was not the only one who leaked this information. Others joined her in this effort. In March 1943, Michael Avjiev, from the city of Kyusendil in Bulgaria, held a party. His purpose was to disguise the invitation of two Jewish guests, Boko Lazarov and his wife, Anka. Avjiev wanted to meet them without drawing undue attention, in order to warn them of the impending deportation.

Avjiev was able to take them aside and tell them in private that a few days earlier he had received a visit in his office from a clerk of the

Commissariat for Jewish Affairs, who demanded he hand over the use of a tobacco warehouse near a train station. At first, the clerk refused to say why he needed it, but Avjiev kept pressing him.

In the end, the clerk swore Avjiev to secrecy and told him about the agreement between Belev and Dannecker, explaining that the warehouse would be used as a concentration center for the Jewish people from Kyustendil and other Bulgarian cities before they were sent to Nazi-occupied Poland. He explained that the trains were on their way to Kyustendil and the deportation was planned for the night between March 9 and 10. Avjiev further explained that he had tried to keep his word and not say anything about the plans, but the closer the date came, the more he felt he could not stand by and do nothing. Avjiev therefore warned Boko and Anka Lazarov of the deportation and passed on to them all he had been told by the clerk from the Commissariat.

Shaken by the news, Boko Lazarov decided to take immediate action and alert the head of the Jewish community. Following this, he turned to Petŭr Michelev, a member of Parliament. Michelev was shocked by the news and said he would do all within his power to prevent the planned deportation. He was one of four people who traveled to the government in Sofia to meet with Dimitar Peshev and other political leaders in order to stop the evil plan before it was too late.

At the same time, Chayim Rachamim, a Jewish man of Kyustendil, heard of the planned deportation from three different sources. The first was Dr. Iosef Vatev, an optician who worked as a medical advisor at the commissary. Vatev had heard the horrific news and told Rachamim that the Jews of Bulgaria were sentenced to be deported soon.

A second source was Vladimir Kortov, one of Rachamim's friends, who told Rachamim that a senior official in the commissariat had told him of the agreement between Belev and Dannecker, and of the planned deportation to Poland. A third source was the local governor of Kyustendil, Miltenov, who told Rachamim there was a verbal order from Alexander Belev to prepare the Jewish people for deportation to Radomir on March

10, when they would be joined by other Jewish individuals from Sofia, Samokov, and Dupnica. From there, they would be sent to their final destination.

And so, despite the secrecy, the news reached several Bulgarian people, who were not prepared to sit idly by while their Jewish friends and neighbors were deported to almost certain death.

CHAPTER 6

Continued Conflict over Deportations

In addition to these courageous Bulgarian citizens working behind the scenes to prevent this tragedy, there were also many public figures, both Jewish and non-Jewish, who became visibly involved. They visited members of the General Assembly and other well-known persons in Sofia and other cities in Bulgaria to plead the cause of the Jewish people. Metropolitan Stefan and Metropolitan Kiril of Plovdiv were among those seeking to intervene on their behalf.

Metropolitan Stefan Intervenes

In March 1943, Metropolitan Stefan was on his way to the Rila Monastery, when he came across a Jewish transport train from Aegean, Thrace. Though he did not know it then, this train was taking the Jews onboard to Treblinka, where not one would survive.

The instant he reached the Rila Monastery, Stefan sent a telegram to Tsar Boris, asking for mercy for the Jews and insisting he not send them to Poland. The tsar promised him he would do all that could legally be done, somewhat assuring the tenderhearted priest.

On Stefan's return trip to Sofia, as he passed through the city of Deupnitspa, he was amazed to find it a ghost town. No one walked the streets because all the Jewish population of the city was under curfew, waiting for the moment they would be deported to Poland. In protest and in a gesture of solidarity, the local Bulgarians had placed themselves under the same curfew.

Upon seeing and learning this, Stefan immediately telephoned Prime Minister Filov and demanded he revoke the curfew and release the Jewish people from their houses. In awe at Stefan's revelation, the prime minister immediately granted his request. Thanks to Stefan's quick and decisive actions, Jewish individuals and families from that town came to his church that same day to recognize his actions and to express their thanks.

After this incident, Stefan returned to Sofia, where a man by the name of Avraham Alphasy, head of the Jewish Consistory, requested his intervention on behalf of the Jewish Bulgarians. He and others in the community had heard the rumors of the impending deportation to Poland and had seen the presence of transport trains in Sofia; they knew their situation was dire.

Stefan did not think twice. He immediately left for the palace to speak with Tsar Boris. At first the tsar claimed he did not feel well and would not be able to meet with him; however, Stefan did not give in but stayed at the palace until the tsar agreed to the meeting. Stefan asked him to defer the decision to deliver the Jewish people to the Nazis. If he refused, Stefan said he would give the order to all the monasteries and churches to open their doors and hide them if necessary, an act that would seriously undermine the monarchic authority in the state.[1] I believe Tsar Boris clearly understood this and decided to defer to Stefan, postponing the deportation.

"Where You Go, I Go"

At the same time, the Jewish people of Plovdiv were rounded up and concentrated in the local school, something that was taking place in other cities throughout Bulgaria. The moment Metropolitan Kiril of Plovdiv heard of this (see photo #15), he ran to the school to speak with those who had been imprisoned. On the way, he saw the transport wagons prepared to load them up, and he declared that if the train carrying the Jewish people left the city, he would lie down on the railway tracks in front of it.

When Kiril arrived at the school, the police would not allow him in. "Try to stop me!" Kiril cried. He scrambled over the fence, jumped down into the schoolyard, and declared to the Jewish people there, "Wherever

---

1 | Stefanov, "Common Misconceptions," pp. 13-14.

you go, I'll go."[2] He also wrote to the authorities in Plovdiv, saying that from henceforth he had ceased to be a loyal citizen of Bulgaria and would act by his conscience.

This was no small matter, as it was the first time in the history of Bulgaria that one of the "Princes of the Church" had ever declared that he would refuse to obey the laws of the state. Kiril warned them he would gather some of the Jewish people under his protection in his church, and if the police dared to try to arrest them, they would have to arrest him first. On March 10, 1943, in the spirit of these words, Kiril sent a telegram to the tsar. It later became known from members of the palace/royal court that his telegram had greatly affected Tsar Boris III.[3]

In the summer of 2017, I had the honor of interviewing David Cohen, the former Israeli ambassador to Bulgaria. He shared with me how both of his parents were Bulgarian Jews, his mother being born in Plovdiv and his father in Burgas, as was he. During War World II, his mother was a young girl. His father, being much older than she, was sent to the labor camps. David explained that his mother's schooling stopped during the war because she was Jewish and had to wear the yellow star.

Then, he told me a story of when he was the Israeli ambassador. In 1997, he was invited to Plovdiv to attend an exhibition that had to do with the Jewish community there. He was stunned to find papers from the Bulgarian Police dating from the time of the war. There in the papers he found detailed information about his mother, including that she was Jewish, where she lived, and her ID number. It also included a picture of her as a young girl. David explained that during the war, all Jewish people were required to report to the authorities to declare they were indeed Jewish and to specifically declare all their property. Seeing this information about his mother made him even more grateful to the Metropolitan Kiril and what he did to save the Jews of his city. It was, in fact, the Metropolitan's actions that enabled his mother not to be deported. This heroic story was

---

2 | Bar-Zohar, *Hitler's Grasp*, pp. 125-127.

3 | Kechales, *The Shoah*, pp. 97-98.

personal to him because he knew Kiril's actions brought forth life to him and to all the Jewish families of that city.

During my interview with David Cohen, he stated that even today, scholars and historians have different opinions and debates regarding who saved the Jewish people of Bulgaria. There are different theories and points of view for this rescue, but he is entirely grateful to the Bulgarian people for their actions during WW II. Many different factors worked together in order to save the Jews of Bulgaria, but in his opinion, first and foremost, he thanks the Bulgarian Church for their interventions on behalf of the Jewish people. He also stated that the good relationship between the leadership of the Church and the leadership of the Jewish community was vital to this rescue.

Four Hours Made the Difference

All of these leaks and actions spurred the leaders of the Jewish community to turn to high-ranking government officials with the request to cancel the evil verdict. One of their means of action was to send a delegation from Kyustendil to Sofia. The plan was to meet at the train station on March 8 at 5:00 P.M. Forty Bulgarian men promised to come, but in the end, only four brave non-Jewish men turned up: Petar Mihalev, a member of Parliament; Ivan Momchilov, a lawyer and former member of Parliament; Vladimir Kortev, one of the leaders of the Macedonian community; and Asen Suichmezov, a businessman. The small but courageous delegation arrived at Sofia on March 9 and immediately applied to the Deputy Chairman of the National Assembly, Dimitar Peshev.

When Peshev learned what was going on, he determined to raise the issue for discussion in the Parliament, stressing the illegality of the decision to deport the Bulgarian Jews. He also decided to meet with Minister of Interior Gabrovski and to discuss the issue with Prime Minister Filov and Tsar Boris.

Peshev and other members of Parliament presented themselves at Gabrovski's office. They warned him that it would be a tragedy if the

Bulgarian Jews were sent to Nazi-occupied Poland. At first, Gabrovski denied that such a thing was being planned, but Peshev insisted and, after a telephone conversation confirming the planned deportation, Gabrovski agreed to temporarily suspend the deportation of Jewish citizens from within the old borders of Bulgaria.

As a result of Gabrovski's and others' intervention, on the evening of March 9, 1943, the deportation order was rescinded, and the Jewish people of Plovdiv, Pazardzhik, Sliven, and other Bulgarian cities from the pre-war borders were released to their homes. The primary reason behind the cancellation of the deportation order was the intent to keep the deportation secret, which obviously had not been fulfilled. The moment the plan was leaked, Filov and Gabrovski knew the issue would cause an uproar in Parliament, and so they felt compelled to rescind the order.

Liliana Panitza, Belev's secretary, recalled the telephone call Belev received from Gabrovski regarding the cancellation of the deportation, followed by Belev's explosion of anger. According to Belev, if the order to cancel the deportation had been given four hours later, the plan would have been carried out successfully. Just four hours made the difference between murder and deliverance for 8,000 Jewish individuals.[4]

A Powerful Letter of Opposition

Following the failure of the plan to deport these Jewish people on March 9, Dimitar Peŝhev remained uneasy, fearing the Jews of Bulgaria would face another attempt to deport them. He decided to write a letter and try to sign as many members from the pro-government majority of the General Assembly as possible. The purpose of this letter was to thwart any future anti-Semitic legislation and to prevent national shame, both political and moral, as well as any attempt to take from the Bulgarian people the moral principles they had always held true.

Peŝhev wrote the letter on March 17, 1943; within two days, forty-two members of the pro-government majority had signed it. Peŝhev wrote the

4 | Bar-Zohar, *Hitler's Grasp*, pp. 131-132.

letter on March 17, 1943; two days later, with forty-three signatures of parliamentary deputies, the letter was placed on Prime Minister Filov's desk. More than a third of the government had joined Pešhev's initiative, resulting in Pešhev being censured and dismissed from his position of Assembly Vice-Chairman. Peshev was politically ostracized for his actions.

In part, the letter reads as follows:

> "We cannot believe that the deportation of these people from Bulgaria has been envisaged; this intention has been ascribed by a malicious rumor to the Bulgarian government. Such a measure is unthinkable, not only because these people, who have not been deprived of their Bulgarian citizenship, cannot be expelled out of Bulgaria, but because it would be a destructive measure, carrying grave political consequences. It would brand Bulgaria with an underserved stain, that not only would burden her morally, but also would void all her moral standing...."[5]

Rabbi Daniel Zion wrote in his book *Five Years under the Fascist Regime*, "... In the meantime, the situation of Bulgarian Jewry grew increasingly worse. The Law of Defense of the Nation was rigidly implemented. All kinds of administrative measures were effected in quick succession. The Jewish streets shuddered at every rumor—and there was no lack thereof. Unfortunately, these rumors plunged us into preemptive mourning. Somehow we had to curb the despair that was gripping our community more and more tightly every day. Desperation peaked when we learned that the Jewish population in Kyustendil had been notified to pack whatever they could carry and make themselves ready for the departure (March 1943). Everybody knew what this meant. At the same time, it was reported that the Jewish community in Plovdiv had been gathered in one school, and at any time they could expect to be loaded onto wagons [trains] and sent to Poland. These two facts brought all Bulgarian Jews to a state of deepest despair. It was clear to all that the Commissariat for Jewish Affairs

5 | Ibid, p. 150.

was determined to destroy us. Prominent Bulgarian public figures from Kyustendil and Plovdiv immediately approached the relevant policymakers and lobbied to repeal the secret order to send part of the Jewish population outside Bulgaria's borders. Fortunately, they were successful. The order was canceled. However, the danger remained. Everyone tried to predict what [who] the Commissariat would target next…. "[6]

Meeting the Führer

The German ambassador went to the King's palace on March 28, 1943, to extend an invitation to Tsar Boris III to visit the "Eagle's Nest," the Third Reich's estate in Berchtesgaden to meet with Hitler. Three days later, on March 31, 1943, the tsar flew to Salzburg and from there traveled to Berchtesgaden.

The very next day, on April 1, he met Adolf Hitler and Joachim Von Ribbentrop, the foreign minister of Nazi Germany, at the Eagle's Nest. The tsar was concerned that Hitler had summoned him to insist he send Bulgarian troops to the Russian front. However, the meeting began well, with Hitler greeting Boris warmly.

The two immediately began speaking to one another in German, since Boris was of German blood and spoke the language fluently. The tsar began to relax and even dared to hope he had nothing to be concerned about. Then Ribbentrop took over and explained that, as far as they understood the Jewish Question, "the only right solution was the radical solution."[7]

In response, Tsar Boris attempted to explain to the foreign minister that the Jews of Bulgaria were Sephardic, not Ashkenazic. The tsar wanted Ribbentrop and Hitler to understand that the Bulgarian Jews were different from those of other countries. It seems King Boris was trying to convey to them that the Jews of Bulgaria were an integral part of society and were not considered foreign. He also explained that they were poorer than the Jewish people in other countries.

Ribbentrop, it seems, was not convinced. "Jews will always remain

6 | Zion, *Nazi Regime*, p. 25.

7 | Bar-Zohar, *Hitler's Grasp*, pp. 157-159.

Jews," was his response.[8] Boris then understood that the meeting was all about what happened in Bulgaria on March 9.

Hitler did not say much at that point, but it was obvious to the tsar that both he and Ribbentrop were not pleased with Boris's actions of sparing the 8,400 Bulgarian Jews, and that they expected more cooperation from him in the future.[9]

After this meeting, according to a report from April 5, 1943, of the Gestapo attaché in Sofia, it was Tsar Boris who had cancelled the deportation orders from March 9.[10] It was no wonder then that Hitler and Ribbentrop were determined to pressure the tsar on this matter. The tsar knew he had to make a move in this dangerous political situation.

On his return to Bulgaria, Tsar Boris decided he must change his policy toward the Jewish people. Some Bulgarian Jews, for various reasons, had been set free from the labor camps, but they would now be re-drafted in an attempt to thwart their deportation. This became his great deception throughout the war—presenting the need for their Jewish population to remain in Bulgaria so they could be involved in the country's construction work.

Around the same time, on April 4, 1943, after the meeting with Hitler, Ribbentrop, and Tsar Boris, Ribbentrop sent a telegram to the German emissary in Sofia stating: "…regarding the Jewish problem in Bulgaria, the King has declared that up to now he has only given his consent for deportation of the Jews from Macedonia and Thrace to areas in Eastern Europe. He only wants to deport a limited number of Bolsheviks-communists from Bulgaria itself. The other 25,000 Jews will be concentrated in camps within the country seeing that he wants to use them to build roads. In my response to the King's statement, I stated with emphasis that according to our concepts of Jews, the only proper solution is the radical one. Ribbentrop."[11]

This telegram implies that Tsar Boris had agreed to deport nearly

8 | Ibid, pp. 157-159.

9 | Ibid, pp. 157-159.

10 | Boyadjiev, *Rescued*, pp. vii-viii.

11 | Nir Baruch, "The Jews in Bulgaria," http://www.thebulgarianjews.org.il/ Uploads/dbsAttachedFiles/TheJewsNirBaruch.pdf, p. 13.

23,000 Bulgarian Jews, considering there were around 48,000 Jewish people living in Bulgaria at the time. It stems from an agreement based on Hitler's and Ribbentrop's conversation with the king on April 1, 1943.[12]

It was during this time that Metropolitan Stefan actively dedicated himself to protecting Bulgaria's Jewish community. In March 1943, he was horrified by what he saw of the expulsion of the Jews of Macedonia and Thrace. He witnessed the transport trains and tried to alert the tsar to have him put an end to this cruelty. Then, after the attempt to expel the Jews of Bulgaria on March 9, 1943, Stefan acted to unify all the leaders of the church against the repressive measures enacted against their Jewish community.

It is worthy of note that despite calls from anti-Semitic organizations for his death, Stefan continued to labor on behalf of Bulgaria's Jews.[13]

A Second Deportation Plan

The first plan for deportation had failed, but the enemies of the Jewish people were not through plotting to destroy them. Following Belev's failure to deport the Jews of old Bulgaria, he initiated a second plan, one that would include all the Jews of Bulgaria. He submitted his plan to Gabrovski in May 1943.

The general plan was to deport 25,000 Jewish people from Sofia and 23,000 from the outlying areas—a total of 48,000. The plan was detailed and comprehensive. First, all Bulgarian Jews were to be brought to transit camps by May 30. Then, beginning on the very day they were brought to these camps, 16,000 of them would be sent each month to the port cities on the banks of the Danube, particularly Lom and Somovit, with the deportations being complete by September 30, 1943. Once all of Bulgaria's Jews had been transported out of the country, they would then be deported to their death in Poland.

Belev, together with Minister of Interior Gabrovski, devised two main objectives for the new plan. The first was to deport all Jewish people from

12 | Ibid, page 13.

13 | Bar-Zohar, *Hitler's Grasp*, pp. 167-169.

the borders of Bulgaria and hand them over to the Germans. The second was to deport all the Jewish population of Sofia (about half of Bulgaria's Jews) to the provincial cities. This second objective was to be put into action in case Tsar Boris rejected the first, though according to Belev, it was in any case simply a stage before the ultimate deportation of all the Bulgarian Jews.

On May 18, 1943, Liliana Panitza once more spoke secretly with Dr. Levi. She warned that his struggle was not yet over and told him of the plans Belev was putting together to deport *all* the Jews of Bulgaria. (This was different than the plan to deport 8,000 Jewish Bulgarians in March 1943, as this latest plan included every single Jew in Bulgaria—man, woman, and child.) Panitza pleaded with Levi not to give up because Belev had plans to continue his war against the Jewish people. Thanks to Panitza's courage, Levi alerted the heads of the Jewish community, and the news quickly spread.

Two days later, on May 20, 1943, Minister of Interior Gabrovski had an audience with the tsar to present him with the deportation plans. This is where the fate of the Jews of Bulgaria was sealed. The tsar rejected the first objective, refusing to authorize their deportation from the borders of Bulgaria. However, he did permit the second objective, which was to banish them from Sofia.

Following the tsar's approval, deportation notices were sent to the Jewish community in Sofia, giving them only three days' notice. All their possessions would have to be left behind, along with their house keys, which would then be handed over to the commissariat. The deportation notices caused confusion and fear among the Jewish population, and the Jewish leaders immediately combined forces to act against the orders.

An article written in 1949, after the war, shows the mood that prevailed at the time:

"In 1943, when Prime Minister Filov and the Minister of Interior Gabrovski, the minions of Hitler, may his name and memory be erased, were about to deport the Jews of Sofia to the furnaces of Poland, the Jews of Sofia elected a deputation headed by the Chief Rabbi Daniel Zion, to intervene for them. As these haters of Israel refused to accept the Jewish delegation the rabbi turned to Tsar Boris and demanded that he cancel the evil edict. Thanks to his assertiveness, the edict was turned over and instead of being sent to Poland—[25,000] Jews of Sofia were sent to the provincial cities…."[14]

At this time, Rabbi Daniel Zion did all within his power to influence the tsar to prevent the deportation. When he was unsuccessful in seeking an audience with the tsar, he turned to Metropolitan Stefan.

Stefan himself related how Rabbi Zion waited for him in his office and told him about the deportation. As Stefan listened, he began to weep. Then he took immediate action, sending urgent messages to the tsar, pleading for him to have mercy on the Bulgarian Jews. "Do not persecute," he wrote, "so that you, yourself, will not be persecuted. With what measure ye mete, it shall be measured to you again. I know, Boris, that God in heaven is keeping watch over your actions."[15]

In addition to sending messages to the tsar, Metropolitan Stefan declared publicly that the church opposed the deportation. Standing opposite the Alexander Nevsky Cathedral and with ministers of the government behind him, he condemned the discrimination against the Jewish people.

After this, Prime Minister Filov addressed Stefan, saying the church had no right to interfere with matters of state. Stefan's response was that he was acting in accordance with Christian principles, under a greater authority than that of the state.

The Miracle of May 1943

According to Rabbi Daniel Zion, the days between "May 24-28 in 1943 were the darkest days for the Jews of Sofia. At this point, the Commissariat, through the police, began sending formal notices to all Jewish homes about an impending forced eviction in the province. No one will ever forget the

14 | David Eizencherg, "Around 40,000 Bulgarian Jews are in Israel," *Hazafa* newspaper, July 8, 1949, p. 6.

15 | Eliezer Ansky, "A Short Biographia of Rabbi Daniel Zion," thebulgarianjews.org.il, http://www.thebulgarianjews.org.il/_Uploads/dbsAttachedFiles/Daniel_Zion_Biografia.pdf.

heart-rending scenes in the Jewish streets and neighborhoods in those hellish days, during which our brothers and sisters were parting with friends and family with tears soaked with blood. We were certain, that this measure [the transfer to the provincial cities] was just the first step towards sending us to Poland. We had to act at the speed of lighting. Eviction notices rained down. The Eviction notices fell on us like rain. For me personally, the 23rd of May 1943 was declared a day of fasting and prayer..."[16]

In his book, Rabbi Daniel wrote of his prayer during this time, which he titled "Our Prayer":

> "Let us love God with all our heart, all our soul, all our mind, and all our strength!
> Let us demonstrate God's wisdom and truth!
> Let us be a model of good!
> Let us be a model of fairness!
> Let us be a model of reason!
> Let us turn to the one true and eternal God, on whom all things depend, and dedicate our lives to work for Him!
> Let us open our hearts and souls to all who are weak and helpless!
> Let us see and enjoy the good and the beautiful in every living being!
> Let us leave the path of unloving and enter God's love; let us think and feel and act like Him!"

He continued by saying, "If we fulfill these ten new rules, salvation will come, and God will show us mercy. He will send peace on Earth and awaken the hearts of all people. He will enlighten their minds, and they will do only good. We all will become bearers of love, and God will be glorified in the world. Amen."[17]

According to the writings of Menachem Moshonov, a goldsmith who supplied the king's jewelry, in May 1943 he turned to Rabbi Daniel for

16 | Zion, *Nazi Regime*, p. 26.
17 | Zion, *Nazi Regime*, p. 26.

help because of the rumors going around in Sofia about the deportations.[18] Rabbi Daniel and Moshonov immediately went to see Colonel Lulchev, advisor to the tsar.

Lulchev agreed that this was indeed a dangerous time for the Jewish people, and he advised them to organize a day of prayer and fasting. On that suggestion, Rabbi Daniel declared a day of fasting and prayer on May 24, the day after his personal fast, and suggested the Jewish community organize a protest against the deportation.

The rabbi then turned to Mr. Vitaly Chaimov, chairman of the Jewish Community Board, for support and authorization for declaring a day of prayer and protest. At this point, the Jewish Council and Community Board finally understood that the threat of being deported was real, so they gave their support and clearance to the rabbi, despite pleading with him a year earlier to do nothing. The leaders of the Jewish community accepted the rabbi's suggestion and decided to march from the central synagogue through the streets of Sofia in protest.

That same day of the march, May 24, was St. Cyril and Methodius Day, a national holiday celebrating Bulgarian culture and literature. On the arrival of Rabbi Daniel Zion to the central synagogue of Sofia where the protest march would begin, he found its gates locked. He therefore led the crowd of protesters to the smaller synagogue in the Yutchbunar neighborhood, where he saw a congregation of several thousand Jewish people, from all strata of society, gathered to pray out loud. Jewish mothers, fathers, children, rich and poor, simple and educated, people of all ages and all political persuasions prayed as one. Gradually, the prayers turned to weeping.

Albert (Avraham) Ben Bassat, Rabbi Zion's son-in-law, wrote a poem while in Somovit camp on how the Jewish people gathered in the main synagogue of Yutchbunar. He wrote how from the youngest to the oldest they came, distressed, depressed, and in shock. Every Bulgarian Jew in the city of Sofia gathered at the synagogue to pray.

In this powerful atmosphere of unity, Rabbi Daniel Zion stepped up to the podium. "Do not despair, brothers and sisters!" he cried out. "Do

18 | Kechales, *The Shoah*, pp. 171-172.

not lose faith in the power of the Most High! Believe in His power and His ability to turn to dust all those who have raised their sword against the defenseless Jewish people! We [The Jewish people] have stared at death before. However, the Almighty has always helped us, even if only at the eleventh hour, to save us from imminent danger. Believe and do not lose heart! No matter what happens, we will overcome all the suffering they pour on us. Keep your heads up! Open your hearts and let the light of God come in; then God too will open his heart and send us salvation ...."[19] According to another source, Daniel encouraged his people with the words, "Put your trust in the Rock of Israel!"[20]

Apparently, my father was in that same synagogue when Rabbi Zion gave his speech, calling on the Jewish people to put their trust in God. My father told me how, at that moment, he prayed with all his soul and might. It was hard for him to trust God in such a dark time. He had lost hope, but in that hopelessness, he cried out to the God of Israel for help. He looked around and saw how the Jewish people were praying. As he looked at them, he remembered his own father and how he went faithfully to synagogue to pray. Encouraged by the memory and by Rabbi Zion's words, he continued praying. It was if, at that moment, the only thing he felt he could do as a fifteen-year-old Jewish boy was to pray.

When Rabbi Zion finished speaking, Rabbi Asher Hananel, Chief Rabbi of Sofia, also gave a speech. After both rabbis spoke, Mr. Menachem Moshonov turned to Rabbi Zion and announced that Metropolitan Stefan wished to meet with him immediately. Rabbi Daniel quickly agreed, and Rabbi Asher Hananel and Menachem Moshonov accompanied him to see Stefan.[21]

The instant Rabbi Zion saw the expression on Stefan's face, he knew his friend had good news. Bringing inexpressible joy to Rabbi Daniel's heart, Stefan told him to go and tell his people that the tsar had given him and the government of Bulgaria his word that the Bulgarian Jews would not be

---

19 | Zion, *Nazi Regime*, p. 27.

20 | Shulam, "Remembering Rabbi Daniel..." https://ffoz.org/discover/yahrzeit/yahrzeit-of-rabbi-daniel-zion.html (accessed: 24.05.2018).

21 | Chary, *Bulgarian Jews*, pp.148-149.

deported out of the country. Then Stefan told Rabbi Daniel, "Go and tell them [the Bulgarian Jewry] the news; reassure them, and let them believe in the good providence of the Almighty, who never forgets His children. Go in peace!"[22]

The rabbi thanked Stefan profusely for the care he had shown and for his efforts to save the Jews of Bulgaria. He assured him they would never forget his valuable intervention and sacrifice.

According to Moshonov's own testimony of this meeting, "We went to the Metropolitan at 8:30 a.m. He wanted to know what we were doing and we told him everything in detail. He received us early and apparently was greatly concerned about our situation, because he was still in his dressing gown. After he had listened to us, he calmed us and promised to continue to do everything in his power to prevent the deportation of the Jews from the country. Metropolitan Stefan added that at the ceremony in honour of the feast of the saints Kyril and Methodius, which was taking place on that same day, May 24, 1943, he would meet the King and would speak to him again about that same matter. He seemed to be very moved and full of hope. He stressed anew that at one of his last meetings with the King, the latter, in the presence of the ecclesiastical high official Kyril, had specifically stated that the Jews would not be deported from Bulgaria. When we parted from the Metropolitan, he reassured us saying: 'Go and calm your brethren, tell them from me that the King has promised, and a King's word is not reversed.'"[23]

Metropolitan Stefan later said that "in these critical moments we firmly took the position in defen[s]e of the mercilessly persecuted Jewry; and we did so strongly motivated by our faith and by the duty, which stems from the civil liberty we enjoy. From the church pulpit we addressed society, the Government and the Head of State with numerous appeals to stop the persecution, to stop the deportation to Poland and to return all the detained in concentrations camps back to their homes."[24]

---

22 | Zion, *Nazi Regime*, pp. 27-28.

23 | Snoek, *The Grey Book*, pp. 189-190.

24 | Protocols of the Holy Synod, Document #26, p. 187.

Rabbi Daniel Punished

When the rabbi returned from his meeting, the people were anxiously awaiting him. He mounted the podium and said, "Here, brothers, our prayers were heard. I have reason to assure you that we will not be deported out of Bulgaria…."[25]

After the prayers in the synagogue and the rabbi's speech, one young man called on the people to march in demonstration in the streets of Sofia. The people agreed, though Mr. Vitaly Chaimov turned to the rabbi and begged him to stay in the synagogue and not to march in the streets with the others. The rabbi answered, "I will join my people. Where they go, I will go."[26]

Some 1,000 Jewish people marched to the central square of Sofia that day. However, when they reached the square, the Bulgarian police swarmed the demonstrators. Many of the marchers were injured, and about 400 of them were arrested and taken to labor camps. In the chaos, two of the marchers grabbed the rabbi and led him to a house to hide. After a while, however, Rabbi Daniel decided it was not his duty to hide but rather to go and find out why the people had been set upon.

When he came to his house in Sofia, he found two policemen waiting for him, and he realized he had been betrayed.[27] The rabbi was immediately arrested and taken to the police station in Sofia, where he was subjected to a violent assault by the Bulgarian police.

After the beating, the sixty-year old rabbi was forced to stand for ten hours straight. At the end of the ten hours, Alexander Belev came to see him and immediately started yelling at him that he was to blame for what was happening to the Bulgarian Jews. According to Zohar's book, Belev said to Rabbi Daniel, "Because of you, these four hundred people will be sent to Poland now!"[28]

In essence, Belev told Rabbi Zion he was to blame for the Jewish

---

25 | Zion, *Nazi Regime*, p. 28.

26 | Avraamov, "Daniel Zion," p. 333.

27 | Zion, *Nazi Regime*, p. 28.

28 | Bar-Zohar, *Hitler's Grasp*, pp. 216-217.

people who would be killed in Poland. Those words must have cut him to the heart because, in reality, he had truly done all he could to save the Jewish community.

In addition, Belev brutally demanded that Rabbi Zion provide information on other Jews, but the faithful rabbi would not betray his brethren. He answered, "Sir, I am not afraid of you! I only fear God!"[29] I can only imagine how much inner strength and courage Rabbi Daniel had to say this. Belev was the most prominent anti-Semite in Bulgaria at that time, and he desperately wanted to annihilate the Jewish people. Rabbi Daniel knew that, yet he spoke boldly and bravely.

Deportations to the Provinces

According to the poem written by Albert Ben Bassat before they were sent to the Somovit camp, all who tried to resist the attack by the police were captured. He wrote that Belev humiliated them, accusing them of treason, saying they had no right to exist. Albert's poem continues to describe the journey to the Somovit camp and the difficult conditions they were subjected to there.

Meanwhile, the poet's wife, Rabbi Zion's daughter Yaffa Ben Bassat and her two daughters were exiled by deportation order to the city of Ruse in Bulgaria. Despite the demonstration, on May 26, 1943, the commissariat began to deport the Jews of Sofia to the provincial cities. Between May 26 and June 7, the commissariat succeeded in deporting 19,153 of Sofia's Jewish population, though they remained within Bulgaria's borders.

Even after the deportations, the tsar continued to receive letters and petitions. Among the petitions was a letter written by sixty-three Bulgarian dignitaries who opposed the transfer of the Jewish people to the Germans. These petitions, along with the fact that Stefan had managed to raise the support of the church to oppose the deportations, were effective in influencing the tsar to refuse permission to hand over the Bulgarian Jews to the Germans.

---

29 | Boyadjiev, *Rescued*, p.vii.

My grandmother Sofie and her younger sons, including my father, Nissim, received deportation orders from Sofia to Plovdiv. (Her oldest sons, Mordechai and Eliezer, had already been drafted into the labor battalions.) She was permitted to take only 50 kilos, or 110 pounds, of belongings with her; she had to leave everything else behind. Once in Plovdiv, Sofie urged Nissim and his older brother David to hide in the forest. My father was only fifteen at the time, and David was seventeen. Sofie was terrified that at any moment they would be deported to the camps in Poland, so she asked them to look after each other and not to worry about her or their younger brothers, Sami and Zako, who stayed with her until the end of the war.

Nissim often told us how his mother made them promise that if he and David saw a train in the area of Plovdiv, they would not leave the forest to come looking for them. He also told us that when they parted, she began to sob.

Joining the Partisans

A few days after Nissim and David had hidden in the forest, they came across a group of partisans and joined them. Thus, at the age of fifteen, my father began to fight against the Nazis.[30] According to my father, he hid in the forest with the partisans for the rest of the war. It was a difficult existence, but he remembers that Christians from the church in Plovdiv gave them food to survive, despite the danger entailed in doing so.

My father didn't talk much about his time with the Partisans, but I do remember one story in particular. He forbade us from eating mushrooms when we were growing up, though I never understood why. But much later on in life, when my daughters were young and were asked to try a cooked mushroom at a restaurant where they were eating, my father got upset. At last, he revealed that his aversion to mushrooms came about from the time he was with the partisans.

30 | It is known that there were at least seventy-eight Jewish young people (both boys and girls) who joined the Partisans, or the Underground Resistance, and died during War World II in Bulgaria. Baruch, "The Jews in Bulgaria," p. 15.

It seems that while my father was living with them in the forest, he and a friend came across some mushrooms. Though they had been warned not to eat certain mushrooms that grew wild in the forest, as some were poisonous, his friend was so hungry that he immediately started eating them, not bothering to take the time to check and see if they were poisonous. Because they were on guard duty at the time and my father was serving as lookout, he did not check the mushrooms either. A few minutes later, he heard his friend start to choke. Nissim rushed to his side, but though he desperately wanted to help, he could do nothing, and his friend died right beside him.

My father sobbed as he shared his story, admitting that it had been too much for a fifteen-year-old to bear. He said that for a fleeting moment, he actually looked at the mushrooms and considered eating them himself. In shock and despair, he held one in his hand and questioned how much more he could handle. *Why do I and my Jewish brethren have to suffer so much?* he wondered. *Perhaps it might be better to give up here and now and end my life.*

Before he could put the mushroom in his mouth, he remembered Rabbi Daniel Zion's words of encouragement, from the many times he heard him at the synagogue and also all the words he told him throughout the war. He remembered looking at the rabbi's ring, with the words *love*, *faith*, and *truth* inscribed on it. No matter what, he told himself, those three things always remain. And with that, he threw the mushroom to the ground. Later in life, he told me that it was as if God had intervened at that very moment by giving him those thoughts and memories.

As he sat there beside his friend, he thought of his mother and brothers, and he reminded himself that he had to continue fighting to live, at least for them. At that moment, he decided not to give up and to do whatever possible to survive. He owed it to God, he decided, and to his family and himself.

This was a turning point for him, he explained as he drew his story to a close. He chose to believe in God and to believe he would survive the war. Needless to say, my daughters and I never again ate mushrooms in front of my father, nor did anyone else in my family.

CHAPTER 7

Final Outcome of Deportations... and a Mysterious Death

After the protest on May 24, Belev gave the order to arrest public Jewish figures, resulting in the arrest of 412 leaders of the Jewish community, including Rabbi Daniel Zion and his son-in-law Rabbi Albert Ben Bassat. Along with other detainees, the two rabbis were taken by transport train to the Somovit concentration camp on the banks of the Danube. Rabbi Zion later wrote that they were starved and mistreated in the camp until they were released. He himself suffered violence and humiliation. Belev did this in order to create panic among the Jewish people, as well as to remove the influential leaders of the Jewish community from Sofia.

Camp Somovit

According to Rabbi Daniel Zion, the detainees, including himself and his son-in-law, were led in the dark of night to the railway and loaded into cattle trains in Sofia. The trains soon began to roll, and no one knew where they were being taken. When they arrived at their destination and the doors to the cattle cars—designed for animals and not for humans—were opened, the stench from urine and unwashed bodies was unbearable. When they arrived at the camp, they were all examined by guards, who took from them anything they might have of value (watches, money, knives, books, and so on). They were then divided into groups of thirty to forty in a room, where they were informed that whoever did not do as he was told would be put to death.

In the first three days, they received nothing to eat and were subjected to cruel treatment. They were not allowed to move around the room and were given only one hour a day to relieve themselves. The rabbi wrote that more than anything else, it was the mental and emotional abuse that was the hardest to bear.

Soon after arriving at the camp, when all the prisoners were standing in a row, Rabbi Daniel turned to the Bulgarian lieutenant and asked whether they were animals or human beings who had been arrested simply because they were Jewish. The lieutenant responded with mocking laughter. The next day, a guard came to him and said, "If you ever again ..." He paused and took his gun out and pointed it at the rabbi's chest before completing his sentence. "...complain, you will get a bullet. Remember that well."

The regime in the camp was cruel and degrading. Many officers and guards beat the prisoners, cursed and berated them, and laid severe sanctions on them. In one instance, an officer forcefully pulled on Rabbi Daniel's ears because he had not called out his name loudly enough in the morning roll call. In addition, the food was mostly inedible and definitely insufficient, and the living conditions were horrific.

The days in the camp were gray, filled with fear and distress, with the detainees' mental anguish growing from day to day. They continually suffered under the fear that at night they would be torn from their beds, put on ferries along the Danube, and transported to Poland where they would be exterminated.

Determined to Pray

In the beginning, they were told they were to receive 100 grams of bread per day, per person, and seven kilograms of beans for 200 people. The rabbi related how he could not bear to see his people suffer, and he was overcome with pity and sympathy for them. He decided that despite the fact that it was forbidden for them to visibly pray in the camp or to leave the yard for any reason, he must pray. And so he found a somewhat secluded place within the camp to be alone with God. In his prayers, which became a daily exercise for him, he pleaded with God to ease the suffering in the camp.

After several mornings of prayer, the guards announced that they had increased the bread ration to 200 grams a day per person. Even so, this was not sufficient, and Rabbi Zion despaired for his people in the camp. He continued to pray, and after some time, the ration was again increased by another 100 grams, and then to 500 grams a day per person.

In his writings, the rabbi spoke of a day when the lieutenant came to the yard and saw him reading a book. He asked the rabbi what he was reading, and the rabbi answered, "A devotional book." The lieutenant laughed, mocking him because he did not have anything to eat, yet there he was, reading philosophy. The rabbi retorted that if it were not for that book, he would react quite differently to the lieutenant. Though I have found nothing to confirm this, I wonder if the beloved rabbi was reading the Bible.

There was also an older guard in the camp, who told the rabbi he could not sleep at night because of what he and the other guards were doing to him and his Jewish friends. In time, the guard and the rabbi became friends, and when this guard was on duty, he would allow the rabbi to go up the hill to pray, a place still within the camp but secluded. However, he warned the rabbi to beware of being seen because if the other guards saw him, both of them would pay a heavy price.

Prayer, Faith, and the Word of God

Rabbi Daniel also wrote about another older guard, who caught the rabbi spilling two drops of water out of his window. As punishment, he made him take a bucket of water and a cloth and clean the whole area. The rabbi bent down and did so, until his son-in-law Albert tried to take his place, but the rabbi would not allow him to do so.

Rabbi Zion wrote that the way the guard treated him and the hatred he had for the Jewish people was nearly unbearable. He explained that of all the things he went through and though this particular punishment was not an extremely difficult one, the humiliation and the hatred he felt from this man caused him unspeakable suffering.

One day, Rabbi Daniel gave a lecture to the other prisoners, listing seven points they could learn through their life in the camp, including the values of equality, humility, and thankfulness. By equality, he meant there was no status among them, as they were all living under the same conditions. He also explained that humility is what they could learn through their suffering and hardship. He told them they could even be thankful in their difficult conditions because life in the camp could teach them to value the simplest things, such as a small slice of bread, and not ask for more than that.

The rabbi tried to look at life in the camp, unbearable as it was, as a learning experience, and he wanted to convey that to his fellow prisoners. In my opinion, this shows how he was able to encourage others and give positive perspective and meaning to the experience of suffering. Although they were all in the same humble position and under constant threat and deprivation, he was truly a spiritual shepherd and leader.

Rabbi Daniel believed that his lecture on finding something good in the middle of their dire circumstances caused people to discuss other subjects as well. As a result, they began to hold lectures on Jewish history, art, and so on. The prisoners also started talking about the Bible, the translation of the Bible, and several of its texts, including the prophets. Rabbi Daniel loved the Bible, and he loved talking about the prophets. Even in such difficult circumstances, the word of God was hidden in his heart and gave him supernatural strength. My mother told me that when Rabbi Daniel talked about this camp, he said it was prayer, faith, and the word of God that got him through.

Life in the camp was hard, but even there the rabbi did not cease to labor on behalf of his people. During all this time and despite their horrific conditions, he did not abandon his faith and continued to pray for his people and his Jewish brethren in the camp, as well as all his people outside the camp, though he did not know their fate. He was finally released from the camp in the autumn of 1943, having spent approximately five months there, the amount of time required of him to pay for his "crime" of being a Jewish leader trying to stop the deportations of his brethren to a place of certain death.

The fear of deportation to the death camps in the east had haunted the detainees from the beginning. However, this never happened. Instead, more Jewish men arrived from other cities throughout Bulgaria. At the end of summer 1943, there were 500 detainees in the camp, all of whom were prisoners of the commissariat, which alone decided who would be arrested and who would be released.[1] After some time, conditions improved in the camp, and several of the prisoners were released. By October 1943, less than six months after their internment, most of the detainees had been set free.

Metropolitan Stefan Confronts the King

Around the time of the deportations of the Jewish population to the provinces and after the arrests of Rabbi Daniel and others (May 24, 1943), a man named Solomon Mashiach went to see Metropolitan Stefan. According to Mr. Mashiach, he told Stefan about the deportations to the provincial cities and of the arrest of the Jewish people, including his good friend Rabbi Daniel Zion. Stefan listened with great emotion and rapt attention, then said he could scarcely believe such a thing could occur. He said that he could not permit this to go on as long as he was alive. With Mr. Mashiach still in the room, Stefan telephoned the king. "Boris, my son," he said, "I am not at all satisfied about you. One hears lately of many things done to our Israelite brethren. Think very hard; it is unworthy of you and of the Bulgarian people."[2]

Stefan did not reveal his source for the information, but he made it clear to the king that he wanted to meet with him personally regarding the matter. The king politely told him that he was not able to do so but would meet with him the following day. Mr. Mashiach informed Stefan that he was worried that might be too late, but Stefan reassured him that he would do everything possible, even if it meant laying down his own life in order to stop such a tragedy.

The next day, Metropolitan Stefan and Mashiach telephoned the

1 | Bar-Zohar, *Hitler's Grasp*, p. 217.

2 | Snoek, *The Grey Book*, pp. 186-192.

palace to speak to the king, but the king's counselor said he did not know the king's whereabouts. Stefan became very angry and refused to hang up until he spoke with the king. When that did not happen, he made inquiries and found out that the king was in the Krichim palace. Stefan immediately telephoned him there. "Boris," he said, "you forget yourself. You elude me and hide… Give the matter serious thought and uproot this demonic influence from your heart."[3] With that, the conversation ended.

An Additional Meeting with Hitler

It seems that because of the failure of the second deportation, Hitler decided to summon Tsar Boris to Berlin. This was given in exactly the same manner as was the summons following the first failed deportation of March 1943.

According to historians, Hitler demanded this meeting because, for the second time, Tsar Boris had revoked the decision to deport the Jews of Bulgaria and hand them over to the Germans. Another cause for this meeting was to ascertain the tsar's loyalty to Germany, since his unwillingness to deport the Bulgarian Jews could be a sign of his waning support of the Third Reich. Hitler did not look kindly on the tsar's disobedience to his demands and feared that perhaps Bulgaria was intending to enter a peace agreement with the Allies.

The tsar went immediately to the Eagle's Nest, though I imagine not without some fear and trepidation. Once there, he asserted before Hitler that the Bulgarian government needed the Jewish work force and thus was not prepared to send them away. In the past, Hitler had exhibited some fondness for Boris, but now he was furious at his lack of cooperation in supporting the deportation of the Bulgarian Jewry to the death camps. He was also angry that the tsar had refused to send Bulgarian troops to fight with the Nazis against the Russians.

Ultimately, Tsar Boris was able to leave the meeting as Germany's ally without giving his word or signing any document that would benefit

3 | Ibid.

the Nazis. By not giving the Führer a straight answer, the king was true to his reputation as "the fox," and he left the meeting pleased that he had succeeded in walking the fine line between remaining a German ally while not committing to actively helping in any way.

Though King Boris was pleased on one hand, on the second hand, I can imagine this meeting with Hitler lay heavily upon his heart. On his return to Bulgaria, he decided to have a meeting with the Holy Synod of the Bulgarian Orthodox Church. The Prime Minister Filov accompanied him to this meeting, which was held on June 22, 1943 and attended by eleven Metropolitans from the Orthodox Church. During this meeting, the king made an anti-Semitic speech, which can be found in the Synod's protocol number 6:

> "…the great damages caused to humanity throughout the generations by the Jewish spirit of profiteering. This spirit caused hatred among nations, despair, moral decay and betrayal between nations everywhere. This spirit of harmful profiteering caused and is causing dissatisfaction, frays, disputes, wars and disasters among nations. The present global cataclysm [e.g., WW II] can also be related to this spirit of profiteering.[4]
>
> "It is true that some great nations make good use of the money accumulated by this Jewish spirit of profiteering, but other nations realized that Jewish profiteering poses a fatal obstacle for their cultural-spiritual and national-economic development. These nations have acknowledged that the sooner they are released from the Jewish influence and exploitation, the sooner they will regain their national feelings and patriotism. This may be achieved when their [Jewish] influence on economic, financial, commercial and industrial institutions is terminated. All over Europe, the appropriate legal conditions have been created. Here too [in Bulgaria] the legal conditions have been fashioned through the

4 | Nir Baruch, "The Jews in Bulgaria," pp. 14-15.

National Defense Law. The Bulgarian Orthodox Church, known for its patriotism, cannot have any other concept."[5]

I assume the king made this speech in order to persuade the Church to change its policy toward the Jewish people, thus making them supporters or at least a quiet voice to the government efforts in deporting the Jews. Another possibility is that he thought these statements would show his loyalties to his German ally, while hoping others realized he didn't really mean them. In all honesty, I don't know what went through the king's mind, but I do believe that if it wasn't for the courageous Christians and others who stood up for the Jewish people, like Rabbi Daniel Zion, the ultimate saving of the Jewish Bulgarians might have ended very differently. I thank God that even after this meeting, the Holy Synod did not crumble but stood its ground for righteousness, godliness, and life, no matter the cost. Their actions brought hope and life to the Jewish people of Bulgaria. May we as Jewish people never forget what they did!

The Third Attempt at Deportation

In August 1943, Belev made one last effort to urge his German friends to pressure Bulgaria into handing over her Jewish population. In that same month, a letter to the Reich Embassy in Sofia arrived from Berlin, demanding aggressive action to cause the Bulgarian government to send their Jewish population to the east. The letter insisted that transferring the Jews of Sofia to the provinces did not satisfy anti-Semitic expectations, and Jewish influence on political and ecclesiastical circles had only grown and made the solution of the Jewish Question yet more difficult.

The Nazi envoy to Bulgaria, Adolf Beckerle, immediately began meeting with various ministers, including Prime Minister Filov. However, this time, the Bulgarian government did not commit to deporting Bulgaria's Jews. In fact, both the government and the tsar refused to deport them from Bulgarian territory.

As a result, Beckerle sent a letter back to Berlin, explaining that the

5 | Ibid, pp. 14-15.

government was not interested in deporting their Jewish citizens to the east. This was the first time a direct answer was given regarding this issue, and it was not the answer the Nazis wanted. This was the third attempt to deport Bulgaria's Jews; like the other two attempts before it, the plan failed, and they remained in Bulgaria throughout World War II.[6] But this decision to openly defy the Nazis did not go unnoticed.

Tsar Boris III's Mysterious Death

Tsar Boris III was once again summoned to the Führer, and so he traveled to the "Wolf's Lair," the Central Command at Berchtesgarden in Eastern Prussia on August 14, 1943. There, he and Hitler had a private meeting that left them both agitated and tense. Besides discussing the issue of the deportation of Bulgaria's Jews, Hitler demanded that Boris send Bulgarian military divisions to assist him in the war against the Allies. Boris refused all of Hitler's demands and returned to Bulgaria.

About two weeks later, on August 28, 1943, Boris fell inexplicably ill and died. Rumors spread following his death that he had been poisoned by Germany, but there is insufficient evidence to prove this. However, if indeed he was poisoned, it would have been because he refused to send the Bulgarian army to war against the Allies, as well as his stand regarding the Jews. (There are others who believe it was the Russians who poisoned him, though no proof exists for either theory.)

The tsar's death was mourned heavily throughout Bulgaria, as he was a beloved and popular figure among his people. My father was sixteen at the time, and he and some of the other partisans decided to risk leaving the forest in order to pay their respects to the king for not handing the Jews of Bulgaria over to the Germans. They were able to see the tsar's body as it lay in the St. Alexander Nevsky Cathedral, and my father remembers thinking at the time that Boris was not entirely guiltless when it came to great harm to the Jews. Nonetheless, Nissim reminded himself, Boris did stand against Hitler and, in his own way, prevented the deportation of the

6 | Bar-Zohar, Hitler's Grasp, pp. 225-228.

Bulgarian Jews to Poland. By doing so, the king had prevented death for my father and his family.

In the end, he was a leader who resisted Hitler and did not let him destroy the Bulgarian Jews. By Boris's word alone, the entire Jewish population of Bulgaria could have been erased. Yet even though he was under tremendous pressure from the Nazis to deport all of Bulgaria's Jews, Tsar Boris did not let that happen. As a result of his resistance, 48,000 Jewish individuals were spared from the death camps, an outcome the tsar did not live to see.

For these reasons, Nissim and others with him felt it was their duty to risk their lives to come and pay their respects to the Bulgarian leader. My father often told me that, upon seeing King Boris's body from a distance, he whispered, "Thank you."

Interestingly enough, only Tsar Boris's heart is now buried at Rila Monastery. King Boris and his heart, separate from one another, were originally buried at this monastery. Later, when the Russian Communists came, they stole the body, which was never seen again, but for some reason they left his heart behind. To this day, Bulgarians are encouraged and comforted by the thought that at least their beloved king's heart remained at the monastery.

Remembering the King

During my interviews in September 2020 with retired Colonel Professor Dimitar Nedialkov and Doctor Daniel Vatchkov, the director of the Chair of History at the National Institute of History in the Bulgarian Academy of Sciences, they both mentioned how smart and courageous King Boris was. In their opinion, he was a key player on the political scene, and Bulgaria has a lot for which to thank this king.

They also stated that Tsar Boris was a strong player, whose death left a big hole in Bulgaria's political realm, a hole that was hard to fill. Boris was able, on one hand, to reap the benefits of a good relationship with Hitler, while on the other hand, cunningly maneuver the situation. He was a leader of a nation allied with the Third Reich, but ultimately he was also a leader who said no to Hitler in a time very few leaders dared to do so.

During my interviews with these two men, they stressed their opinion that the Bulgarian Jews were saved because of the collective effort of the Bulgarian nation from the head, Boris, to the church, as well as to others throughout the Bulgarian population. At any point during the war, the deportation and extermination of the Bulgarian Jews could easily have become a reality.

On September 29, 2020, I had the honor of interviewing Simeon Borisov von Saxe-Coburg-Gotha, better known as King Simeon II (the son of King/Tsar Boris III), at the Royal Palace in Vrana, Sofia. He told me he had been crowned king of Bulgaria at the age of six. He explained that he was playing on a swing when the king's personal secretary came and addressed him as "your majesty." Even at his tender age, when Simeon heard those words, he knew his father had passed away.

Like any young boy who had lost

his father, he grieved, but he was now king of a country. That was a lot for a six-year-old to grasp. Knowing it was his duty to follow his father and do whatever was necessary for their country, the young boy tried as best he could, his heavy heart a constant reminder of why such things were required of him.

During my time with the king, I had a special opportunity to share with him about this book and why I was writing it. My family and I had decided to honor him with a gift, a piece of artwork made by one of our dear friends, Grace Alon, displaying the Aaronic blessing in Hebrew and in English (the blessing with which Aaron the priest blessed the people of Israel, as recorded in Numbers 6:23-27, TLV):

> "Speak to Aaron and to his sons saying: Thus you are to bless *Bnei-Yisrael*, by saying to them:
>
> '*Adonai* bless you and keep you!
> *Adonai* make His face to shine on you and be gracious to you!
> *Adonai* turn His face toward you and grant you *shalom*!'

In this way they are to place My Name over *Bnei-Yisrael*, and so I will bless them."

A Divine Appointment

I gave the piece to him and thanked him and his family, particularly his father, on behalf of me and my family. I thought of my father's story about coming out of the forest to pay his respects to King Boris, and there I was, seventy-seven years later, standing before the king of Bulgaria, the son of King Boris. I was able, on behalf of my family, to say thank you that his father did not deport my family to the death camps during the war. As an Israeli Jew, I was grateful for this divine appointment to be able to give a blessing to the king and to the Bulgarian people from Israel. It was a door that had been opened to us and for which I would be forever grateful.

Following the interview, I asked his majesty if he would like to meet my family. I told him they were waiting outside, and I even had my grandchildren with me—four generations beyond the Holocaust. His majesty was very generous and came out of the palace to meet them all. We were even granted permission to get a picture with him and the whole family. This picture will always be a family treasure (see photos #16, #17, and #18).

Upon returning to Israel from my meeting with King Simeon, I received word from his majesty that the gift we presented to him had found a place in the royal palace. This was indeed a great honor for us as Jewish people to have this time with the king and to be so honored by him.

While there, I also asked his opinion of why the Bulgarian Jews were saved when so many others were not. His one-word answer surprised me: "God." He was absolutely right. There is no doubt in my mind that my family was saved because of God and because of the people who believed in Him and were willing to risk everything in order to do what was right. I believe God orchestrated this rescue, where people from all levels of society worked in order to save lives.

After the interview with his majesty, my family and I were allowed access to King Boris's private office in the Vrana Palace. We went in through the main entrance of the palace and walked down the hall to the private office, eyeing the many magnificent paintings of the royal Bulgarian family along the way. I was amazed to think of how it must have been for Rabbi Daniel and Metropolitan Stefan to walk those very halls seventy years earlier.

The palace guard told us that the office was where the king accepted people and held meetings. As I scanned the impressive room and spotted a military uniform prominently displayed, many thoughts raced through my head, as once again I thought of my parents telling me about those two incredible men who risked everything to get an audience with the king. There are not enough words to describe how I felt at that moment. It was as if we had walked those halls and stood in that office along with those two beloved heroes, Rabbi Daniel Zion and Metropolitan Stefan.

A Great and Miraculous Event

Following the tsar's death, Prime Minister Filov and Minister of Interior Gabrovski were replaced. Filov soon became one of the members of the Regency Council established to help the young king rule the country, and Dobri Bojilov was nominated as Prime Minister. Bojilov replaced most of the ministers, including Gabrovski. Soon after the swearing in of the Bojilov government, Docho Christov, the new Minister of Interior, convened the regional directors of Bulgaria and announced, "The Jewish Question is becoming more and more difficult." He continued by saying, "...this is a result of the fact, that we didn't succeed to deport them. To send them back is unthinkable. The question [for us] is how we can use their work; [how] to free the Bulgarian society from the influence of the Jews." Later in the meeting, he said, "We shall not deport Jews anymore... wherever they are, there they shall remain."[7] The new Prime Minister Bojilov and his government, after being briefed and discussing the matter

7 | Bar-Zohar, *Hitler's Grasp*, pp. 238-239.

of the Jewish people, agreed with Christov and declared they would not deport them from the borders of Bulgaria.

Dr. Daniel Vatchkov, director of the Chair of History at the National Institute of History in the Bulgarian Academy of Sciences, believes that the greatest event in Bulgarian history, second only to liberation from the Ottoman Empire, was the rescue of the Bulgarian Jews during World War II. This miraculous event, he declared, came about because of the people of Bulgaria who acted on behalf of the welfare of its Jewish citizens. In a time of universal madness and evil, when the Jewish people were persecuted all over Europe simply because of their race, many Bulgarians opposed this persecution and did not allow their Jewish population—including my family—to be destroyed. Although there were those in Bulgaria who wanted to carry out the Final Solution for the extermination of their Jewish communities, the Bulgarian people took a strong and courageous stand against it, despite the fact that the Jews made up less than 1 percent of the country's total population. As a result, I am here to tell this story today.

CHAPTER 8

The End of World War II in Bulgaria

One of the many things I have learned while working on this project is that not all people felt the same about the Bulgarian Jews. Though many were determined to see them exterminated, others were just as determined to help preserve their lives.

Upon the death of Tsar Boris III, his young son became the tsar, and Filov was one of the regents of the newly formed Regency Council. Dobri Bojilov was prime minister for less than one year when a deteriorating situation caused him to resign on May 31, 1944, and a new government was formed under Ivan Bagrianov. The new Prime Minister opposed former Prime Minister Bogdan Filov's policies regarding the deportation of Bulgaria's Jewish population, and the moment he entered his position, he acted on their behalf. When Bagrianov came into office, Filov met with him and advised him to "take the necessary measures concerning the Jews, but quietly, without noise...." But Bagrianov did not listen. Instead, he took unprecedented steps to help the Bulgarian Jews.[1]

The first step Bagrianov took was to appoint Judge Protich to head the Commissariat for Jewish Affairs (a candidate that the Jewish leadership proposed). Then, on July 27, he cancelled the Law for the Defense of the Nation, perhaps the most significant of all his acts pertaining to the Jews. He also declared that the Jewish people were no longer required to wear yellow stars. In September of 1944, he released all Bulgarian Jews, including Mordecai and Eliezer Mizrachi, my father's older brothers, from the work camps. It was indeed a time of rejoicing for Bulgaria's Jews.

But circumstances changed yet again when, on September 9, the Red Army crossed the Danube and invaded Bulgaria. The fascist government fell, and a pro-Soviet government was established in its place. Many

1 | Ibid, p. 242.

Bulgarian officials were tried by the new communist regime, and many were executed, including Bagrianov, Bojilov, and Filov.[2] In the final stage of the war, the Bulgarian army joined the Soviets in the battle against Nazi Germany and fought by their side until World War II ended in Europe on May 8, 1945.

Honoring the Protectors/Deliverers

Many leaders, such as Dimitar Peshev, Metropolitan Stefan, Metropolitan Kiril, Liliana Panitza, Colonel Tsvetan Mumdzhiev, and, of course, Rabbi Daniel Zion, acted to save the Bulgarian Jews from deportation, powerfully and fearlessly influencing the government on the issue. It is important to note yet again that not one Jewish citizen who lived in Bulgaria during the Holocaust was sent to the death camps in Poland. Bulgarian Jewry was the only Jewish community in Nazi Europe whose numbers actually grew during World War II.

As a result of their assistance in protecting and delivering the Bulgarian Jews from certain death, both Metropolitan Stefan (his niece Mrs. Maria Nikolova Popova representing him) and Metropolitan Kiril of Plovdiv (his nephew Professor Kiril Markov representing him) posthumously received the title "Righteous Gentile" on March 12, 2002, at Yad VaShem, the World Holocaust Remembrance Center in Jerusalem. (Stefan died in 1957 at the age of seventy-nine, and Kiril died in 1971 at the age of seventy.)

Throughout the years preceding, as well as during World War II, the pressure placed by the Bulgarian Orthodox Church on the nation's government was one of the decisive factors that delivered the Jewish people from the death camps in Poland. As stated earlier, this can also be attributed to the good relations between Metropolitan Stefan and Rabbi Daniel Zion.

2 | Chary, *Bulgarian Jews*, pp.178-179.

Rabbi Daniel Zion a Hero

Rabbi Zion was indeed a hero, and he is remembered for his courage and selfless actions on behalf of Bulgaria's Jewish community, which he loved dearly. He took to heart the fate of his brethren and left no stone unturned in his efforts to support and deliver them from despair.

A letter sent by the chief rabbinate to the Minister of Religion in Jaffa-Tel Aviv on January 28, 1949, confirms that Rabbi Daniel Zion was indeed Bulgaria's chief rabbi, thus entitling him as "the distinguished rabbi." The letter also states that "Rabbi Zion, according to reliable accounts from the time of the Nazi occupation, labored with self-sacrificing courage, and by means of his friendly relations with the Bulgarian church, to save his flock from the claws of the Nazis...."[3]

Following this letter from the rabbinate, the Minister of Religion, Rabbi Fishman, wrote on February 3, 1949, to the Ministry of Finance, Custodian of Absentee Property, to say that "The Rabbi Zion is one of those who have distinguished themselves, particularly during the Nazi occupation of Bulgaria. He labored in courage and at personal risk for the sake of his Jewish community. Thanks to his relations with the leaders of the Christian church in Bulgaria he was able to save many Jews from the claws of the predators...."[4]

A further letter, sent on February 28, 1949, to the Jewish Agency by the Minister of Religion, Rabbi Fishman, described Rabbi Daniel as a "*Gaon*" (genius and brilliant one), the chief rabbi of Bulgaria. The use of the term "Gaon" was Rabbi Fishman's way of showing respect and honor for Rabbi Daniel Zion's outstanding role in benefiting the Bulgarian Jewry.

"I write to you concerning housing for the Gaon Daniel Zion, who was formerly the chief rabbi of the Jews of Bulgaria...," he wrote. "I wish to note that he was one of the distinguished rabbis of Bulgaria, and laboured with courage and at personal risk to save the Jews of Bulgaria during the Nazi occupation. Thanks to his connections with the Christian church and the respect with which they regarded him, he was successful in delivering

3 | Israel State Archives, 00113ol, G-19/4742.
4 | Ibid.

many Jews from the claws of the predator. He is therefore deserving of special consideration…."[5]

Rabbi Daniel endured many threats during WWII, yet he confronted ministers of government, representatives of the people, intellectuals, and politicians in order to save the Bulgarian Jews from destruction. He did all that was in his power to reach the tsar himself, in order to present Boris with the devastating situation facing the Jewish people. The rabbi also warned the tsar that whoever harmed the Jewish people would find his days were numbered, and the time would come when he would have to stand before God and pay for his actions.

A Time of Judgment

Rabbi Zion also warned that the day would come when those responsible would pay with their lives. As it turned out, many of them did die at the hands of the Communists, both those who were guilty and those who were not. After September 9, 1944, partisans, Communists, and large numbers of the Russian Agrarian Party summarily executed a considerable number of Fascists. Some say the number of people killed in these acts of vengeance numbered in the thousands.[6] A few weeks later, when the Communist "Fatherland Front" government established the People's Court to try the leaders of the former regime—many at the height of their political power—for war crimes, many were sentenced to death or life in prison.[7] It is likely the Soviets simply wanted to kill all the leadership in order to eliminate any opposition to their control. It is still unclear how many were killed after the Soviet coup.

Rabbi Zion had foreseen this, even in the days of the Jewish people's worst suffering. Although he was saved from the Holocaust, not all of his family was as fortunate. His parents, Solomon and Flora, died in Saloniki in 1940; his brother, Shmuel, and sisters, Dodon, Rikta, and Rashel, were sent to Auschwitz in February-March 1943, where they perished in the gas

5 | Ibid.
6 | Bar-Zohar, *Hitler's Grasp*, p. 249.
7 | Ibid.

chambers. We will always remember those who perished in the Holocaust. Thankfully, two of the rabbi's sisters—Julie, who was living in Bulgaria, and Tamar, who had moved to Turkey—survived.

According to a 1965 article that appeared in the newspaper *Ma'ariv*, Rabbi Daniel was the chief rabbi until the day he emigrated from Bulgaria to Israel. He was known to be an honest man, courageous, uncompromising in his fight for righteousness, and a vigorous anti-Fascist. He was the only religious Jew who organized a protest against the fascist authorities during the Second World War. As mentioned earlier, he appeared before the tsar and warned him that if he failed to protect the Jews, he would pay for his actions in heaven. Following this, the rabbi was interned in the Somovit labor camp, much more severe than the other camps and therefore reserved for the "rebellious Jews" with the intent of deporting them to the death camps of Poland. Thanks be to God, this never came about.

Return to the Promised Land

Rabbi Daniel Zion made *aliyah* (immigration, literally, "to ascend") to Israel with his family in 1948, where he established a synagogue in Jaffa on Yefet Street 75. The synagogue was named "*Shaar HaShemayim*" (The Gates of Heaven). As with any synagogue, morning, afternoon, and evening prayers were held there daily, as well as on Shabbat and the Holy Days. Josef Shulam, my mother, Rivka, and my sister, Simcha (her name in Hebrew means "joy"), all remember how the rabbi would pray *shacharit* (morning prayer) or *aravit* (evening prayer) in the synagogue. Then, after the prayers, he would open his home to whoever wished to come and study the Holy Scriptures, both the *Tanach* (Old Testament/Covenant) and the New Covenant.

After the war, my father returned to Sofia, where he found his mother, Sofie, and was delighted to see that she was still alive. We have a picture of Nissim's brother David in British uniform. It seems he joined the Jewish Brigade, also called "The Jewish Fighting Unit," which fought alongside the British during World War II. (We don't know his exact role, only that he joined at some point.) My uncle Sami remained with my grandmother for most of the war, where he worked from a young age in order to bring food home to the family. The rest of my uncles also survived.

Most of the Jewish population of Bulgaria, including my father's family, immigrated to Israel after the war. On the day the State of Israel was declared, May 15, 1948, the Jewish population numbered 600,000. Some 7,000 of those Jewish people were from Bulgaria. Between May 15, 1948, and December 31, 1949, 35,089 more Jewish individuals immigrated to Israel from Bulgaria. Of the 48,000 in Bulgaria prior to the war, only 6,000 remained there after 1949. As a result, the vast majority of Bulgarian Jews immigrated to Israel and comprised a significant percentage of the demography of Israel at that time.

As stated earlier, my father made the journey alone on a clandestine ship, coming with the Zionist Youth Movement, HaShomer HaTsa'ir. After World War II, he told his mother that he felt in his spirit and in his heart that he must go home to the Land of his fathers, the Land of Israel. He felt that his family had lived in exile for almost 2,000 years, and the time had finally come to return. Though my father was not a very religious person, he said he felt something he could not explain. The best way he could describe it was that he felt hope and excitement about going back to the Land of the Bible, from which his forefathers had come. It was time, as he said, to go "home."

MAPS & PICTURES

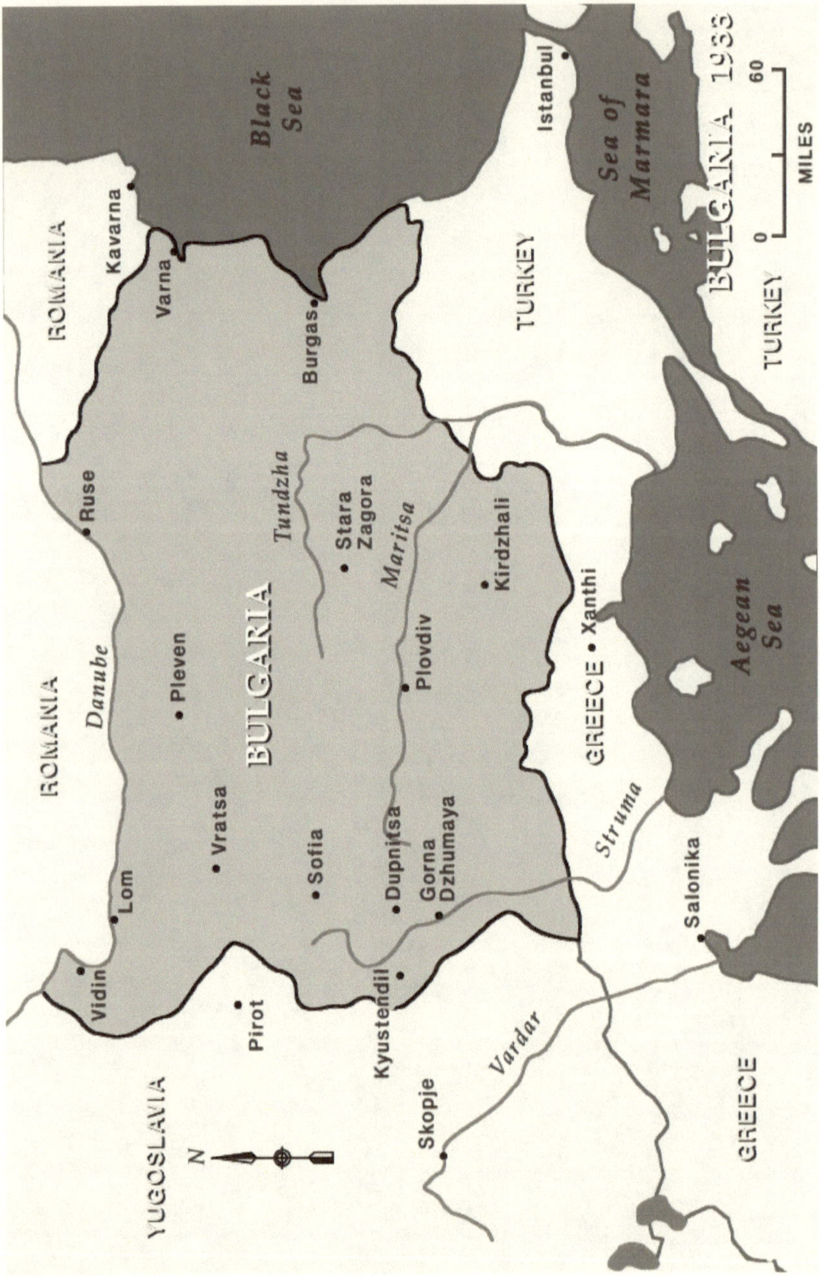

Bulgaria, 1933, pre-World War II borders.[1]

1 | United States Holocaust Memorial Museum, used by permission.

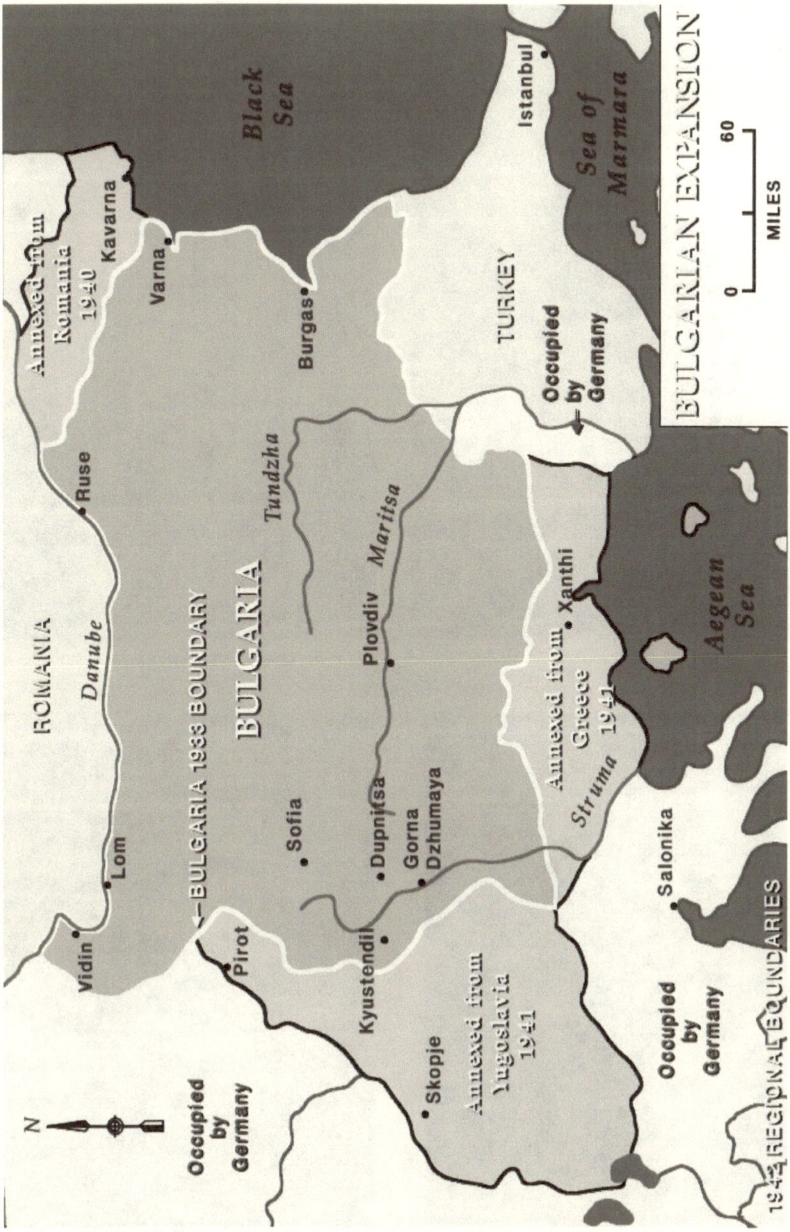

Bulgaria's border changes, 1939-1942: Bulgarian borders during War World II. In 1940, Southern Dobruja was given to Bulgaria. In 1941, Germany bestowed on Bulgaria the territories of Macedonia, part of conquered Yugoslavia, and Thrace, part of conquered Greece.[2]

2 | Ibid.

03 | Rabbi Daniel Zion, Bulgaria

04 | Rabbi Daniel Zion, Israel

05 | Daniel's brother and sisters with their parents. Sitting down are Daniel's parents (Rabbi Solomon and his wife, Flora); standing up are Daniel's brother (Shmuel) and sisters (Dodon, Rashel, and Rikta). Daniel's siblings in this photo were all killed in the Holocaust.

06 | Rabbi Daniel Zion at his office, Sofia, Bulgaria

07 and 08 | Rabbi Daniel Zion and others leading a funeral procession through the streets of Sofia.

09 | Metropolitan Stefan of Bulgaria was one of the most charismatic yet controversial figures of the Bulgarian Orthodox Church. Yad Vashem Photo Archive.

10 | Rabbi Daniel Zion's family, Sofia, Bulgaria, 1939. Daniel Zion is on the far right, standing.

11 | Mizrachi family, Sofia, Bulgaria, 1942: Nissim (top left), Samuel (Sami, top right). David (second row on left), Sofie (middle), Roza, Mordecai's wife (second row, right), Yitzhak (Zako, third row, left) and Avraham Kedem (Mordecai and Roza's little boy). Mordecai (Nissim's oldest brother) is not in this picture because he had been sent to Bulgaria's labor camps.

12 | The Zion Family, WW II, Sofia, Bulgaria. This picture was taken at the wedding of Rabbi Daniel's son, Michael Zion. Daniel Zion is on the far right, bottom row.

13 | The gathering and deportation of the Macedonian Jews, March 1943. Yad Vashem Photo Archive, FA 213/42.

14 | Loading the Macedonia Jews on the trains to the extermination/death camps, March 1943. Ibid, 213/6.

15 | Metropolitan Kiril was literally willing to lay down his life (on the train tracks, if necessary) to protect his beloved Bulgarian Jews. Yad Vashem Photo Archive.

16 | The Mizrachi family with his majesty, King Simeon II, September 29, 2020, at the Royal Palace in Vrana, Sofia.

17 | Avi and family interview the king.

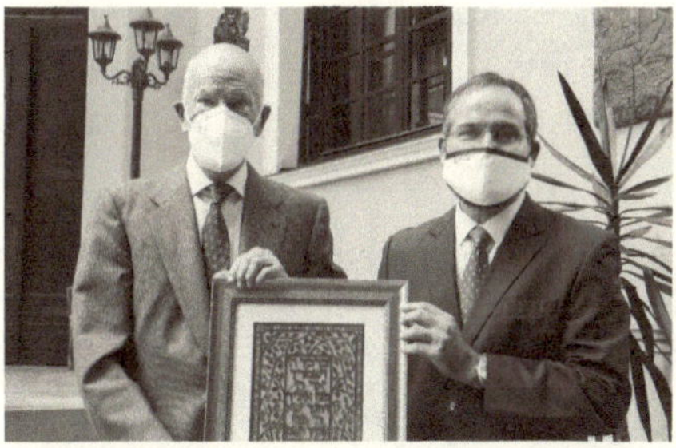

18 | King Simeon and Avi (with the gift the Mizrachis brought from Israel)

19 | Bintivey Ha'apala Information Center, Atlit Ma'apilim Camp, The Council for Conservation of Heritage Sites in Israel, Item ID 725.

20 | Bintivey Ha'apala Information Center, Atlit Ma'apilim Camp, The Council for Conservation of Heritage Sites in Israel, Item ID 725.

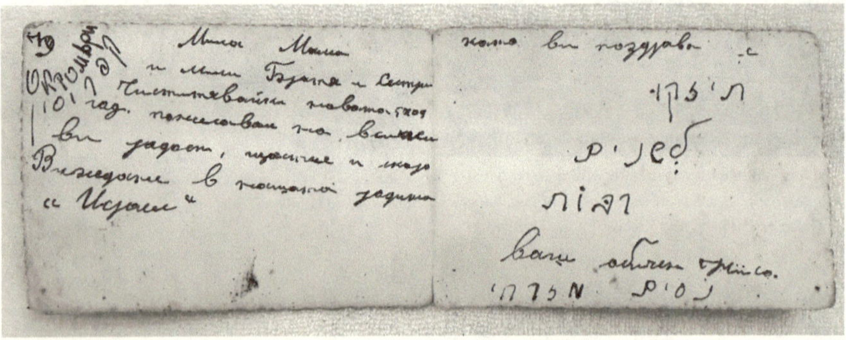

21 | Bintivey Ha'apala Information Center, Atlit Ma'apilim Camp, The Council for Conservation of Heritage Sites in Israel, Item ID 725.

22 | Rivka in her Hagana uniform.

23 | Nissim in the IDF, 1949

24 | The Bar Mitzvah of David Zion, the grandson of Rabbi Daniel Zion.

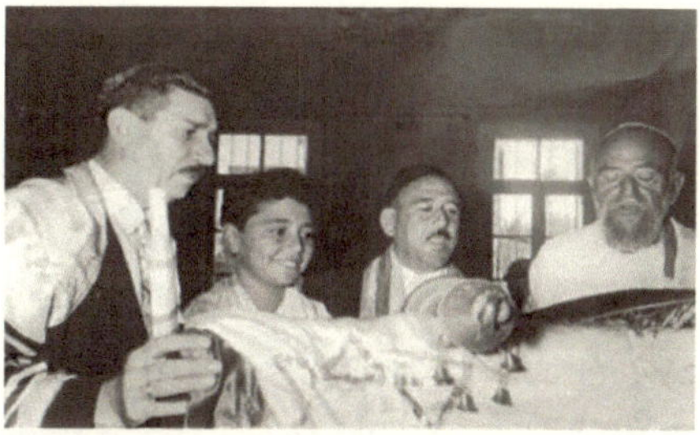

25 | The Bar Mitzvah of David Zion, the grandson of Rabbi Daniel Zion.

26 | The Bar Mitzvah of David Zion, with his grandfather, Rabbi Daniel Zion, at Daniel's synagogue, 1960, Jaffa, Israel.

27 | Rabbi Daniel Zion blessing his grandson, David Zion, at David's Bar Mitzvah, 1960, Jaffa, Israel.

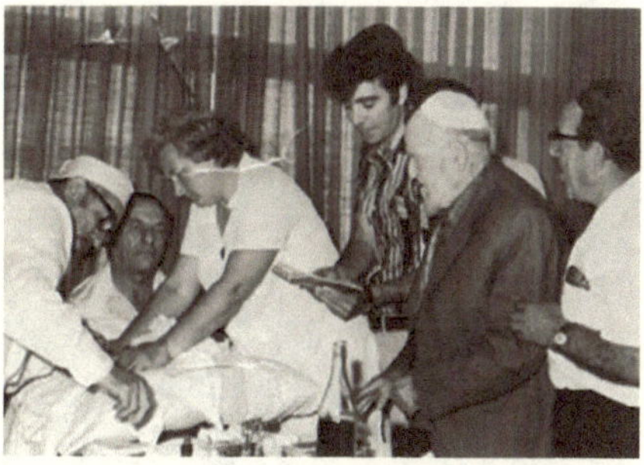

28 | Rabbi Zion pronouncing a blessing at his great-grandson's brit milah, 1974.

29 | Nissim and Rivka at their wedding, July 16, 1951, Jaffa.

30 | Nissim and Rivka in Jaffa, 1951.

31 | Nissim and Rivka at the Tel Aviv-Jaffa beach, 1951.

32 | Nissim and Rivka in Jaffa, 1951.

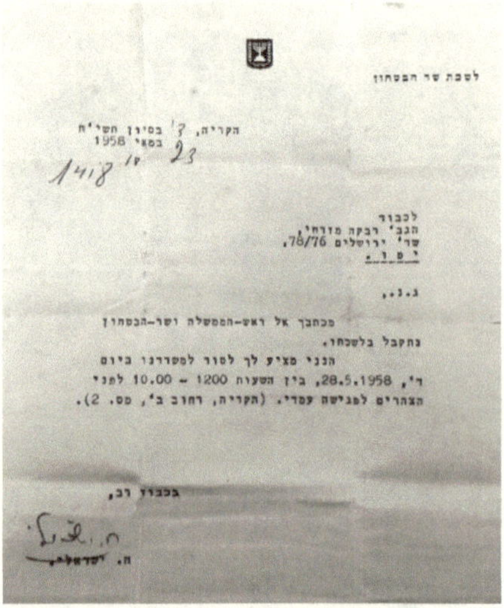

לשכת שר הבטחון

הקריה, ז' בסיון תשי"ח
23 במאי 1958

לכבוד
הגב' רבקה מזרחי,
שד' ירושלים 78/76,
יפו.

ג.נ.,

מכתבך אל ראש-הממשלה ושר-הבטחון
נתקבל בלשכתו.
הנני מציע לך לסור למשרדנו ביום
ד', 28.5.1958, בין השעות 1200 - 10.00 לפני
הצהרים לפגישה עמדי. (הקריה, רחוב ב', מס. 2).

בכבוד רב,

ח. ישראלי

34 | The letter addressed to Rivka Mizrachi, confirming she gave a letter to the offices of the Prime Minister and to the Ministry of Defense, May 1958.

33 | Nissim, Rivka, and baby Simcha; Jaffa, 1954.

35 | Avi as a young boy at the fountain on Yerushalamin Blvd. Jaffa (beginning of the 1960s). This fountain is known today as Dimitar Peshev roundabout (in honor of his acts in saving the Bulgarian Jews during WWII).

36 | Mizrachi family photo autumn 1967: Simcha, Nissim, and Avi standing; Rivka sitting down, holding Immanuel.

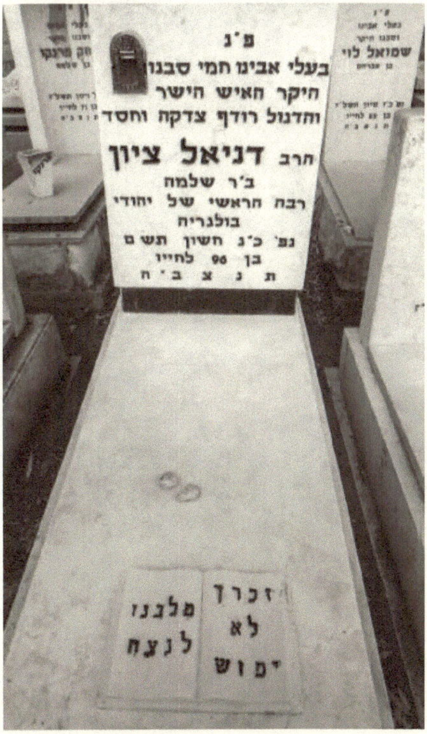

41 | The tombstone of Rabbi Daniel Zion, chief rabbi of Bulgaria, Holon, Israel, July 21, 2021.

37 | The Mizrachi family before the Yom Kippur War (Socrates St. Jaffa).

39 | Nissim, Rivka, Avi and Immanuel in front of their house in Zichron Yaakov.

40 | Avi Mizrachi and Shlomo Zion (grandson of Rabbi Zion) at the rabbi's grave, Holon, Israel, July 21, 2021.

38 | Simcha in the IDF (Israel Defense Forces).

42 | Avi at the age of 18 in the IDF (1979).

צבא ההגנה לישראל

בזה ניתנת לך הזכות לענוד את
אות המערכה
ברצועת הביטחון בלבנון

רב־אלוף אביב כוכבי
ראש המטה הכללי

התשפ״א, 2021

מזרחי
שם משפחה

אברהם
שם פרטי

מ״א / ת״ז

מס׳ 075244

43 | Campaign medal for Avraham (Avi) Mizrachi honoring him for his service in the First Lebanon War.

44 | Avi Mizrachi doing reserve duty in the IDF.

45 | Avi Mizrachi doing reserve duty in the IDF.

46 | Avi Mizrachi doing reserve duty in the IDF.

Claims Conference

"עָלֶיהָ, לִבְנֵיכֶם סַפֵּרוּ; וּבְנֵיכֶם, לִבְנֵיהֶם, וּבְנֵיהֶם, לְדוֹר אַחֵר"

פרח לניצול

תעודת הוקרה והערכה
מוענקת ל:

מזרחי ניסים

תעודה זו מוענקת לך ניצול/ת שואה
ברגשות כבוד והערכה עמוקים,
על ידי חיילי צבא ההגנה לישראל ומפקדיו,
על חלקך החשוב בבניין הארץ ותרומתך
להמשכיות קיום העם היהודי בארצו.

ג'וליוס ברמן
אלי שרמייסטר
פרופ' יחזקאל טלר

47 | The certificate given to Nissim Mizrachi by the Foundation for the Benefit of Holocaust Victims in Israel, acknowledging him as a Holocaust survivor.

48 | Avi in reserve duty and Chaya visiting him in front of Rachel's tomb.

49 | Mizrachi girls with Grandfather Nissim.

51 | Avi and Emanuel with their father, Nissim.

50 | Three generations of Mizrachi's celebrate Nissim's 90th birthday.

52 | The Mizrachi family (1990)

53 | Three generations of the Mizrachi family living in the land of Israel.

From generation to generation.

PART II

Post-War, the Journey Home to Israel

CHAPTER 9

The Bulgarian Jewish Community after WWII

I have often wondered what I would have done had I been one of my ancestors who survived World War II and then had to decide what to do and where to go from there. It was no doubt a question considered by thousands of Bulgarian Jews at the war's end, as well as by any other European Jews who miraculously survived the Holocaust.

Remembering Those Who Perished

On July 17, 1946, special memorial prayers were held in the Great Synagogue of Sofia to commemorate all those who had perished in the war, as well as the Jewish victims in Europe. In addition, a day of fasting and prayer was proclaimed for the Jews of Bulgaria. The chief rabbi, Rabbi Daniel Zion, "appealed emotionally to the throngs to repent and return to the ways of our God, who would lead us back to the land of our fathers."[1]

A couple weeks later, on August 1, 1946, the United Zionist Union held a convention in Sofia, with Chief Rabbi Daniel Zion among the guests. One of the primary events of the convention was the offering of remembrance prayers for the people of Israel who had perished during the war, as well as for the Jewish soldiers in the liberating forces, and the fallen members of the Jewish Brigade of the British army, established in September 1944. The brigade was disbanded in the summer of 1946, as a result of souring relations between the Jewish settlement in the Land of Israel and its British rulers. These soldiers, including my uncle David, returned to the Land, experienced in battle and highly motivated to join the Jewish army that was established with the declaration of the State of Israel.

1 | "The Bulgarian Jewry also fasted yesterday," *HaMashkif*, July 18, 1946.

Rabbi Daniel was an ardent Zionist, so it was no surprise when, on December 16, 1948, he immigrated to the Land of Israel with his family. At that time, they were part of a wave of 3,000 Jewish immigrants, 2,500 of whom came from Bulgaria, sailing in three ships to Haifa Port. Upon arriving in the Land, Rabbi Daniel settled in Jaffa with his family and was soon nominated the Rabbi of Jaffa.

Nissim Sets Sail for the Promised Land

As previously stated, at the end of the war, my father told his mother that he felt in his heart and soul that he needed to return home to Israel. His call to return to the Land of his fathers was affirmed in his heart on November 29, 1947, as he and his family gathered around the radio and heard an international proclamation about establishing a Jewish state in the Land of Israel. No doubt, nearly every Jewish person in the Land of Israel and around the world was listening. As the roll was called at the United Nations, my father said it felt as if time had stopped, as he carefully recorded the "yay" and "nay" votes of the countries. Every time a country voted YES, everyone in the house rejoiced. At the NO votes, they held their breath. Throughout the vote, Nissim thought to himself, *I am experiencing a turning point in history!* At the conclusion of the vote, with the "yays" winning, my father formally began his preparations to return to the Promised Land.

With other members of the Shomer HaTsa'ir, my father began to take practical steps for his aliya, going up to the Land of Israel. He was told he could take only one backpack so as not to arouse suspicion, and all his preparations were to be done secretly and with great care. His instructions were to come to a specific meeting place in Sofia, quietly and not in groups, in the early hours of the morning. He came, as did the others who planned to sail with him, at the frigid end of December.

After arriving, they were loaded onto trucks that took them to the train station. In sharing his memories of that time, my father always stressed the bitter cold he felt while boarding the train at the Bulgarian station with his friends. What he remembered most about that train ride was traveling farther and farther from the home he had always known toward his new home far away, to the "land of milk and honey."

From there they traveled to a port in north Yugoslavia, where the illegal immigrant boat *Bonim ve'Lochamim* (Builders and Warriors) was anchored. The boat was crowded, packed with some 1,000 immigrants, most of whom were from Bulgaria (see picture #19). It sailed on February 18, 1948, my father's twentieth birthday.

My father often told me how frightening and heart-wrenching it was to leave the only home he had ever known and to step into the unknown and the unfamiliar, to follow an idea and a hope. Although he knew in his spirit that he was called to make this journey, he also knew it would not be an easy one. How right he was.

Hardships along the Way

From Bulgaria, the train traveled to the small port of Bakar, in the north of Yugoslavia, where the "Builders and Warriors" was anchored.[2] As the Jewish refugees boarded silently, shivering from the cold as they hesitantly walked along the creaking plank that led to the ship's deck, their emotions ricocheted between excited and terrified. The ship had one big warehouse below the deck, where most of the immigrants were housed, and another six cabins for the crew, as well as a cabin in the bow and a dining room.

Once onboard, the refugees made their way down into the belly of the ship to inspect their accommodations. They were horrified when they saw wooden bunks, originally built with the intent of transporting goods, now stacked in threes and filled with young people. The ship was built for a maximum of 300 passengers, rather than the 1,000 now onboard. Most

2 | The ship was built in 1944-1945, then purchased by Yehuda Arazi and Ada Sereni, members of *Ha'Mossad Le'Aliya Bet* (the Institute for Aliyah B, a branch of the Haganah). The ship was actually a wooden motorized freighter, built in Savona, Italy, and registered under the name "Pinter," meaning a Jewish individual who lived in Italy. After the ship was purchased by the two Jewish Mossad members, it sailed under the name "*Enzo Sereni,*" but it was soon captured and confiscated by the British authorities. Later, after a legal battle, it was released to Ha'Mossad Le'Aliya Bet and sailed back to Italy, where its name was changed from "Enzo Sereni" to "*Bonim ve'Lochamim.*"

were under thirty, with only a few older people, but all were fired with the same desire: to reach the Land of Israel. Of the 1,002 passengers, 204 were from the Shomer Ha'Tsair.

The ship's crew, which consisted of the captain/commander, Moshe Rabinovitz, and seven sailors, were all Italian. On February 18, 1948, when everyone was on board, the ship set sail at 8:30 A.M., headed in the direction of the Land of Israel.

The ship's route began in Bakar and went first to Spalto in Yugoslavia. From there, the ship continued through the Strait of Otranto between Albania and Italy, along the Greek coast, the Isle of Cephalonia and Zante, along the coast of Peloponnese Peninsula, Cape Metapan, to the island of Sapientza before going to the island of Kithira Sidheros on the northeastern tip of Crete. From there, it went directly to the shores of the Land of Israel.

Nissim recalled that the journey was crowded, suffocating, dark, and cramped, with a few lamps whose light did not reach the lower shelves. He also told us about the three toilets for a thousand people, placed at the bow of the ship, far from the bunks, requiring long waits in line. When it rained and the winds blew strongly, the trek to the toilets was particularly arduous, as the storm rocked the boat. There were no showers on board, with only a row of taps lined along a metal trough on the deck, which could be used for washing one's face or brushing teeth, similar to those used by the military. In addition, the water was briny because it came from the sea, and it sloshed from side to side with the rocking of the boat so that washing one's face or brushing teeth was no easy task.

Nissim described the food on the ship as consisting primarily of a sort of porridge, prepared in a corner of the ship. A few cans of preserves occasionally broke the monotony, but for the most part they ate porridge every morning and every evening. It was not long before the passengers suffered from nausea, and most were seasick. Vomiting became the norm.

As the boat progressed farther out into the sea, the weather became particularly bad. It rained constantly, the winds raged, and it was very cold. Storms rocked the ship, making walking on the deck feel like climbing mountains. The passengers would struggle their way up a steep path, and then the boat would tilt downwards, sending them slithering backward so that it took many attempts to reach their destination.

A few days into the voyage, the ship halted and let down its anchor, though no reason was given to the passengers. Fueled by the unknown, rumors spread as fearful passengers recalled stories of other immigrants drowning on previous voyages. By means of a special radio, the home port and others in Bulgaria were made aware of the problem, causing rumors to spread there as well. The parents of one of the women on board were so convinced the ship had gone down that they considered sitting *shiva* (the week-long mourning period in Judaism for close relatives or immediate family) for their daughter. In the end, it turned out the boat had run onto a reef. Thanks be to God that after two days, inexplicably, the boat freed itself and continued its voyage.

My father often expressed the relief he felt when they hoisted anchor and started sailing again. The trip was not easy, he explained, but it was worth everything for him to see the Land of Israel that he and generations before him had yearned and hoped for. At that moment, he realized he would be one of the first from his family, after 2,000 years of exile, to return to the land promised to his forefathers, Avraham, Yitzhak, and Yaakov. He thought of how the Jewish people felt while returning to rebuild the temple after the first one was destroyed. Now, nearly 2,000 years later, he was on his way to *Ha'Aretz*, that same land, with a hope to rebuild it yet again.

So Close...and Yet So Far

Despite the difficult conditions, Nissim clearly recalled the joy and excitement that filled the ship as they finally drew closer to the Promised Land. Everyone was excited to come at last to the Land of their fathers. After ten days of being rocked from side to side through stormy weather and difficult conditions, the immigrants onboard grew more and more hopeful as they realized they were about to reach their destination.

One day toward the end of their voyage, however, Nissim described how the emissaries from the Land, Jewish individuals from Palestine[3] (as the Land was identified at that time—see footnote) who served as organizers and leaders during the journey, began to exhibit strange behavior. The rain had stopped and the sun began to shine, but as the emissaries shouted to the passengers to get down below the deck, it soon became clear that the British had discovered the ship.

Absolute silence fell on the crowd as they hovered below deck, feeling their dream turn to dust. As the horns of the British ship drew louder and closer, the emissaries came below and gave instructions to the passengers. Among other things, they were asked to hide anything that had Bulgarian script on it, including coins. They were told to throw into the sea anything that could betray where they had come from. Further, they were asked not to speak with the British when they boarded the ship—an easy task for my father since he didn't know a word of English.

It was not long before they heard shouts, and a few English soldiers appeared in the opening to the crowded warehouse. They had been discovered.

On February 28, 1948, the ship was forced to sail to the shores of Haifa. When the passengers saw the shore from the ship, their hearts were broken as they realized how close they had come to the Land of Israel. Their dream stood right before them, but they were not allowed to disembark. Instead, the soldiers ordered the immigrants to move from

---

3 | In reference to the term "Palestine," it is important to understand that during the British Mandate, the term "Palestine" was associated with the geographical area that currently covers the State of Israel and the Gaza Strip. For that reason, at this time in our story, the land is identified as Palestine. In addition, the word "Palestine" was not birthed in an Arab or Middle Eastern home; its origins are actually Greek. About 2000 BC, a wave of invaders and merchants swept out of Greece and crossed the Aegean and Mediterranean (see Deuteronomy 2:23; Amos 9:7). Greek military colonies and trading posts were then set up on the coastlands of what is today modern Syria, Lebanon, Israel, and Cyprus. These settlers on the southern coast of Israel are identified as Philistines in the Bible. When the Roman Emperor Hadrian succeeded in crushing the Jewish Bar Kokhba Revolt in 135 AD, he decided to rename the province of Judea, giving it the name of the Jewish people's biblical enemies, the Philistines. The Latin name *Palaestina* was then joined to the word *Syria*, and the region of Syria and Judea become *Provincia Syria Palaestina* after 135 AD. (Avner Boskey, *Jews, Arabs, and the Middle East; A Messianic Perspective*, David's Tent Publishing, Nashville TN, 2017, pp. 149-150.)

their ship to a British ship surrounded by five destroyers that would escort them to Cyprus.

Just moments before boarding the British ship, Aliza Haroati, one of the refugees, later wrote in her book, *Bonim ve'Lochamim —Builders and Warriors*, "In these moments, in the heat of emotions at the sight of our homeland—we all went on board, and stood at attention and sang *Hatikvah*, "the Hope" [a 19th-century Jewish poem and later the national anthem of Israel—see words below]. Our singing was choked with tears, but full of pride and sorrow…."

Translation of the Hatikvah

As long as in the heart within,
The Jewish soul yearns,
And toward the eastern edges, onward,
An eye gazes toward Zion.

Our hope is not yet lost,
The hope that is two-thousand years old,
To be a free nation in our land,
The Land of Zion, Jerusalem.[4]

The British ship was huge and seemed palatial compared to the immigrants' ship. It was spacious, its deck was shining, and they could sit and stand without being pushed into the shelves. They suddenly found themselves opposite one another, rather than on top of one another. The emissaries who had come from the Land to warn them managed to escape. The immigrants, however, had not been so fortunate.

In frustration and despair, the Bulgarian guides decided to go on a hunger strike. Though the immigrants had opted not to fight physically against the English, as it seemed pointless, they willingly participated in the hunger strike but were soon exhausted and starving. The strike lasted sixty-two hours but accomplished nothing, as they were ultimately taken to the camps in Cyprus, regardless of their efforts.

4 | Taken from the Knesset website: https://knesset.gov.il/holidays/eng/hatikva_eng.htm.

CHAPTER 10
The Camps in Cyprus

The older I get, the more I appreciate the call my father felt to return to the Land of our fathers. Though he had never set foot on Israeli soil when he left Bulgaria, he knew he was coming home. It was a call so strong that even hardship could not dissuade him. And, of course, he wasn't the only one who felt that way.

Soon after World War II, the British government found itself with a dilemma: what should it do with the Jewish people streaming into the Land of Israel, people they considered "illegal immigrants."[1] On August 7, 1946, they decided to intercept the ships carrying Jewish refugees from World War II, deport them to Cyprus, and house them in detention camps.[2] Their intended purpose was to discourage other immigrants from coming and to put an end to the illegal immigration. However, the decision failed to deter anyone, and the would-be immigrants, or *ma'apilim*, continued to try and reach the shores of the Land of their fathers.

Life in the Camps

When the British authorities chose to send the immigrants to camps in Cyprus, they had not determined how long these immigrants would be interned there and how long they would be prevented from fulfilling their hope of reaching the Land of Israel. In December 1946, the government allotted 750 certificates for aliyah per month, but this was not enough, as thousands of ma'apilim (refugees) continued to try to reach the Land.

The camps on Cyprus were opened on August 13, 1946, and operated until February 10, 1949. During this time, some 52,000 refugees were

1 | After World War I, the British were granted control, by the League of Nations, over the area of Palestine. The British Mandate lasted until May 15, 1948.

2 | Deportations to Cyprus, *Yad Vashem*, https://www.yadvashem.org/odot_pdf/Microsoft%20Word%20-%201036.pdf.

removed from thirty-nine different boats and held in the detention camps, where approximately 2,200 babies were born. By the end of this period, the last of the detainees finally came home to what was by then the legally constituted State of Israel.

There were two types of detention camps in Cyprus. One was composed of five "summer camps" near the port city of Famagusta in the region of Karaolos. The camps in this area were numbered: 55, 60, 61, 62, and 63. The second was composed of seven camps, called "winter camps," in the region of Dekalia, north of Larnaca. The summer camps housed the people in tents, while the winter camps provided tin huts.

Conditions in the camps were harsh. They were overcrowded, and the quality of the food was poor. There was a lack of clothing and shoes, as well as a shortage of water, particularly in the summer months. Despite these difficult conditions, the people tried to adapt and to prepare the younger generation for their immigration to the Land. Many Holocaust orphans were housed in the camp and aided by guides and emissaries who came from the Youth Aliyah movement and the Jewish Agency to help them prepare for their ultimate move to Israel. The majority of the detainees were indeed young, with 80 percent of the refugees between the ages of thirteen and thirty-five.

Like my father, many of the ma'apilim had belonged to several of the Zionist youth organizations and had sailed together from Europe. Once they were in the camps, they joined up once again with their own youth organizations and prior acquaintances. This improved the internal organization of life in the camps and helped the detainees better adapt to their difficult conditions.

During this period of the British Mandate, members of the *Palmach*, the elite fighting force of the *Haganah*, the Jewish underground army in Palestine, came to the camps and worked with the young people to prepare them for their future army service in Israel. Despite all their difficulties and the harsh living conditions in the camps, the immigrants were successful in organizing and participating in activities under various auspices, which gave them order, support, purpose, and hope. Although there were no written laws or real sanctions within the camps, crime was not reported in any of them. Everyone worked together cooperatively, despite differences of opinion, and waited together for the day they would finally be allowed to immigrate.

My Father in Camp 61

My father, Nissim, was taken to Camp 61 in Cyprus, one of five camps in Karaolos considered a summer camp. It was established during the months of August and September 1946. The site was set up next to the village of Karaolos, some 3.5 kilometers west of Pamgusta. Of the five camps located in the vicinity of Karaolos, Camps 60, 61, 62, and 63 were separated by internal fences, whereas Camp 55 was farther away.

Conditions in Camp 61 were particularly harsh. The internees lived in crowded conditions and lacked privacy. There was poor sanitation and a shortage of clean water. The British army provided food, which mainly came in tin preserves and was seldom sufficient to ease the internees' hunger. Emissaries from the Jewish Agency and the American Jewish Joint Distribution Committee (the "Joint") were allowed to provide medical services and education.

Waiting and Dreaming

My father often told us how, while in Camp 61, he remained close with his friends from the Shomer HaTsa'ir movement. While there, he sent a postcard to his family for the Jewish New Year in 1948, showing a picture of him with several of his friends from the group. A translation of his words, written in Bulgarian, said, "Dear Mother and dear brothers, I bless you all for a Happy New Year and wish you much joy and happiness, may we meet soon in our land of Israel. Yours, Nissim. (October 30, 1948.)" (See photos #20 and #21).

As stated earlier, by using tips my father had learned from his mother, Sofie, who was extremely talented in turning meager ingredients into tasty meals, he proved his worth in the camp's kitchen. He was soon added to the kitchen staff and helped prepare food for the internees, working there until he was able to go to Israel.

When the State of Israel was declared on May 14, 1948, the institutions in Israel began to plan evacuation of the camps on Cyprus. The British forces also prepared themselves for the immigration of the ma'apilim to Israel. The fledgling state was in the middle of a difficult war and did everything possible to bring the immigrants to the country. In February of 1949, the last of the detainees immigrated to Israel, and Camp 61 was closed. According to the records I received from the Zionist Archives, my father made aliyah in February 1949 and was among those last detainees to leave the camp on Cyprus.

I often think of those who went before me and of the price they paid to find their place in the new State of Israel. Whether by working in the kitchen or through various other methods, these hardy and determined immigrants found ways to adapt to their difficult but temporary lives in the Cyprus camps. Regardless of their personal methods of coping, they kept their dreams alive by continually focusing their hearts and minds on finally moving from the camps to the Promised Land of their fathers.

CHAPTER 11

The State of Israel

"I will bring them out from the peoples. I will gather them from the countries. I will bring them back to their own land. I will shepherd them upon the mountains of Israel, by the streams and in all the habitable places of the land" (Ezekiel 34:13, TLV).

May 14, 1948 (5th of *Iyar, Tashach*), the day when the Provisional State Council voted for the establishment of the State of Israel, was a day of great rejoicing for the Jewish people living in the Promised Land and around the world. It was a historic occasion they had longed for and dreamed of for nearly 2,000 years.

The establishment of the State of Israel is a story I never tire of listening to or of telling over and over again. One of the events that helped create the establishment of that state was the resolution passed by the United Nations General Assembly on November 29, 1947, calling for the establishment of a Jewish state in the Land of Israel. This recognition by the United Nations gave international legitimacy to the state and became a part of Israel's Declaration of Independence. After the UN declaration, as mentioned earlier, my father made preparations to immigrate to the Land.

November 29, 1947

A number of events led to the declaration of November 29, but I will mention only one. Prior to the declaration of the United Nations, a special committee known as UNSCOP (The United Nations Special Committee on Palestine) was formed to deal with the matter of what was then Palestine. This committee was formed following Britain's request regarding the continuation of its mandate in Palestine. The committee recommended that two states be established in Palestine: a Jewish state and an Arab state. Further, it recommended that Jerusalem be united under international rule. UNSCOP brought its recommendations to the UN, and those recommendations ultimately led to the decision of November 29, the UN Resolution 181.

The Jewish leadership readily accepted the UN Resolution, but the Arab leadership rejected it. The next day, the Arabs in the Land of Israel responded by attacking Jewish settlements, the first step toward the War of Independence. The vote taken at the UN Assembly, however, was very exciting for the Jewish people, as it was more than a two-thirds majority (thirty-three states/countries in favor, thirteen against, ten abstained, and one absent from the vote), thus ending the British mandate in the Land.

No Jewish individual in Israel or around the world who was alive on November 29, 1947, could ever forget this memorable day, which happened some two years after the end of World War II and the Holocaust. On this day, my mother, Rivka, was in Israel, and my father, Nissim, was in Sofia. Both were glued to the radio and listened to the countries of the world voting "yes" or "no" to the Partition Plan. Once they realized the Jewish State was going to be established, the Jewish population around the world erupted into shouts of joy and dancing. Although everyone in the Land knew this declaration would result in fighting and bloodshed, none of them was unhappy to hear that the decision was made to establish a Jewish state in the Land of Israel.

Two days later, the UN issued the Resolution of November 29, expressing for the first time the worldwide recognition of the right of the Jewish nation to establish a sovereign Jewish state. The excitement was indescribable, a milestone in the life of the Jewish people. There are no words to describe the excitement in the Jewish world, which after 2,000 years of exile, was finally able to return to the Land of their fathers.

The Declaration of Independence

The State of Israel was established on May 14, 1948, and the date was no coincidence. With May 15 nearly upon them and the end of the British Mandate growing closer, everyone knew war was about to erupt. However, because the 15th was a Sabbath and the Jews cannot "work" on the Sabbath, the ceremony for the declaration of Israel's statehood was pushed forward a few hours to Friday afternoon on May 14, just before the beginning of the Sabbath at dusk.

The signing of the Declaration of Independence took place in Tel Aviv, Rothschild Street number 16. At 4:00 P.M., the members of the council, along with other distinguished guests, convened in the hall of the Tel Aviv Museum of Art. They sang HaTikva, the new national anthem, and listened to David Ben Gurion, the chairman of the *Moetzet HaAm* (People's Council), who became the first Prime Minister of Israel, read the Declaration of Independence out loud. The final sentence in the Declaration states, "PLACING OUR TRUST IN THE 'ROCK OF ISRAEL', WE AFFIX OUR SIGNATURES TO THIS PROCLAMATION AT THIS SESSION OF THE PROVISIONAL COUNCIL OF STATE, ON THE SOIL OF THE HOMELAND, IN THE CITY OF TEL-AVIV, ON THIS SABBATH EVE, THE 5TH DAY OF IYAR, 5708 (14TH MAY, 1948)."[1]

Rabbi Fishman stood to bless the people with a recitation of "*Shehecheyanu*," a prayer thanking God for sustaining the lives of the people so they could experience that historical moment. Rabbi Fishman also signed the proclamation, which was the first legislation of the Provisional State Council. The Declaration of Independence was signed by thirty-seven people, members of the People's Council.[2] The members of the People's Council signed the scroll (leaving room for those who were not present). And at the end of the ceremonial signing, David Ben Gurion stood up and proclaimed, "The State of Israel is established! This meeting is adjourned!" The entire ceremony lasted thirty-two minutes, and at its end—in one day, as prophesied in the Bible—the Jewish State of Israel was born.

1 | Mordecai Naor, *The Friday That Changed Destiny 5th Iyar 5708 (May 14, 1948); The Drama of the Establishment of the State of Israel* (Tel Aviv, published by the Yehuda Dekel Library, 2014), pp. 12.

2 | The Declaration of Independence was signed by thirty-seven people, members of the provisional People's Council and representatives from all of the *Yishuv's* various communities (those Jewish people present in the Land prior to the Declaration). Of the thirty-seven, thirty-five were men and two were women, including Golda Meirson (Meir), who later became the Prime Minister of Israel from 1969 to 1974.

Groundwork Laid for Statehood

One of the events, prior to the signing of the Declaration, occurred on May 12, 1948, two days before the British Mandate was terminated. The People's Council convened in the Jewish Agency building in Tel Aviv. The session lasted thirteen hours, with the purpose of discussing what steps to take once the last of the British soldiers had departed.

At this time, emergency meetings were held between David Ben Gurion and military commanders, with Ben Gurion receiving their statistics regarding the neighboring countries. For instance, there was only one weapon for every three to four Israeli soldiers. In addition, their ammunition was limited, and they had only two tanks and one helicopter. These were meager defense mechanisms against their enemies' huge stockpile of weapons, ammunition, tanks, helicopters, and more.

Golda Meir, who at that time managed the administrative department of the Jewish Agency but would one day become Israel's Prime Minister, returned from a secret meeting with King Abdullah of Jordan. Golda brought the unwelcome news that Jordan would join the war against Israel, adding even more to the fear and pressure surrounding the declaration of the state.

Moreover, the members of the People's Administration had to decide whether to accept the American proposal to postpone the declaration of the Jewish state. When the decision was made to press ahead and immediately declare independence, the majority of the *Minhelet HaAm* (People's Administration) agreed with the decision.

Ben Gurion and other key figures worked together on the text of the declaration until, on Friday, May 14, the finished version was brought before the People's Administration for approval at 2:00 P.M. (just two hours before the ceremony). The session took place in the Jewish Agency building, with twenty-five of the thirty-seven members of the People's Administration in attendance.

Time to Vote

Close to 3:00 P.M., Ben Gurion stood up and said the time had come for a vote. He read the text, from start to finish, before all those present. At the first vote, sixteen members were in favor of it, whereas eight wished to make changes and therefore abstained. However, once Ben Gurion pointed out that everyone had already had the right to express their opinions, they decided to hold a re-vote. In this second vote, the draft of the declaration was unanimously accepted, with all twenty-six members voting in favor of it. All this activity was going on just one hour before the official ceremony.

During this time, preparations were being made for the declaration ceremony at the hall of the Tel Aviv Museum of Art (Rothschild Street, number 16). The organizers soon realized there were not enough chairs in the main hall, so they decided to go out to the local coffee shops to get more. They went out onto the streets and asked to borrow chairs for a meeting, without giving many details of that meeting. During this time, there was a desire to keep the ceremony a secret so the enemy would not bomb the building during the declaration. Even so, news of the meeting passed through the grapevine, and many people showed up outside the Tel Aviv Museum before 4:00 P.M to hear the declaration.

The occasion of the Declaration of the State of Israel was a historical moment in the history of the Jewish people. On May 14, 1948, even as the last British troops were departing, the leaders of the Jewish settlement in the Land of Israel met and decided to declare independence. "This was an historic day; a day that the Jewish People had longed for and awaited for two thousand years…."[3]

I remember, as a child, hearing my parents talk about how, in the Diaspora, at every Passover evening meal, the Jewish people would say, "Next year in Jerusalem." They also explained that at the close of every wedding ceremony, a moment before the groom smashes a glass with his foot, he quotes Psalm 137:6: "If I forget thee, O Jerusalem, let my right

3 | Naor, *Changed Destiny*, p. 23.

hand forget her cleverness. If I do not remember thee, let my tongue cleave to the roof of my mouth; if I prefer not Jerusalem above my chief joy..." (KJV).

According to General Yosef Avidar, head of logistics in the Israel Defense Forces and one of those present at the ceremony, there was a very special feeling in the museum of Tel Aviv that day. There was solemnity and joy, of course, but also concern and anxiety regarding the dangers of war, and a sense of hope as well as great challenge. Dr. Herzog Vardi (Rosenblum), one of the thirty-seven signers, said, "After the blessing of '*Shehehiyanu*' [a prayer thanking God for sustaining the lives of the people so they could experience such a historical moment] by Rabbi Fishman-Maimon we went up to sign our names. At that moment I was particularly struck by the unity between us.... The ceremony ended and we were all left in a state of tremendous tension. We were waiting for the offensive [attacks] to begin."[4]

God's Call to Come Home

This was the moment when the Jewish nation could at last return freely to the Land of their fathers. In our family, we know my mother was already there at the time of the declaration, and my father, Nissim, was still in the detention camp in Cyprus. Nissim recalled it as a deeply emotional moment, with tears streaming down his face as he listened to the Declaration of Independence over the speakers in the camp. As they all sat silently, listening to every word of the proclamation, my father felt a tightening of his throat and an excitement in his spirit. He could not believe that he had lived to hear the nation of Israel born, for prophecy to come true in his lifetime. In his heart, he knew this was only possible by God above, that a nation would be born in a day, a dream and a hope become a reality. A Jewish nation was born, after 2,000 years, in half an hour.

4 | Ibid, pp. 54-55.

Can a land be born in one day?
Can a nation be brought forth at once?
For as soon as Zion was in labor,
she gave birth to her children (Isaiah 66:8, TLV).

Following the declaration, my father joined his fellow inmates joyfully dancing the "Hora" (a circle dance originating in the Balkans) in the middle of the camp. I can easily imagine how he and the others, including the rest of my family, felt as they listened to the birth of the state.

I personally believe that the Declaration of Independence, which established Israel's claim to statehood, was a fulfilment of the prophecy in Ezekiel 36:24: "I will take you from the nations and gather you from all the countries and bring you into your own land" (TLV).

CHAPTER 12

The War of Independence

Surviving World War II and then struggling to return to the Land of our fathers weren't the only hardships faced by my Jewish family. In many ways, they were only the prelude to what was to come, beginning with the War of Independence. Now, in 2023, we Israelis continue to defend the Land of Israel. I am comforted knowing that "... the Keeper of Israel neither slumbers nor sleeps" (Psalm 121:4, TLV).

A "Total War"

The War of Independence was a critical war, both nationally and on a personal level. My mother, Rivka, fought from the very beginning. She was just sixteen years old when she trained with the Haganah Organization (the Jewish underground army, which later became the Israeli Defense Forces) on a kibbutz in the north (see photo #22). She fought in the Palmach (an elite fighting force of the Haganah during the period of the British mandate) and later in the Israeli Defense Force (IDF) on the northern front.

My father left the detainment camp on Cyprus and arrived in Israel toward the end of the war, in February 1949. He clearly remembered the emotion of leaving the camp behind and landing on Israeli soil. According to the Central Zionist Archives, he came to Israel from Cyprus on the boat *Independence* on February 2, arriving near Binyamina and Pardes Chana.

The moment he landed, he was so overcome that he fell to his knees and kissed the ground. He truly felt he had come home. From the moment he arrived, after being welcomed by the Jewish Agency, he was enlisted and sent to join the battle in the Negev (see photo #23). Thanks be to God, both my parents survived this war.

Bleak Beginnings

The War of Independence is divided into two main phases: the first, after the events of November 29, 1947, and the second, after the Declaration of Independence on May 14, 1948.

The first phase followed the UN Resolution of November 1947 when a civil war broke out in Israel between the Arab and the Jewish population. On November 30, 1947, five Jews were killed when local Arabs attacked a Jewish passenger bus near the Lod Airport, as well as a bus in Petech Tikva. In this stage, most of the Arab attacks, snipers, and bombs, were on the roads, which also placed Jerusalem under siege. At this time, Jerusalem had 100,000 Jewish and 60,000 Arab inhabitants.[1]

April 1-May 14, 1948, marked an interim period, when the army moved from a defensive posture to an offensive one. The Haganah's *Plan Dalet* (Plan D) indicated this change in strategy. According to the plan, fighters sought to gain control of all the territory that had been allotted to the Jewish state, and to establish a continuous line that would give control to the Jewish forces between the Jewish settlements. For instance, the Haganah captured the city of Tiberias, in which the Jewish people had been under siege.

At the start of the war, Israel had about 13,000 fighters, many of whom were women, including my mother. The Arab fighters numbered 14,000, but at the beginning of 1948, their numbers quickly rose to 21,500, including the mercenaries who arrived from other Middle Eastern countries.[2]

The Haganah began their fight with approximately 10,000 rifles, 4,000 sub-machine guns, 800 light machine guns, 150 medium machine guns, and close to 800 mortars.[3] Most belonged to the various settlements and were intended for their own defense. Only a few of the soldiers were armed; there was only one gun for every three to four soldiers, and each gun was allotted 500 bullets. From a military standpoint, it was a bleak beginning.

---

1 | Adrian Wolff, *Israel: A Chronology from Biblical to Modern Times* (Israel: ISBN, 2017), p. 384.

2 | The Independence War from the Knesset website https://main.knesset.gov.il/About/Occasion/Documents/IndependenceWar.pdf.

3 | Mordechai Bar-On, "Balance of Forces in Combat Reality and the David-and-Goliath Myth in Israel's War of Independence," *Israel*, 20 (2012), p. 119.

The *Yishuv* (Jewish People Already in the Land)

Between October 1947 and May 1948, however, the clandestine arms industry of the Yishuv produced 15,468 Sten sub-machine guns, some 200,000 hand grenades, 125 mortars, 130,000 explosives, and forty million bullets. Still, despite the efforts made by the Jewish settlements, enlisted soldiers were not always supplied a uniform or provided sufficient food and water. They would set out into combat with just ten bullets per gun. Surviving soldiers testified that they could not understand how they managed to stay alive and how they were able to fight when overrun by hordes of well-armed Arabs. According to one soldier, Yoram Kaniuk, "The war was more terrible than can be explained. What is a war without tanks, without an Air Force, just a few small, rickety Primus planes in the sky, no weapons, no food, no water, no mortars, no changes of clothes…?"[4]

The general opinion in the world was that the Jewish Yishuv would not survive, and the Jewish army headquarters gave only a 50 percent chance of success. But the Yishuv fought valiantly and managed to hang on. Kaniuk, the soldier mentioned above, had enlisted at the age of seventeen. At the time, he thought of all the Jews who perished in the Holocaust and of the thousands of survivors waiting to come to Israel. He said he felt he was fighting for all of them, both the victims and those who were still alive.

On April 6, 1948, the future Prime Minister of Israel, David Ben Gurion, said, "From the start this has been a war against every Jew in the country, both young and old, big and small, women, children, and babies. There is no difference between the home front and the front lines. Every baby is in the front lines, and no Jewish baby is safe even though he sleeps with his mother in his bed…."[5]

4 | Zeev Galili "What Really Happened in the Independence War," *The Logic in Madness*, May 3, 2014.

5 | Moshe Naor, "The homefront and the recruitment in the Independence War," *Israel*, vol. 4, 2003, p. 52.

Against All Odds

The second stage of the war began with the Declaration of Independence on May 14, 1948. Some hours later, on May 15, as the Egyptian Air Force bombed Tel Aviv, an invasion of Israel began by armies of Egypt, Lebanon, Syria, Jordan, and Iraq, two contingents from Saudi Arabia and Yemen, and possibly another from Algeria.[6]

In a press conference on May 16, the Secretary General of the Arab League stated, "This will be a war of extermination and a momentous massacre."[7] Three of the five armies (Lebanon, Syria, and Iraq) attacked in the north with thirteen battalions of seasoned soldiers, heavy weapons, artillery, armored vehicles, and an air force. Against these formidable foes stood nine battalions of the Haganah (which later became the Israel Defense Forces, or IDF). In the middle of May 1948, the Arab forces had 39,500 combat soldiers, not including combat support, staff soldiers, and others who were not at the front. Israel, on the other hand, had 32,000 soldiers, only half of whom had been trained for active combat.[8]

At the same time, only some 60 percent of the Jewish military corps was equipped with weapons.[9] The newly born state of Israel had no military aircraft and was desperately short of weapons, but the citizens of Israel understood that their very existence was at stake. In the fateful weeks following the declaration, though mightily outnumbered, they fought with determined courage born of desperation.

It is noteworthy that some 5,000 volunteers from overseas enlisted in the Jewish war effort. The significant contribution of these volunteers, referred to as *Mahal*, the Hebrew acronym for "volunteers from abroad," was crucial in the fall and winter operations of 1948. "The most significant contribution of *Mahal* to the IDF was in shaping and developing the Air Force. Many of the pilots in the airforce (sic), as well as officers and technical personnel came from among these same volunteers. In these units

---

6 | Wolff, *Israel*, pp. 393-394.

7 | Ibid

8 | Ibid.

9 | Assaf Agin, "Balance of Powers in the Independence War," *Ma'rachot*, vol. 390, July 2003, pp. 60-64.

the main operational service language was English...."[10] These volunteers came from fifty-six different countries, and 122 of them were killed.[11] According to Yitzhak Rabin, "They came to us when we needed them most."[12]

The IDF was officially inaugurated on May 26, two weeks after the Declaration of Independence.[13] At the onset of the war, Israel had only three tanks, five cannons, and no military aircraft. The Arab armies had more than 200 tanks and hundreds of cannons.[14] The first two tanks the IDF obtained were Cromwell tanks. The advantage of these tanks was that they were relatively low, making them more difficult to see, but they had no armor and had already disappointed the British army during WWII. As it turned out, they were a disappointment in the War of Independence as well. The third tank obtained by the IDF was an M4 Sherman. The British army had ordered it to be destroyed, but the driver tasked with towing the tank to its final destination was Jewish. He instead drove it directly to Tel Aviv and into the hands of the IDF.[15]

From the Lowest Point to Victory

The state of Israel did not have military aircraft until the end of June, when its first four planes were brought from Czechoslovakia. In the end, their effect on the battlefield was negligible. The Egyptian and Syrian armies used their air force to bomb various targets in Israel. Despite the odds, the IDF managed to conquer the Galilee and the Negev. My mother fought in the north front, near Galilee, and my father fought in the south front in the Negev. He fought in Uvdah, one of the last offensives of the 1948 war in which Israel conquered the southern Negev in March 1949.

The war was officially ended on July 20, 1949, with the signing of

---

10 | Shay Levi, "Improvising and Winning: Weaponry during War of Independence," *Mako*, April 22, 2015; Bar-On, "Balance of Forces", pp. 145-146.

11 | Wolff, *Israel*, p. 395.

12 | Yitzhak Rabin said this sentence during a memorial service while he was Prime Minister of Israel.

13 | Wolff, *Israel*, p. 398.

14 | Ibid, p. 394.

15 | Ibid.

a cease-fire agreement with neighboring Syria, Egypt, and Lebanon.[16] The cease-fire lines (also known as the Green Line) were not considered boundaries by the Arabs, who continued to deny the existence of a Jewish state. They were not considered boundaries by Israel, either, who knew these lines were not easily defended. Jordan had gained control of the west side of the Jordan River, including East Jerusalem and the Old City. The name "The West Bank" was so called by the Jordanians because it was west of the Jordan River; however, its biblical and ancient names are Judea and Samaria. Syria remained on the Golan Heights, and Egypt retained control over the Gaza Strip. But Israel had gained about one-third more territory than had been allocated in the UN Partition Plan (all of Galilee and Negev), so Israelis were relatively satisfied with the outcome and were busy building their new state.

Ending this chapter, I would like to honor all those who have served in the defense of the nation of Israel. Thank you for your service. I especially want to thank and honor my parents, Nissim and Rivka, for defending the nation and its people. I want to thank all my family members and friends who have served in the IDF, including all four of my daughters.

Finally, I want to honor the memory of all those who gave their life for the defense of the nation. I honor the memory of all the fallen soldiers of the wars of Israel and victims of terrorist acts. May their memory be for blessing!

---

16 | "Israel's War of Independence (1947-1949), *Israel Ministry of Foreign Affairs*, http://mfa.gov.il/MFA/AboutIsrael/History/Pages/Israels%20War%20of%20Independence%20-%201947%20-%201949.aspx (accessed: 26/11/2017).

PART III

The Rabbi's Legacy in Israel

CHAPTER 13

Rabbi Daniel Zion in the Promised Land

"But the righteous will live by his trust" (Habakkuk 2:4, TLV).

Although the situation in the newly established State of Israel was violent and dangerous from its declaration on May 14, 1948, until the war ended on July 20, 1949, life continued in the midst of it. Much, in fact, went on behind the scenes regarding Rabbi Daniel Zion.

A Place to Live

As the war raged on, on December 16, 1948, Rabbi Zion immigrated (made aliya) to Israel with his family. (One daughter and her family were already in Israel.) The rabbi arrived with another 3,000 immigrants, most of whom came from Bulgaria. They had sailed in three ships and arrived at the Haifa port, where three of Rabbi Daniel's children were immediately recruited into the army. Rabbi Zion settled in Jaffa as the rabbi of the city, where there was a large community of Bulgarian immigrants. Daniel and Rachel moved in with their daughter, who was living in Jaffa, because they could not find an apartment in Jaffa for themselves.

A few months later, according to an article published in the *HaTzofe* newspaper on July 13, 1949, Daniel and his wife still had not found an apartment. According to the article, Rabbi Daniel Zion had given his heart and soul on behalf of the Bulgarian Jewish community, and it is likely that his courage saved the Bulgarian Jews from the Nazis. Yet when he arrived in the land, he was unable to find an apartment and was obliged to move in with his daughter. The article addressed how absurd this ordeal was and called for the Israeli authorities to get involved.

The chief rabbinate had promised to appoint Daniel Zion the rabbi of the Jabalia neighborhood of Jaffa (located in the south part of Jaffa), where there was a concentration of immigrants from Bulgaria, and his fellow Bulgarians sought to obtain a two-room apartment for him in Jaffa. They wrote letters on his behalf to the military governor, to the Jewish Agency department of housing, to the Ministry of Religion, and others. The various ministries were telephoned numerous times, with requests to find a solution for Rabbi Daniel. All their efforts were in recognition of the fact that he had done all he could to save the Jews of Bulgaria.

Letters were sent again and again to the authorities, some from the Ministry of Religion and the Chief Rabbinate, requesting accommodation in the neighborhood where Rabbi Daniel was appointed rabbi in recognition for the "national efforts" of the "distinguished" rabbi. For example, on January 28, 1949, a letter was sent to the Minister of Religion, explaining that Rabbi Daniel Zion had been the chief rabbi of Bulgaria and should be recognized as a distinguished rabbi. The letter also said, "The Rabbi Zion, according to reliable sources during the Nazi occupation, acted with courage and with the help of his friendly relations with the heads of the Bulgarian church, to deliver the sheep of his fold from the claws of the Gestapo..."[1]

On February 25, 1949, an additional letter from the Chief Rabbinate was sent to the Ministry of Religion in the District of Jaffa-Tel Aviv, regarding accommodation for this brilliant and self-sacrificing rabbi. In this letter, the rabbinate insisted that housing be found for the distinguished rabbi who was suffering because he had nowhere to live since his aliyah to Israel. The letter declared, "In the eyes of the population of Bulgarian immigrants who know of his great national efforts...."[2]

Yet another letter from the rabbinate was sent to the Ministry of Religion in Tel Aviv-Jaffa on June 10, 1949, in which they requested that the situation regarding the rabbi be taken into consideration. The letter noted that Rabbi Zion was to receive a position as rabbi in the Jabalia neighborhood, where most of the Bulgarian immigrants were concentrated.

1 | Israel State Archives, 00113o1, G-19/4742.

2 | Ibid.

The letter also stated that improvement in his living conditions would bring greater spiritual benefit to the people in the neighborhood.[3]

The Union of Immigrants from Bulgaria also sent a letter to the Jewish agency, seeking assistance in finding more appropriate accommodation for Rabbi Daniel Zion in the Jaffa area. The letter noted that an apartment was found for the rabbi in the area of Tel Arish (area in the city of Holon, south of Tel Aviv-Jaffa); however, there was no synagogue there, and this apartment was not within walking distance of a synagogue. (There was no public transport on Holy Days or Shabbat, as according to Jewish law vehicles are not allowed to be operated on Holy Days.)

The letter requested an apartment be found for the rabbi, even if only one room, in the area of Jaffa between Tel Aviv and Jabalia. Again, the point was made that Rabbi Zion had been their chief rabbi, and these Bulgarian Jews appreciated his efforts from the past.[4]

In the end, the rabbi felt he had no choice but to agree to move to Tel Arish, despite the fact that his wife's health was frail, and the apartment had no water or electricity and was far from their community. Soon after, Rachel died in July 1949, just eight months after their arrival in Israel.

Questioning the Rabbi's Faith

Sadly, that was not the end of the rabbi's trials. Though he was indeed appointed to be one of Jaffa's rabbis and finally moved there in 1950, problems about his faith soon arose. In 1950, the rabbinate in Tel Aviv began to receive word of his faith in *Yeshua HaMashiach* (Jesus the Messiah).

According to an article in the Hebrew newspaper *HaMaariv*, high-ranking officials in the Tel Aviv Rabbinate were divided in their thoughts about Rabbi Daniel.[5] Some thought he was going through a spiritual crisis; others claimed he had been in crisis since his arrival in Israel because of financial difficulties and the death of his beloved wife. Another article, in the newspaper HaTzofe, mentioned that Rabbi Daniel Zion had been

---

3 | Ibid.

4 | Ibid.

5 | Moshe Meisels, "The Chief Rabbis are investigating Rabbi Daniel Zion," *Maariv*, June 12, 1950.

the chief rabbi of Bulgaria and was living in Jaffa.[6] According to this article, written on June 12, 1950, the Chief Rabbinate convened to discuss some of the rabbi's ideas.

Another article in the *Maariv* newspaper also referred to Rabbi Zion as the chief rabbi of Bulgaria.[7] According to this article, the rabbi had announced that he was taking off a month for reflection and introspection, in the neighborhood of Givat Shaul in West Jerusalem. Following this time, he would publish his response to the different rumors about him.

At the same time, the chief rabbi of Tel Aviv, Rabbi Unterman, gathered testimonies from a number of Sephardic Jews. According to these, Rabbi Daniel had expressed heretical views and frequently traveled to Jerusalem to meet with Christian missionaries. Further, the article stated that the rabbi fasted for three days and nights and claimed the "messianic spirit was on him during this time."[8] Further, the article claimed the rabbi had determined that the Jewish people were obliged to follow the principles of Yeshua.

This article asserted that the rabbinate had been about to appoint Rabbi Zion as rabbi of one of the neighborhoods in Jaffa; however, in light of these disclosures, the rabbinate withdrew their appointment. They did, however, continue to gather testimonies and eventually summoned the rabbi to testify and declare his beliefs.

Declared Insane

Some days later, the *Herut* newspaper published the verdict of the rabbinical court, to the effect that Rabbi Daniel Zion had lost his mind.[9] The article stated that the rabbi had joined himself to Christian organizations and to a missionary lady in Israel. It claimed he regularly traveled to Jerusalem in order to fellowship with Christian organizations

6 | "Inquiries made about Rabbi Daniel," HaTzofe, June 12, 1950.

7 | "Rabbi Zion taking a month for reflection and introspection, following this time he will publish his response," *Maariv* newspaper, June 13, 1950.

8 | Ibid.

9 | "Rabbi Daniel Zion has lost his mind; The verdict of the Tel Aviv-Jaffa," *Herut* (June 15, 1950).

and that, while there, had collected New Covenants (New Testaments) to distribute to the Jewish people.

Further, the court said he preached beliefs that "oppose Judaism" and often spoke of how Yeshua had appeared to him in a vision. Finally, the article stated that the rabbinate demanded the public in Israel "distance themselves from him and from his teachings."[10]

On the day this article appeared in the newspaper *Herut*, another article was published in *HaTzofe.*[11] Many of the points raised were repeated from the *Herut* article but with the addition of other comments. *HaTzofe* wrote that all efforts had been made to restore Rabbi Daniel Zion to the right path, but he had obstinately clung to his faith and continued to preach Yeshua as Messiah. Therefore, the Ministry of Religion had decided to cease financial support of the rabbi and gave an order to the synagogue to end his sermons. Further, the rabbi was warned to cease preaching about Yeshua.

On June 16, 1950, yet another article appeared in *Herut*, saying the rabbinate had determined the rabbi was insane and that, according to the testimony of some Bulgarian Jews, there had been several instances of mental instability in his family.[12] The writer of the article, Yoel Marcus, criticized the chief rabbinate's verdict, which was based on the rabbi's beliefs rather than on his mental state.

Marcus also noted that the rabbinate declared a *cherem* (ostracizing or censure, or expulsion from the Jewish community) on the rabbi based on his beliefs and sermons. The article noted that Daniel Zion could have proved otherwise to the rabbinate by bringing other witnesses, including doctors, to prove he was not insane, but he did not do so. The rabbi believed a committee should have been formed based on integrity, righteousness, amity, and truth. Marcus stressed the fact that Rabbi Daniel had served as a chief rabbi and was a devout man. In the end, the verdict of the rabbinate

10 | Ibid.

11 | "Public Statement about Rabbi Daniel Zion," HaTzofe (June 15, 1950)

12 | Yoel Marcus, "Within the Volume," (June 16, 1950).

regarding the rabbi's sanity did not deter him or his acquaintances, and it would not prevent him from expressing his belief in Yeshua.

A Stressful Year

Not only was June a critical month for the rabbi, but the entire year between when his wife, Rachel, died (July 1949) and the hearing before the rabbinate (June 1950) was highly stressful for him. According to his own testimony, the rabbi received a vision from God, saying the Jewish people must believe in Yeshua the Messiah. As a result, he felt he must preach his faith publicly and cease to be a believer in secret.[13] This vision changed the rabbi to become fearless in speaking openly of his faith, something the Orthodox rabbis were unable to deal with.[14] In the newspaper *HaTzofe*, the rabbi spoke of this vision, which took place during the months of January-February 1950, when he spent an extended time in prayer and fasting. He said he was "in a consuming fire, I could not move from my place." After the revelation, he wrote a letter to the Knesset in which he stated that if the people of Israel received Yeshua as their Messiah, "they would receive the Old City of Jerusalem; and if not, they would suffer great hardships…."[15] According to this same article, several Jewish individuals from the Bulgarian community testified before the chief rabbi of Tel Aviv, Rabbi Unterman, regarding Rabbi Daniel's thoughts. Rabbi Unteran hoped that "this matter" would pass; however, in the end, he understood the rabbi would continue to declare his faith as a Jewish believer in Yeshua.

Joseph Shulam, whose family members were from Bulgaria, has written about Rabbi Daniel and graciously granted me an interview. He recounted how the rabbi told him personally that he was to stand before the chief rabbinate, which indeed he did. The rabbis were prepared to allow Rabbi Daniel to serve as the rabbi of Jaffa on condition that he would not mention "*his* name" (they could not bring themselves to say the name, but

13 | "Rabbi Zion Preaches on The Voice of Israel," *HaTzofe* (September 15, 1952).
14 | Jacob Gartenhaus, "Rabbi Daniel Zion," *Messianic Good News*, http://www.messianicgoodnews.org/rabbi-daniel-zion/ (Accessed: 03/26/2018).
15 | "Hallucination of Rabbi Daniel Zion," *HaTzofe*, (June 13, 1950).

they were clearly referring to Yeshua). They said they would not take from him the title of "rabbi" as long as he would cease to speak of "that man," that is, Yeshua.

According to Shulam and my mother (both of whom knew Daniel personally), the rabbi answered that he was not ashamed of the Messiah Yeshua and that "what God gave me, no one can take from me." He left the rabbinical court singing songs of praise to Yeshua the Messiah. It is not clear the exact date that this happened, but it was during the spring-summer of 1950. One thing is for sure: the rabbi was prepared to give up his title and his livelihood for the sake of the gospel and his faith in Yeshua.

Taking a Stand for Yeshua

Then, in July 1950, a shortened version of the rabbi's story was published in New York,[16] stating that he had been the chief rabbi of Bulgaria. Further, the story said the rabbi was known as a historian and writer, as well as for his extensive knowledge. He was highly respected in pre-war Bulgarian society and was known to a number of cabinet ministers and people in high positions as one who had served his people devoutly and faithfully for many years as chief rabbi in Bulgaria. He was also an ardent Zionist all his life, and he made aliyah to Israel immediately after the establishment of the state.

After Rabbi Daniel had declared his beliefs publicly in Jaffa, the chief rabbinate in Tel Aviv decided to strip him of his title of rabbi and thus reduce him to poverty. Following this, without the rabbi being present and without any medical evidence to substantiate their claims, the rabbinate declared him mentally unstable and in need of commitment to a psychiatric institute. However, they were unable to accomplish this as the wider public loved and respected the rabbi.

According to an article written in 1950 by Avraham Polak, the founder of the Union of the Messianic Jews in Israel, Rabbi Daniel Zion had indeed made aliyah and was appointed a chief rabbi of the Jaffa area. Polak

---

16 | William Zukerman, "Why a Rabbi Was Declared Insane in Israel," *Jewish Newsletter*, 5.2, July 28, 1950.

testified that in 1950, the rabbi publicly declared his faith in Yeshua, the Messiah of Israel. Following this, many determined his "insanity," while others accepted his faith and honored his status as rabbi.

The Union of the Messianic Jews in Israel

The first conference of the Messianic Jews in Israel was held on December 8 and 9, 1950.[17] More than 200 Messianic Jewish believers from all over Israel, including Daniel Zion, attended this meeting. I, for one, was amazed to realize that a Messianic conference was held in the Land of Israel less than three years after its rebirth in 1948. From this conference, Avraham Polak, Moshe Ben Meir, Daniel Zion, and others established The Union of the Messianic Jews in Israel (*Ichud Yehudim Meshichim belsrael*). Rabbi Zion was elected chairmen of this organization. In addition, the leaders called on all Messianic Jews in Israel to join in a single union, under the slogan "Together we stand, divided we fall."[18] The official languages of the conference were Hebrew and Yiddish.

During this conference, Rabbi Daniel was asked to lead the Shabbat Evening Service, which he recited and sang the prayers passionately. (Zion was known throughout the Messianic community as someone who wasn't willing to give up his Jewish identity and so declined any job or connection from the Church.) The service was closed with the singing of the Hatikvah, the national Israeli anthem.

A Bridge Between Israel and the Nations

According to an article written by Avraham Polak, Rabbi Zion had a synagogue that operated according to Halacha (Jewish law). At the Jewish New Year, some 250 worshippers, Jews of Bulgarian background who still loved and respected the rabbi, gathered at the synagogue to participate in the High Holy Day prayers. This testimony is corroborated by Pirchiya Cohen, the granddaughter of Rabbi Daniel. She recalled that during the

17 | Boyadjiev, *Rescued*, pp. xi and 57.
18 | Ibid.

High Holy Days, the synagogue on Yefet Street was filled to capacity, and the Jews of Bulgaria, now living in Jaffa, deeply cared for and honored the rabbi.

Polak further wrote that in the year 1950, the rabbi was sixty-seven years old, of average height, and had a gray beard. He spoke several languages: Hebrew, French, Ladino, Turkish, and Bulgarian. Polak described him as someone who spoke pleasantly, with patience and wisdom. In his own words, "He [Rabbi Zion] is quiet and reserved, however, a high intelligence, sagacity, energy, sense of purpose, and warmth and kindness will soon be apparent: a natural fighter with extraordinary courage."[19]

Polak went on to explain that although Christian organizations offered him financial aid, the rabbi refused to receive any. He claimed he had no need of aid as his children had grown, he was a widower, and God would provide all he needed. Polak explained that the rabbi had been sent to serve the Lord among his people, the Jewish nation, and Christians should respect that because he was sent to Israel and not to the Gentiles.

The rabbi refused the requests of Christian organizations to join them as he continued to see himself as a Jew, observant of the Law, and a testimony to his people in the State of Israel. He clearly did not consider himself a Christian but, rather, a Jew who loved Yeshua as his Messiah. According to Polak, the rabbi was one who sought the foundation of the faith, the roots taken from Judaism. He was also an example of one who sought the common language of his Jewish brethren in order to touch as many Jewish hearts as possible.

Rabbi Daniel Zion said that he wished to be a kind of bridge between Israel and the other nations, in order to fulfill the prophecy that "God will reign for ever and ever." Furthermore, he emphasized that if the rabbis were to pray to God with all their heart and soul, read the New Covenant, and consider whether Yeshua really was the Messiah, God would most certainly take away the veil from their eyes. Polak claims that Rabbi Daniel should be considered one of the greats, a Jewish hero of his time. He says Daniel

19 | Abraham Polak, "Daniel Zion 1," *JCG*, 168, November 1950.

was one of the pioneers who set the wheels turning for the gospel in Israel in this day and age.

Family Memories

The same is true for my father's family. Nissim and his brothers all attended Rabbi Daniel's synagogue in Israel, just as they had done in Bulgaria. Though they knew he believed in Yeshua as the Messiah, the synagogue was run like any other Orthodox Jewish synagogue. My parents, Nissim and Rivka, attended his synagogue, as did countless other Jewish people, especially those from Bulgaria.

Rabbi Daniel also held home-group meetings. According to my interview with Joseph Shulam, it was there that the rabbi taught from the New Covenant and spoke of his love for the Jewish Messiah, Yeshua. Shulam got to know my parents at these meetings and remembers hearing my mother share her testimony during one of them. He also remembers how much she loved reading the Psalms. It was encouraging to him to realize how Jewish-Israeli believers remained Jewish in every aspect of their life and faith, even while believing in Yeshua as the Messiah.

According to Shulam, after what happened to Rabbi Daniel with the rabbinical court in 1951, he still led the synagogue. An article written by Yair Dekel told how Sephardic Chief Rabbi Toledano and Rabbi Zion made an agreement between themselves.[20] Rabbi Daniel agreed not to talk about Yeshua during the synagogue services and prayers, but he would be free after the service to speak about his belief in Yeshua with anyone who wished to hear it.

In Tel Aviv on June 19, 2017, I also had a chance to speak with David Zion, another grandson of Rabbi Daniel Zion, about his memories of this remarkable man. It was obvious that David had been deeply impacted by the life and faith of his grandfather. One of those impactful experiences was when his grandfather Daniel blessed him and prepared him for his Bar

20 | Dekel, "Stiff Annex."

Mitzvah (see photos #24-27) Hearing this blessed my heart, since my own father also prepared for his Bar Mitzvah with Rabbi Zion.

One of David's clearest memories was of how little Rabbi Zion ate. The rabbi had received a beehive from Kibbutz Yad Mordechai, and he ate from it daily, along with some dried fruit. In keeping with his modest, humble lifestyle, he ate little else but always seemed satisfied. He owned no property and wanted or needed nothing beyond his basic needs. If he received donations, he passed the majority of them on to the poor.

David recalls his grandfather's deep devotion to the Torah and the Tanach. He loved talking about the stories contained in the Tanach, particularly to his grandchildren and other children as well. It was vitally important to him that his grandchildren grow up knowing the Scriptures. He also impressed on them the importance of keeping Shabbat and observing the commandments between God and man, and between man and his neighbor. "Always love and be good to your neighbors," the rabbi admonished.

David also remembered his grandfather telling him, "You are not to take vengeance nor bear any grudge against the children of your people, but you shall love your neighbor as yourself" (see Leviticus 19:18). What we often refer to today as the "Golden Rule," Rabbi Daniel repeated often to his children and grandchildren: "Do to others what you would have them do to you." Those words, in David's opinion, were the motto of Rabbi Zion's life.

And yet, though the rabbi was a kind and gentle man, always ready to love and forgive, he was also a brave man who did not back down in the face of danger. Nothing exemplified the man's courage so much as when he went to the king of Bulgaria and interceded on behalf of his people, regardless of the possible repercussions to himself. Saving the lives of his beloved Jewish kinsmen was paramount in his heart and mind.

One of David's fondest memories is of his childhood was when, after every Yom Kippur when the day's fast was over, it was his job to build a *sukkah* (a temporary dwelling or booth connected to the holiday of *Sukkot*) for his grandfather to celebrate the Sukkot holiday (Feast of Booths/Feast of Tabernacles). David took great pride and joy in building that sukkah for his grandfather every year until he went into the army at the age of eighteen. He stressed that he was careful to make sure he built a kosher (satisfying the requirements of Jewish Law) sukkah for Rabbi Daniel.

Another of David's favorite memories is when his grandfather prayed and blessed David's son, Miki Zion. This happened at David's son's *brit milah* (the covenant of circumcision). For him as a father, having his grandfather bless his son was of significant meaning. This important generational blessing was captured in a photo (see photo #28).

Later, when the rabbi was too old to walk or even come to the synagogue, David remembers hearing him sing to the Lord. Regardless of how old or feeble he became, he never stopped singing to *Hashem* (God). One of the Hebrew songs David clearly remembers went something like this: "It doesn't matter if trouble comes your way; pray to Yeshua and comfort will come."

David stressed that his grandfather dearly loved the Torah and believed in Yeshua as the Messiah. "If I had to sum up my grandfather in one word, it would be *love*. He had immeasurable love for others, regardless of the circumstances."

Joseph Shulam once told me how, for approximately six years, he would regularly meet with Rabbi Daniel during the end of the 1960s and beginning of the 1970s. Shulam met with him every Shabbat and Tuesdays to study Hebrew Scriptures. He sometimes joined the rabbi in the synagogue prayers and then his Bible studies at home.

During this time, Rabbi Zion still had his synagogue and apartment in Jaffa where he held his Bible studies. Shulam was amazed how the rabbi, who was then nearly ninety years old, gladly taught him with so much knowledge and love for the Torah and the Hebrew scriptures. Shulam was honored and blessed to have had the time during these years to spend and learn from this esteemed rabbi, a time when Shulam really got to know Rabbi Zion on a personal level. Shulam saw that the rabbi was a simple man who loved God and his Jewish nation. He was a Zionist and loved the nation of Israel to the end of his days. He said that Rabbi Zion was grateful to God to be living in the state of Israel, and that he remained Jewish in every aspect of his life, even while believing in Yeshua. Anything Rabbi Zion was given he donated to others, living simply and with a humble and giving heart.

While Shulam studied with the beloved rabbi, he got to know the Mizrachi family. He told me how he remembered seeing me as a young boy and teen near Rabbi Zion's synagogue in Jaffa. He got to know my father in the synagogue and my mother in the Bible studies, and their children when we were running around outside. He told me that he remembers how much my mother loved reading the Psalms. Each day, she would read a part from Psalms. I smiled when he told me this because I also remember her reading the Psalms to me.

Dr. David Stern's Memories

Dr. David Stern, author of the *Complete Jewish Bible* and other books on Messianic Judaism, met with Rabbi Daniel Zion in 1974 and had the chance to hear his testimony firsthand. At this meeting, the rabbi told Dr. Stern about the time in Bulgaria when he had a vision of Yeshua, and of consequently coming to faith in Him. He then told David it was because of his faith in Yeshua that he was able to influence the king, as well as other key people in the government and the church, not to deport Bulgaria's nearly 50,000 Jews.[21]

In 2016, I was able to interview David Stern about his meeting with Rabbi Daniel, and he described the rabbi, who was ninety-one at the time of the meeting, as having a gentle face, full of compassion. He told Dr. Stern that he believed in the God of Israel, the God of Avraham, Yitzhak, and Yaakov, and that everything he did was out of care and love for his people.

Rabbi Daniel told David that he never ceased being Jewish and always felt that he was an inseparable part of the nation of Israel. Despite hearing everything Rabbi Daniel went through with the chief rabbinate in Israel,

21 | David H. Stern, *Messianic Jewish Manifesto* (Clarksville: Jewish New Testament Publications, INC, 1988), pp. 213-214.

David was deeply touched when the rabbi said that he continued to pray for the rabbinate and for their well-being.

In his old age, Rabbi Daniel loved singing to the Lord and praying for the people of Israel. David remembers ascending the spiral staircase at the rabbi's home and hearing Rabbi Daniel's voice as he sang praises to his Messiah. In his lifetime, the rabbi wrote nearly 200 Messianic Jewish poems and songs, most of which have been lost, but David Stern had five of them. When I interviewed the doctor, he and his wife, Martha, were very gracious to give us a copy of these songs so we could include them at the end of this book. More than my words written in this book, these songs illuminate the heart and soul of this noble rabbi.

One of the things that stood out most to David was how faithfully the rabbi prayed for his people, whom he loved so dearly, right up until his last breath. David told me that even when the rabbi was old and struggling, he was wholly dedicated to fulfilling the Torah of Israel and continued to help those around him.

In Dr. Stern's book *Messianic Jewish Manifesto,* written in 1988, he states that "many autobiographies, testimonies, and testimony collections..." have been written over the years, but suggested that "a modern update including the lives of this century's believers would be welcome. Otherwise, we will forget them." [22]

Rabbi Zion's Testimony in His Own Words

The rabbi best described his faith in Yeshua in a letter to *The Pentecostal Evangel* in 1951, in response to a letter from Dr. Keith Brooks, editor of *Prophecy* magazine, asking him for a personal testimony. The rabbi's original letter was written in Hebrew but later translated into English. I include most of that English translation here.

> "I received your dear letter and hasten to reply, giving you the true story of how I found my Messiah....

22 | Ibid.

"It was over the course of twenty years that faith gradually developed in me. I was of course, educated in an environment quite hostile to the name of [Yeshua]. I myself—now much to my sorrow—once tore up a copy of the [New Covenant]. But after that I was troubled and prayed much that God would show me the way of truth.

"In His great mercy He answered my prayer. The very Spirit of the Messiah came upon me. The Holy Spirit began speaking to me by an inner voice. He gave me many signs by which I should find *the Saviour.* His likeness as He hung upon the cross frequently came before my mind. There were miracles wrought in answer to my prayers in His name. Thus I knew in my soul that He was the Messiah.

"Despite all these things, causing me to believe in Him, I was in a high position among the Jews and I was not yet moved to go before them and before the world to publish my faith. Since I was the Chief Rabbi of Bulgaria, it took some time for me to be emancipated.

"Finally, I left this rabbinate and came to the land of Israel. There were many afflictions and disappointments to humble me. The inner voice of Messiah finally sent me to Jerusalem and there I remained a full month in solitude. The Spirit told me to read the [New Covenant] constantly and with devotion.

"At the conclusion of this month, the Spirit came mightily upon me. He was in my heart as a burning fire. For some time I was unable to speak, then the Lord definitely led me to go to the two secretaries of the Chief Rabbinate of Tel Aviv and tell them that [Yeshua] the Son of God is our Messiah, our Redeemed. I could find no rest until I started for Tel Aviv. God enabled me to witness to them with power.

"From thence the message went forth over all the land. There was great confusion among the Jews.... There came to me also journals from other lands with strange reports about me. It seemed my faith had been broadcast to all the world.

"But despite all the insults, misrepresentations and persecutions—and some friends turned to bitter enemies—God gave me great strength to withstand all the slander and Satanic temptations. I had debates with noted Rabbis in the land, as well as with many learned people who dwell in the darkness. I was never so happy in my life. I was dwelling in the light of [Yeshua], and God, through the Spirit, empowered me so that none were able to prevent my speaking....

"My one hope now is that my remaining years may be devoted to bringing this same wonderful faith to my brethren, and that He may empower me to sound the trumpet with no uncertain sound. ...

"Yours in the peace of the Messiah—Daniel Solomon Zion, Jerusalem."[23]

Rabbi Daniel's Broadcast on The Voice of Israel

The rabbi was once again in the news in 1952. At 3:45 P.M. on September 14, he spoke on "The Voice of Israel" (Israel's official radio broadcasting station) regarding his faith.[24] This was during the weekly Protestant prayers in the Jerusalem YMCA, which were broadcast on the program. His speech was in Hebrew, and he spoke of his belief and testimony of the divine revelation he had experienced three years earlier, by which he understood that the Jewish people must believe in Yeshua as Messiah. In other words, the rabbi gave his testimony in Hebrew on a well-known radio station that was broadcast throughout the country.

The rabbi's speech on the radio was a decisive event, as this was the first time anyone had shared that Yeshua was the Messiah on The Voice of Israel. He gave his testimony that in the 1930s, prior to WWII, he had

---

23 | "Israel's Christian Rabbi," *The Pentecostal Evangel*, September 2, 1951, Number 1947, p. 11, Public Domain.

24 | "Rabbi Zion Preaches on The Voice of Israel," *HaTzofe* (September 15, 1952).

begun reading the New Covenant and learning of Yeshua's teachings. He began to believe in Yeshua and spoke of this with a few people. He went on to say that Yeshua had done only good for the Jewish nation. He expressed his regret that Yeshua had been made distant from the Jewish people and also spoke of the heavy price his people had paid for rejecting Him. He explained that because of his status as rabbi, he was prevented from sharing his faith openly until God, in His grace, delivered him from all fear so he could share his faith in Yeshua as Messiah without restraint. He further explained that he had to give up his authority as an orthodox rabbi in Jaffa because of the cherem placed on him by the Chief Rabbinate of Tel Aviv.

In this same broadcast, the rabbi explained that during January and February 1950, he had traveled to Jerusalem for a month in order to fast and pray. In his prayers, he requested that God would show him the right way, and he proclaimed that God answered his prayers. The Holy Spirit revealed to the rabbi that Yeshua is indeed the Messiah; He has borne our griefs and carried our sorrows; He was wounded for our transgressions and bruised for our iniquities; by His stripes we are healed (see Isaiah 53:5). In Him, the Lamb who bore the sins of the world, we have the forgiveness of sins. After his revelation, the rabbi explained, he could not continue to believe in secret. He had to openly proclaim that Yeshua was the Messiah, declaring Him to be the Messiah of all Israel.[25]

He then went on to explain that despite the difficulties, the suffering, and the persecution he had endured, he thanked God that he had remained strong in faith. His heart belonged to God, he declared, and he proclaimed that he turned to Him in the hard times for the strength to overcome all the difficulties and continue in his witness. He told how God directed him to the Scriptures, particularly Isaiah 41:10, where he read, "Fear thou not; for I am with thee: be not dismayed; for I am thy God: I will strengthen thee; yea, I will keep thee; yea, I will uphold thee with the right hand of my righteousness" (KJV).[26]

Toward the close of the broadcast, Rabbi Daniel reiterated that he had

---

25 | Gartenhaus, "Rabbi Daniel Zion."

26 | Agnes Waldstein, "Ein Radioansprache Daniel Zions", *JCG*, 193 (January 1953).

not left Judaism; he was simply a Jew who had found the Messiah, and Yeshua had Himself been and remained a Jew. The rabbi stressed that he kept the laws of the Torah, and there was no contradiction between what is written in the Law (Bible) and his belief in Yeshua as Messiah. Yeshua, after all, declared that He did not come to destroy the Law but to fulfill it. Rabbi Daniel noted that if anyone wished to learn more of his faith, they should read 1 Corinthians 8:5-6 (TLV), which says, "… yet for us there is one God, the Father, from whom are all things, and we exist for Him; and one Lord, *Yeshua* the Messiah, through whom are all things, and we exist through Him."[27]

Rabbi Daniel said it was his desire that the world would know Yeshua and believe in Him. There is no doubt this was a tremendous occasion for a rabbi to testify before all Israel, via the radio, of his faith in Yeshua. It is no wonder that his testimony raised such a widespread response in the country.

Controversy over Broadcast

Two days after the broadcast, a storm was raised in certain sectors in the state. According to the newspaper *Davar*, the Ministry of Religion investigated the background to the broadcast and found it had taken place through the new broadcasts of the Protestant church.[28] According to the ministry, the broadcast had violated existing agreements, whereas those responsible for the broadcast insisted it followed all the rules and the accepted protocol. The ministry opposed the broadcast because the rabbi had spoken in Hebrew, rather than in English, and because he had appealed to the Jewish-Israeli population to believe in Yeshua. However, those who were responsible for the broadcast believed they had acted within their rights as an autonomous party. They also felt justified in light of the fact that they had submitted the program to The Voice of Israel beforehand and received permission for the content.

Some months later, an article in the *Maariv* newspaper stated that Mr.

27 | Ibid.

28 | "Investigation of the Protestant Broadcast," *Davar* (September 16, 1952).

William Hull, the head of the Christian Zion delegation, under whom the rabbi had broadcast his speech on The Voice of Israel, sent a letter of apology to the Minister of Religion, M. Shapira.[29] Hull noted the sharp reaction of the Israeli press against the speech and claimed the speech had been directed at Christians rather than the Jewish people. However, because the speech was broadcast in Hebrew, it was the general opinion that it was addressed to the Jewish population.

Most likely, the reason Mr. Hull wrote the letter was that he was pressured to do so. The press was vehement in its criticism of the broadcast and in its opposition to the rabbi's words. Although it did not break the law because it was broadcast by a Jewish person in Hebrew, it raised a commotion, and Hull tried to calm things down by sending the letter.

According to writer and historian Dr. Agnes Waldstein, Rabbi Daniel Zion continued to share about Yeshua at every possible opportunity. He gave lectures in various Jewish synagogues and also to congregations of believers throughout Israel, including a synagogue in Haifa. Waldstein claimed that the synagogue in Haifa honored and respected the rabbi, inviting him to come and teach them after hearing him speak on The Voice of Israel broadcast. The writer also confirmed that the rabbi composed several songs, including Jewish-Messianic ones.[30]

Ultimately, Rabbi Daniel reaped as much criticism over the broadcast as he had over his other statements about Yeshua, but he knew in his heart he had done what God had called him to do. It was, after all, God's approval the rabbi had always sought, rejecting the fear of man even in the most difficult of times.

29 | Y. Aden, "Thousands of Israeli Children in the Missionary Network: 400 Missionaries in Israel—New Methods, New Rationales—Conversions in order to Move to Canada or to Avoid Military Service," *Maariv* (December 19, 1952).
30 | Agnes Waldstein, "Israel," *JCG*, 194 (February 1953).

CHAPTER 14

The Mizrachi Family Meets Yeshua

O Israel, trust in *Adonai*—
He is their help and their shield! O house
of Aaron, trust in *Adonai*...
He will bless the house of Israel (Psalms 115:9-10).

I learned long ago that God often works behind the scenes. Of course, we've all experienced those rare times when we see something absolutely amazing happen right before our eyes, and we know it's a miracle from the Lord. But many times we don't see the wondrous work God is doing in our lives—bringing people and situations together, weaving them into a beautiful tapestry that will bless us and honor Him—until much later. The Mizrachi family coming to know Yeshua as Messiah and Savior is one of the latter. Though our family came to the Promised Land full of hope and wonder at what God was doing, we had no idea we were about to meet the One who had walked those same dusty roads of Jerusalem and beyond 2,000 years before.

Settling in Jaffa

As mentioned earlier, my father, Nissim, immigrated to Israel during the War of Independence and joined the fight toward the end of that war. According to my younger brother, Immanuel, after the War of Independence, my father was stationed in *Kibbutz Ein HaMifratz*. However, when he learned his family had arrived in Jaffa, he requested a transfer to Jaffa in order to reunite with them.

Some months later, my mother Rivka's family, the Bahats, also immigrated to Israel from Turkey. Her parents, Yehuda and Rachel Bahat, and her sister, Sarah, arrived on the boat *Anna Marie* on April 4, 1949.

However, the Central Zionist archives and the Israel Ministry of Interior have no registration of my mother immigrating after the birth of the state.

My wife, Chaya, recalls that my mother once mentioned she had arrived in the Land illegally with the Haganah organization before the declaration of the state and lived in a kibbutz in the north of Israel. She told her this right after we got married and were living with them in Zichron Ya'acov. My wife tried to get more details from her, but my mother became very secretive and wouldn't say anymore.

This confirmed for me that my mother immigrated before the establishment of the state and explains why there is no record of her immigration afterward. In addition, my wife recalls a conversation with my mother when she mentioned fighting in the Haganah during the War of Independence. My older sister, Simcha, also remembers my mother saying this, as well as mentioning about her time in the Palmach, though with little detail.

Both my parents' families settled in Jaffa, relatively near one another, which is how Nissim and Rivka met. It seems Rivka had noticed Nissim and began waiting next to the gate each Friday when he came home from the army, to return again on Sunday. In time, my father noticed her and decided to initiate a conversation. From there, the romance took root and blossomed, and they were married by an orthodox rabbi in Jaffa on July 16, 1951. My mother was just nineteen, and my father was twenty-three.

After their wedding, they lived in an apartment in Jaffa, moving some years later to a one-bedroom apartment with a living room and kitchen, also in Jaffa (see photos #29-32). A section of the apartment served as a pet fish shop. It was there in 1954 that my sister, Simcha, was born, the eldest of my parents' children (see photo #33). Not long after that, my mother's father, Yehuda Bahat, died in 1955.

A Period of Austerity (*Tsena*)

In the 1950s, following the War of Independence, Israeli society was exhausted, worn down from coping with security problems and a struggling economy. We must not forget the waves of immigration they experienced, when the local Jewish population doubled in size. From the day of the Declaration of Independence on May 14, 1948, to the end of 1951, approximately 700,000 immigrants arrived in Israel. Within the space of four years, from 1948 through 1953, the population grew from half a million inhabitants to 1,484,000.[1]

These waves of immigration presented difficult problems for the fledgling nation. The immigrants were housed in crowded conditions, including tents, shacks, tin huts, or anything else the new Israeli government was able to obtain for them.

The immigrants, including the Mizrachi family, were made up of Holocaust survivors, homeless and without family, as well as Jews from the Middle East and Africa, whose cultural and traditional backgrounds were very different from those of Israeli society. Most of the new immigrants arrived with nothing at all, needing food, clothing, a means to earn a livelihood, accommodations, and so on. This immigration exacerbated Israel's existing economic hardship, the shortage of food, the difficulties of assimilation, and the challenges of creating a melting pot in Israeli Society, while at the same time coping with security concerns, the lack of quiet on the borders, and terrorism.

Only about 10 percent of the land of Israel was cultivated by Israeli farmers; therefore, the government sought to establish an agricultural base that would provide basic food to the population. From the birth of the state until 1954, some 350 *kibbutzim* and *moshavim*, mostly agricultural settlements, were established in order to help provide food to the local population.

Moreover, the conflict and security problems did not cease with the end of the War of Independence because, in the eyes of the Arab nations, the state of Israel was not legitimate. One of the goals of establishing these settlements was to spread the Jewish population throughout all vital areas in order to create a defensive belt and fortify the porous borders. The

1 | Zeev Drory, "Army and Society in Israel in the 1950s," Iyunim [Studies] in the Establishment of Israel Journal, Vol. 16 (2006).

Ministry of Defense's statistics of terror and sabotage in the 1950s paint a picture of mortal danger to the citizens of Israel, in addition to their economic woes. The Israeli society lived in fear of terrorism, robbery, and economic troubles.

During the War of Independence, the Israeli government enforced a regime of austerity. This involved rationing of food and other basic products, including clothing and shoes. A modest food ration was determined, and citizens were required to register in the food shops in their neighborhoods. The authorities enforced the rationing by means of ration books and food coupons.

This period of austerity, or tsena, made life difficult for everyone, particularly women, who were obliged to stand in line for hours at the local grocery to receive the rationed goods. During this period, there was a lack of essential products, and each woman had to fight to get what her family was legally entitled to receive. Moreover, some products were of inferior quality or defective, but the women had to make do with them. It was no easy task to prepare satisfying meals out of the meager rations they were given. In the 1950s, almost no one had a refrigerator at home, and it was rare to find even an icebox. Therefore, the struggle to obtain adequate food was a daily challenge. The financial needs of this time influenced, to a large degree, the consolidation of the society, where all were made equal. This period of austerity continued through to the mid-'50s.[2]

Rivka's Testimony

During the tsena, my mother began to struggle with depression. She was frustrated at her inability to feed my sister, Simcha, who was still a toddler and needed a lot of care. In addition, the security situation lay even more heavily on her. We later learned she had lost a great many of her close friends when she fought in the War of Independence. By the time Rivka was twenty-five, her mental state had deteriorated to the point that she decided to end her own life. Before following through on her decision,

2 | "The Period of Austerity: The State, Women, Food and Young Israel," *The National Library of Israel*, https://www.nli.org.il/he/discover/israel-culture-and-society/israeli-food/tzena.

however, she determined to talk with a rabbi. She chose Rabbi Daniel Zion, as she and her husband prayed regularly in the local synagogue in Jaffa, where most of the worshippers were Bulgarian Jews.

My mother highly respected the rabbi and finally managed to drum up the courage to speak with him. She began the walk from her house on Jerusalem Boulevard toward the synagogue on Yeffet Street. After about fifteen minutes of walking, carrying her baby in her arms, she began wondering if it was worth continuing. After considering the possibilities, she decided to walk just as far as the synagogue. She poked her head in the door and saw that Rabbi Zion was still at prayer, so she sat on a bench outside, waiting for him to finish.

Following his prayers, the rabbi left the synagogue and saw my mother sitting outside. He approached her and asked in Ladino, *"Ke koza Iga?"* ("What is it, my daughter?")

Rivka shot him a glance and said simply, "Rabbi, I do not wish to live."

The rabbi's jaw fell, then he told her, "My daughter, my daughter, do not do such a thing!" Then he told her to wait while he went to get something. He returned a few minutes later with a book and said, "Before you do something you may regret, please read this book."

Out of respect for the rabbi, my mother agreed. She returned home, and after putting her little one to bed, began reading the book. To her amazement, she saw it was the New Covenant, something she had never considered opening, let alone reading, because it was a forbidden book for the Jewish people. However, again out of respect for the rabbi, she pushed ahead. Soon she was stunned to find that the New Covenant was a Jewish book in every way, a book full of quotes from the Tanach, particularly from the Law of Moses.

Then, with her heart full of questions, she returned the next day to the synagogue to meet the rabbi. In the end, through reading the book and through the personal testimony of Rabbi Daniel Zion, my mother chose to live. After this meeting with the rabbi, she also recognized Yeshua as the Messiah of the Jewish people, the son of David, and became a Jewish believer. The very moment she came to faith in Yeshua, her depression lifted, never to return. While still alive, my mother would say, "Rabbi Daniel Zion, who introduced me to Yeshua, my Messiah, saved me, and this brought life to our family."

A New Life in Many Ways

As I said, my mother held the rabbi in the highest regard, and this experience only increased her respect for him. Whenever she had a question of the Law or the Scriptures, she would ask him about it. It was not long before the rabbi noted her gift of expression, both verbal and written, and asked her to be his personal secretary. Naturally, she was delighted to accept, and she became his secretary in 1958, working until 1976 when the family moved from Jaffa to *Zichron Ya'acov.*

During this time, she dealt with his correspondence, administration, the organization of social events, and assisting Sephardic Jews—Ladino speakers—to make aliyah to Israel. Simcha recalls that my mother would write the rabbi's letters to those who were abroad in order to assist them in moving to the Land. The moment these new immigrants arrived in Israel, she assisted them in their settling in and acclimatization.

Both Simcha and I recall our mother talking about a particular letter the rabbi asked her to write and deliver to then Prime Minister of Israel, David Ben Gurion. We had always heard that my mother had personally handed a letter to Ben Gurion, but we did not know the content of the letter.

While conducting research for this book, my family and I came across a letter among my mother's belongings that confirms she did indeed send or hand such a letter to the offices of the Prime Minister and to the Ministry of Defense. The letter was written by Chaim Israeli, head of the department of defense, confirming receipt of the letter from the rabbi in May 1958 (see photo #34). When my daughter later traveled to the state archives in May 2018, she was told that as far as they knew, my mother had indeed met Ben Gurion personally.

At this time, my parents and sister lived in the one-bedroom apartment in which a portion of it served as a pet fish shop. Simcha slept on the couch in the living room, while my parents slept in the bedroom. My sister recalls that every time someone came to the shop, regardless of the hour or whether or not the shop was already closed for the day, our parents would open it up. Even in the middle of meals, if someone came, my parents got up from the table and attended to their customer because every lira (Israeli *shekel*—basic monetary unit in Israel—at the time) made a difference. They were used to making do with very little, so every bit of money helped to make ends meet.

In addition to the fish shop, my father worked in construction and also as a gardener in Jaffa. One of the projects he was responsible for was the garden of the Immanuel Hostel, called *Beit Immanuel*.[3]

I was born in 1960 and given the name Avraham Mizrachi, which was shortened to Avi. Born in the French hospital in the old city of Jaffa, I was named after my grandfather Avraham, who died during War World II in Bulgaria. Eight days later, in accordance with Jewish tradition, I was circumcised by Rabbi Albert Ben Bassat, a *mohel* (a Jewish person trained in the practice of brit milah, the covenant of circumcision) and Rabbi Daniel Zion's son-in-law, who had married the rabbi's daughter, Yaffa.

Most of my childhood was spent in Jaffa (see photo #34). Being raised by parents from the Holocaust generation wasn't easy. Growing up during WWII and then living in a struggling pioneering state had affected my parents deeply. I remember them acting in a way that was common to other homes of Holocaust survivors. For one thing, they did not trust banks or the authorities. They hid money under the kitchen tiles and later in other parts of the home. They took books they did not need any more and cut out the pages so they could hide bills of money in them. Every time I took out a book from our library in the house, I had to remember not to take the

3 | Located in a spacious and picturesque mid-19th-century structure that once served as the glittering Baron's Palace, home to the grandfather of British actor Sir Peter Ustinov, Beit Immanuel was first occupied by CMJ (Church's Ministry Among Jewish People), pioneers dedicated to the return of the Jewish people to the land of Israel and the restoration and proclamation of the Messianic Jewish hope in Yeshua.

ones with the money inside. As a result, I grew up thinking you needed to hide money in your house for fear someone would take it away.

Also, we could only shower once a week so we wouldn't waste water or money. And because food was scarce, I grew up with the idea that you never threw away food. Because I was raised not to waste anything and to hold on to all you had for fear that it could be taken away, to this day I use everything I have and have a hard time throwing away anything. My parents struggled with this survivor mentality their entire life.

Along with these memories, however, I also remember how passionate they were about our Jewish heritage. They were Zionist parents who loved going to Synagogue and living in the Land of Israel with their Jewish people.

My grandparents' mother tongue was Ladino, and they knew very few words in Hebrew. It was my parents' generation who actually learned to speak the language. My father and mother knew some Hebrew words before they came to Israel, but it was only after they made aliya that they were able to adopt it as their main language. This meant a lot to them because they, like so many Israelis, wanted to keep the language alive for generations to come. I am blessed and touched in my heart that not only do I speak Hebrew, but my daughters and grandchildren also speak it.

My mother regularly took Simcha and me to the synagogue of Rabbi Daniel on Shabbat, and in the middle of the week to his home for a Bible study. I remember going to the synagogue as a child, as well as to the rabbi's house, where he would place his hands on my head and pray for me. The memory is so clear, as I recall the kind old rabbi laying his hands on my head and blessing me with his soft, kind voice. I remember him as a peaceful, joyful person whom I respected and honored.

My father also attended the rabbi's synagogue, but he had no interest in my mother's new faith in Yeshua. He saw that she had "returned to life," as it were, and no longer suffered from depression, so he was obviously happy about that. And as long as she kept her faith to herself, he allowed her to go to the rabbi's home studies, which focused on that faith. However, the moment Simcha also decided to believe in Yeshua as her Messiah, my father was upset. He became angry and sometimes shouted at his wife and his daughter. When he saw his daughter could not be dissuaded, he decided he wanted to hear no more of their faith at home.

Simcha remembers one particular day when her father shouted at her, but she also remembers her mother's response. She recalls that after Nissim left the room, Rivka turned to Simcha, and together they prayed for him. Rivka asked Simcha to keep from nurturing anger or resentment in her heart toward her father, and so Simcha began to pray daily for the salvation of her father and brother (me). I am eternally grateful for her continued prayers.

CHAPTER 15
Post-Independence Wars

It seems the tiny State of Israel has experienced very little peace since their 1948 declaration of statehood. Even between actual wars, deadly skirmishes and terrorism from surrounding nations threatened their tenuous peace. Two wars in particular, which I remember as a young boy, stand out as events that highlighted the miraculous intervention of the God of Israel.

Leading up to the Six-Day War

For several months before the Six-Day War in June 1967, Israel's security situation was tense. The Syrian army had perched on the edge of its territory on the Golan plateau overlooking the Galilee and was shelling Israeli villages and kibbutzim around the Sea of Galilee. Then, on May 15, President Nasser of Egypt, in a radio broadcast, called for the destruction of Israel: "This is our chance, Arabs, to deal Israel a mortal blow of annihilation, to blot out its presence in our holy land."[1] He also moved 100,000 troops, 1,000 tanks, and seven divisions toward the Israel-Egypt border.

Between May 16 and May 19, while efforts were being made to resolve this escalation via diplomatic means, the IDF began to call up its reserves. On May 18, Egypt demanded that UN forces be removed from its territory along the Israel-Egypt border. The next day, UN Secretary General U Thant acquiesced. The UN flag was taken down in Gaza, and UN troops ceased operations, with troops withdrawing ten days later.[2] On May 20,

1 | Wolff, *Israel*, p. 434.

2 | "2 Report of the Secretary-General on the Withdrawal of the Emergency Force: A/6730/ Add 3, 23 June 1967," *Israel Ministry of Foreign Affairs*, 26th of June, 1967, https://mfa.gov.il/mfa/foreignpolicy/mfadocuments/yearbook1/pages/2%20report%20of%20the%20secretary-general%20on%20the%20withdrawa.aspx [accessed on June 20th, 2021].

Syrian Defense Minister Assad claimed Syria's forces were "ready not only to repulse the aggression, but to initiate the act of liberation itself, and to explode the Zionist presence in the Arab homeland. The Syrian army, with its finger on the trigger, is united.... I as a military man, believe that the time has come to enter into a battle of annihilation."[3]

On May 22, Egypt closed the straits of Tiran and the Suez Canal to Israeli ships, an aggressive act against recognized international law, further escalating the situation. Despite these provocations, on the following day, May 23, the Israeli government voted against going to war, and the ministers of the government continued to seek an alternative to resolve the conflict.[4]

But the pressure continued to mount. On May 24, President Charles de Gaulle of France, Israel's only ally at the time and the only country providing them with weapons, threatened that if Israel attacked an Arab state, France would declare an embargo on Israel. The United States also refused repeated requests for military aid and approval for a preemptive strike.[5]

On May 27, the President of Egypt proclaimed, "Our basic objective will be the destruction of Israel."[6] Three days later, on May 30, 1967, the king of Jorden signed a military defense agreement with Egypt, thus joining the Egyptian-Syrian front. On May 31, the president of Iraq declared, "The existence of Israel is an error.... Our goal is clear—to wipe Israel off the map."[7] The armies of Egypt, Syria, Jordan, Iraq, and Saudi Arabia were in a state of high alert. On June 3, the President of France declared a military embargo on Israel.

---

3 | "The Six-Day War: Precursors to War, Arab Threats Against Israel," *CAMERA*, http://www.sixdaywar.org/content/threats.asp [accessed on June 20th, 2021].

4 | Wolff, *Israel*, p. 435.

5 | Warren Bass, "Case II: The Six-Day War, 1967," *A Surprise Out of Zion? Case Studies in Israel's Decisions on Whether to Alert the United States to Preemptive and Preventive Strikes, from Suez to the Syrian Nuclear Reactor* (RAND Corporation: Santa Monica, 2015), pp. 15-23.

6 | Wolff, *Israel*, p. 435.

7 | Ibid.

The Six-Day War

At the time, the tiny state of Israel had 2.8 million inhabitants with 260,000 troops, many of whom were women and civilian reservists. They faced 415,000 soldiers of the neighboring Arab countries of 48.2 million inhabitants. The Arab forces had several times the amount of military equipment, tanks, and aircraft as Israel.[8] The only chance for survival was a surprise attack.

On June 5, at 7:45 A.M., Israel responded and conducted a preemptive strike on Egyptian airfields, destroying most of Egypt's air force. Following this, Nasser called for *jihad* (a struggle or fight against the enemies of Islam) and vengeance. Meanwhile, from its vantage point on the Golan Heights, Syria attacked Israeli cities and towns in the north. Despite Israel's assurance that it wanted no fight with Jordan (who had annexed the West Bank and East Jerusalem after expelling the Jews from East Jerusalem and the Old City in 1948), Jordanian forces opened another front in Jerusalem. There, from its strategic position on the hills of Jerusalem and the West Bank, they began attacking Israel in West Jerusalem and cities along the coast.[9]

Israel had gone to war knowing that like 1948, this was again a war for its very existence. So pessimistic was the mood in Israel that plans were made to turn parks into gravesites, as many believed these areas would soon be needed as the result of this war. However, in six short days, Israel's armed forces miraculously conquered the entire Sinai Peninsula, the West Bank, Jerusalem (Judea and Samaria), and the Golan Heights. From June 5 to June 10, 1967, Israel won this defensive war against a mighty enemy dedicated to nothing less than Israel's elimination.

A Personal Perspective

When the Six-Day War broke out in 1967, my parents were still living on Jerusalem Boulevard 78 in Jaffa. My sister was thirteen years old

---

8 | They had 2,350 tanks, 491 fighter airplanes, and 90 bombers, about four times Israel's numbers.
9 | Wolff, *Israel*, pp. 436-438.

and had moved to a boarding school called *Beit El* (The House of God) in Haifa, a school that taught Yeshua as Messiah. My younger brother, Immanuel, and I still lived at home with our parents. I was six years old during the war, and Immanuel was almost two (see photo #36). As the only bedroom in our home was used by our parents, we boys slept on the couch in the living room, as Simcha had done for years before.

Just as my father had been called to the front in the previous wars, so now he was called up to the reserves. The moment he received his call-up notice, my mother called Simcha at school and asked her to come home. She explained that war had broken out, and since she was alone with the two little boys, she was unable to get to the bomb shelter or to any good shelter in time. She told Simcha that her little brothers (Immanuel and myself) were afraid and anxious because their father had left for the war, and she would truly appreciate if Simcha could come home and help out until the situation calmed down.

Naturally, my sister did as her mother asked and caught a bus from Haifa in the direction of Jaffa. After being on the bus for a while, she heard shouting. Soon, all the passengers were ordered to get off the bus and take cover. Simcha described the experience as terrifying, and she believed at that moment that she was going to die. She quickly found cover in a ditch, where she heard bombs falling just a few meters from her.

Simcha later told me that most people, particularly those living outside Israel, do not understand how dangerous the pre-1967 borders were. For instance, the fact that the Jordanians occupied the hills not far from the coast gave them a strategic advantage in the war, enabling them to attack Israeli cities with artillery and mortars.

As Simcha hid in the ditch with bombs falling all around her, she prayed to God for protection in the name of Yeshua, crying out to Him to save her. Finally, there was a lull in the shooting and bombing, and the passengers were told to get back on the bus to Tel Aviv-Jaffa.

When my sister finally arrived in Jaffa, she spotted us and realized how absolutely joyous we were to see her. From then on, every time the sirens sounded the alarm, we all hid together underneath the sink because there was no shelter near enough to reach in time, even though my mother grabbed Immanuel and Simcha grabbed me. This comforted me that my sister was with me and always grabbed me to hide from the bombing.

Historic Unification of Jerusalem

On June 7, 1967, the third day of the war, a historic event took place. This is the day the paratroopers fought their way into the old city of Jerusalem, liberating the Jewish Quarter and the Western Wall. The IDF entered the Old City through the ancient gates, on the same site where the Bible describes King David's conquest of Jerusalem 3,000 years earlier. Since that time, the Jews have been living in the Land of Israel and Jerusalem, though they were periodically expelled from and returned to Jerusalem by some of its various conquerors—the Persians, Greeks, Romans, Byzantines, Arabs, Crusaders, Ottomans, and the British. When the British Mandate ended in 1948, the Jewish community was again expelled from the Old City of Jerusalem and their homes and synagogues destroyed by the Jordanian army.

One of the most moving things I recall my father telling me was how he had gone through a great deal in his life, both difficult times and happier ones. But while fighting, when he heard in Hebrew *"Har Habayit Be'yadeinu!"* ("The Temple Mount is in our hands!") and in English "The Old City is ours!" his heart overflowed with excitement and joy. Even years later when he told me this, his eyes lit up, and his face seemed to shine.

Divine Intervention

As a Jewish person born during the Diaspora, my father described his deeply emotional experience when, for the first time, he was able to see and pray at the *Kotel* (Western Wall) in the city of David in Jerusalem. He realized that having this longing to return to the Jewish homeland fulfilled in his lifetime could only be possible by the hand of God. He wanted me to grow up appreciating how momentous this event was, so I would never take for granted that today we live in the nation of Israel, and our capital is Jerusalem.

I remember when, as a child, I heard my parents speak of Jerusalem and read from the prophet Zechariah 8:1-8, when they spoke of the reunification of Jerusalem: "And the word of the LORD of hosts came, saying, 'Thus says the LORD of hosts: I am jealous for Zion with great jealousy, and I am jealous for her with great wrath. Thus says the LORD: I have returned to Zion and will dwell in the midst of Jerusalem, and Jerusalem shall be called the faithful city, and the mountain of the LORD of hosts, the holy mountain. Thus says the LORD of hosts: Old men and old women shall again sit in the streets of Jerusalem, each with staff in hand because of great age. And the streets of the city shall be full of boys and girls playing in its streets. Thus says the LORD of hosts: If it is marvelous in the sight of the remnant of this people in those days, should it also be marvelous in my sight, declares the LORD of hosts? Thus says the LORD of hosts: Behold, I will save my people from the east country and from the west country, and I will bring them to dwell in the midst of Jerusalem. And they shall be my people, and I will be their God, in faithfulness and in righteousness'" (ESV).

Surprisingly, in six days, the IDF had successfully conquered the territories of the Sinai and Gaza Strip from Egypt, the West Bank and Jerusalem (Judea and Samaria) from Jordan, and the Golan Heights from Syria. These territories and their borders (technically only armistice lines) had never been agreed upon, internationally or locally, as recognized borders. As a result, Israel had been left vulnerable, but now these territories and borders were controlled by Israel. Nevertheless, on June 19, 1967, the Israeli government voted unanimously to withdraw from the Sinai Peninsula and from the Golan Heights in return for a peace agreement and negotiation of the West Bank border with Jordan. The Arab states flatly rejected this offer. Furthermore, on September 1, 1967, the Arab League at the Khartoum Summit in Sudan passed three resolutions, which became known as the "Three No's": "No peace with Israel, no recognition of Israel, and no negotiations with Israel."[10] So Israel had no choice but to retain control of these strategic territories, including all of Jerusalem and Judea and Samaria. This allowed Jewish people to return to rebuild their homes, to pray at their homes and synagogues in the Old City, and to pray at their most holy site, the Western Wall of the Temple Mount.

Though I believe the IDF fought with a fierce desire to succeed, statistically speaking, Israel should not have won the war, particularly in such a short time. I believe it was a Higher Power that protected Israel; as a Jewish Israeli, I give God all the honor and glory for protecting me, my family, and the nation of Israel during this conflict.

The Yom Kippur War

Six years after the Six-Day War, another war broke out. At 2:00 P.M. on October 6, 1973, on Yom Kippur (the Day of Atonement), Egypt and Syria invaded the Sinai and the Golan Heights.[11] The outbreak of the war came as a total surprise to Israel and her citizens, as neither the IDF nor the government had considered outright war a possibility. The country was unprepared for war and for the mobilization of reserve soldiers. As a result, Israel paid a very high price, losing 2,800 soldiers, with a further 8,800 wounded.

The Yom Kippur War was the war of the *tsabarim*, literally meaning a prickly but sweet cactus fruit; also, a term used to denote a native-born Israeli; and a generation born in Israel, which had not gone through the horrors of the Holocaust. Before the outbreak of that war, I was preparing for my Bar Mitzvah celebration in the local synagogue. I was twelve at the time, about to turn thirteen. My younger brother, Immanuel, was only eight, and my older sister, Simcha, was nineteen and serving as a soldier in Kibbutz Beit HaEmeq in the north of the country (see photos #37-#38).

Simcha and I were tsabarim, as we were both part of that generation

10 | Ibid, p. 440.

11 | Yom Kippur is the holiest day in the Jewish calendar. On this day, the whole country is on shut-down (radio and TV off the air, no cars or buses on the roads), and most Israelis fast and go to pray at the synagogue.

that had been born in Israel—the first generation born there after the birth of the state—and did not go through the horrors of the Holocaust. And now we would fight in the Yom Kippur War. Those like Simcha, born in the first seven years of the state, were considered the "Golden Generation of Zionism." They were raised in a climate of the joy achieved for the Jewish people who had suffered 2,000 years of exile, with each generation yearning to return to the Land of their fathers. But now the war was to be fought by a generation who had never experienced that level of joy because they never experienced the same level of suffering as their predecessors.[12]

Personal Effects on Our Family

On the day the war broke out, my mother, brother, and I had just returned from prayer at the synagogue. Suddenly, we heard the wail of the sirens, and we knew we were at war. My mother turned on the radio, even though it was forbidden by Jewish law on a holy day. We heard that Israel had been attacked, and indeed, we were at war. Everyone was taken by surprise, and I remember that my father had no sooner returned from prayers at the synagogue than he immediately left to fight. He was forty-five years old, and he was gone to the front before I could say a word.

Because of the war, my Bar Mitzva celebration was canceled and, in fact, never took place. Rabbi Daniel, at the age of ninety, was brought to the synagogue on a stretcher to pray for the soldiers and citizens of Israel. Once again, he was interceding for my family and for the Jewish people, who were struggling for survival.

I was also there, fervently praying that God would take care of my father and sister and bring them back to us alive. This was the last time Rabbi Daniel entered his synagogue. Joseph Shulam recalled how this war affected the rabbi deeply. After this war it was physically difficult for him to get out of bed. However, he also remembered how the beloved rabbi prayed for Israel, singing songs of worship to God. Though Shulam

---

12 | Ariel Hirschfeld, "The Yom-Kippur War – The Silence," *Ot: Journal for Theory and Literature*, (4), 2014, pp. 9-10.

remembered him as frail, he also remembered how he interceded on behalf of his nation and people.

Simcha was doing her national service as a soldier on Kibbutz Beit HaEmeq where she had met some young Dutch people who came to volunteer for Israel. Among them was Erwin Freund, the son of a Jewish Holocaust survivor and a Christian mother. While volunteering at the kibbutz, Erwin caught sight of Simcha as she sat reading a book. To his amazement, he saw that it was the New Covenant in Hebrew. Curious and pleased, as he too was a believer in Yeshua, he spoke to her, and soon after they began to date. Simcha often spoke of the time when, late one night, Erwin surprised her when she was home visiting her family in Jaffa. He had jumped over the neighbor's fence to reach the backyard, and our mother woke Simcha in the middle of the night to tell her that Erwin had come to visit. Of course, Simcha was mortified to be caught in her pajamas and with cream on her face, but she was also pleased that he missed her and made such an effort to see her.

Erwin was back in Holland when the Yom Kippur War broke out. Concerned for Simcha and her family, he told his parents that he was returning to Israel. His parents were understandably anxious about him flying to a country at war, but they believed God would protect him if he felt he was doing the right thing. Erwin set off with a suitcase filled with chocolate bars for his friends and the soldiers on the kibbutz. When he arrived at the Ben Gurion International Airport in Israel, the security people were so suspicious of his luggage full of candy that they opened each chocolate bar to make sure he wasn't smuggling something. Simcha was on duty when Erwin suddenly appeared. As she had no idea that he was coming, how surprised and delighted she was that he had returned to Israel at such a time. It touched her deeply that despite the danger, he had come to be by her side and to help his Israeli friends in their time of need. With all the men fighting at the front, Erwin worked very hard taking care of all the difficult tasks on the kibbutz. Among other jobs, he fixed toilets, worked on the sewage, and took care of any other difficult or unpleasant tasks that came along. And, of course, everyone was most happy and grateful for the chocolates, even though already opened.

Throughout the war, Simcha held an important position as lookout. She was to sound the alarm of an attack or incoming bombs in the area of the kibbutz, hopefully in time for people to take cover in the bomb shelter. In addition, she was the one who received the first notice about soldiers from the kibbutz who had been hurt or killed in battle. This was an especially difficult duty, as many of them were friends and colleagues.

Two Fronts

Following the success of the Six-Day War and the sense of security that came with that victory, as well as the territorial buffer of the Sinai and Golan, the IDF was taken by surprise by the attack. In the first days, the Israeli army came close to collapse. With only 320,000 soldiers, the IDF faced two fronts with a combined force of 700,000 soldiers. The joint Egyptian and Syrian forces had 4,500 tanks, and 695 fighter planes. The Israeli army had 1,700 tanks, and 391 planes.[13]

On October 6, 1973, the Yom Kippur War began with a large airstrike. More than 200 Egyptian aircraft conducted simultaneous strikes at Israeli targets, while the Egyptian assault force of 32,000 infantry began crossing the Suez Canal in twelve waves.[14] The Egyptian Army successfully crossed the Suez Canal and constructed five bridgeheads within twelve hours. The Egyptian army attacked Israel's *Bar Lev* line, which had sixteen forts along the eastern side of the Suez Canal. On the day the war broke out, Israel had only about 500 soldiers, supported by seven batteries of artillery and 266 tanks deployed along the length of the canal.[15] The Egyptian army attacked the canal with 550,000 soldiers, close to 2,500 tanks, 1,500 artillery pieces, and anti-aircraft batteries with Scud missiles. Within forty-eight hours, the Egyptian army had conquered all Israel's fortifications along the canal,

13 | Wolff, *Israel*, pp. 450-451.

14 | Edgar O'balance, "No Victor, No Vanquished: The Yom Kippur War," *Hativa 14*, http://www.hativa14.com/wp-content/uploads/2014/03/Edgar_Oballance.pdf (accessed: 02/08/2018).

15 | Edgar O'balance, "No Victor, No Vanquished: The Yom Kippur War," *Hativa 14*, http://www.hativa14.com/wp-content/uploads/2014/03/Edgar_Oballance.pdf (accessed: 02/08/2018). Identical

with the exception of the Budapest fort.[16] Most Israeli soldiers defending this line became casualties.

For the next several days, the Israeli air force played a minimal role in the fighting, largely because it was needed to deal with the simultaneous, and ultimately more threatening, Syrian invasion of the Golan Heights.[17] And yet, despite the Egyptian victories, the Israeli navy managed to sail patrol boats to the Gulf of Suez. They then attacked numerous Egyptian boats, sinking many of them. Following this exceptional assault, the Egyptian plans to cross the Suez Canal were derailed. Further, throughout the war, the Egyptian army was unable to transport sufficient military supplies through the canal, which led to their eventual defeat.[18]

In the north of the Golan, with just 113 tanks, Israel faced the Syrians who had over 570 tanks and 360 pieces of artillery. After four days of battle in what became known as *Emeq HaBacha* (the Valley of Tears), Israel destroyed over 500 Syrian tanks and armored vehicles, and hundreds of Syrian soldiers were captured. But not one Israeli tank remained undamaged, with only seventeen of them still active. In addition, 131 soldiers were killed, and twelve were declared missing. In the center of the Golan, with only fifty-seven tanks, Israel fought against more than 600 Syrian tanks and artillery. After one day of battle, 90 percent of Israeli officers were killed or wounded. Things indeed looked bleak for Israel.[19]

Despite the surprise attacks, the reserve forces reported for duty immediately. This was possible simply because they had been at home or at the synagogue, observing the fast of Yom Kippur, when the war broke out. Such rapid deployment of the reserves took the Syrian army by surprise, and they were caught unprepared. Because of this, many of their forces were trapped in different areas of the Golan before they had achieved their goal of destroying the IDF and invading to the north of the Jordan River.

16 | Wolff, *Israel*, pp. 450-451.

17 | Kenneth M. Pollack, *Arabs at War: Military Effectiveness, 1948-1991*, (University of Nebraska Press, 2004), p.112.

18 | Benny Michelsohn, "Not All was Black: IDF's Accomplishments During the Yom Kippur War," IDF (August 2013), pp. 57-58.

19 | Wolff, *Israel*, pp. 450-451.

Another factor that helped Israel during this war came from the United States under President Richard Nixon, who sent weapons and ammunition to Israel.[20] American aircraft, in 567 missions, dropped over 22,000 tons of supplies. In addition, 90,000 tons of materiel were delivered by sea. These deliveries kept Israel fighting. After the war, Prime Minister of Israel, Golda Meir, said to Nixon, "For generations to come, all will be told of the miracle of the immense planes from the United States bringing in the materiel that meant life to our people."[21]

Ceasefire

After some weeks of heavy fighting on both fronts, the Israeli army in the north succeeded in recapturing the Hermon post on the Golan and pushed forward toward Damascus. On the southern front, the IDF pushed the canal toward Cairo. After a series of battles, in which both sides suffered heavy losses, the UN negotiated a cease-fire on October 22, though there were a number of skirmishes afterward.

Throughout the war and until his return home, we heard nothing from our father who was fighting in the Sinai. We didn't know whether he was dead or alive, or if he had been injured. He returned wounded after three weeks of war and never spoke of his experiences. My sister tried to talk with him about it, but he refused to say a word. All we knew is that most of his fellow soldiers had been killed. The Yom Kippur War is branded into the Israeli consciousness as a horrific war. In contrast to the tremendous victory of the Six-Day War, this war took a huge toll in Israel. Even so, the IDF managed to rally and fight to victory. The war itself had many political consequences, including Egypt's decision in 1979 to make peace with Israel.

---

20 | Ibid, p. 453.

21 | Jim Byron, "How Richard Nixon Saved Israel," *Richard Nixon Foundation*, October 8, 2010 < https://www.nixonfoundation.org/2010/10/how-richard-nixon-saved-israel/> [accessed on June 27, 2021].

The Mizrachis Resettle after the War

Following the Yom Kippur War, my parents moved from Jaffa to Zichron Yaakov. They purchased an old rundown house with a big garden, and with help from Immanuel and me, renovated the house on their own (see photo #39). My father worked in the fishponds near *Moshav Dor*, which belonged to the Ministry of Agriculture, and my mother worked as a seamstress and also volunteered in an organization for the elderly. Following her army service, my sister went to Holland, where she and Erwin were married. Today they live in the United States. They have two married children and one grandson, who is now the fourth generation of Holocaust survivors.

Throughout all these difficult years, because of Rabbi Daniel, my mother and sister lived with their hope in Yeshua the Jewish Messiah, while the rest of the family lived as conservative Orthodox Jews. My sister said that if she had not become a believer in the Messiah, she might well have become a very bitter woman, in light of all the difficult experiences she suffered in her youth. Instead, Yeshua brought peace and grace to her heart. My mother always pointed out that if Rabbi Daniel had not given her the Bible with the New Covenant, she would have ended her life. The faith of this rabbi in Israel's Messiah is what enabled my mother to continue to live and to raise her family in Israel. I often wonder, when I think of all that my family has gone through since World War II, what might have happened if Rabbi Daniel had not stood in the gap and interceded for them and many others throughout those difficult times. We certainly do have much for which to thank the Almighty God.

Rabbi Daniel Zion Honored at His Death

Some years after the Yom Kippur War, at the age of ninety-six, Rabbi Daniel Zion died. May his memory be blessed! The Hebrew date was 23 Cheshvan 5740, or by the Gregorian calendar, November 13, 1979. The announcement to the Bulgarian community, written in Bulgarian, described his courage in delivering the Jews of Bulgaria during World War

II. He was called the shepherd and hero of the Bulgarian Jews, and the community did not forget him.[22]

I remember the day my mother called when I was a soldier in the air force. It was my nineteenth birthday, and she was finally able to reach me at my base to wish me a happy birthday. But I could tell that something was wrong. She then told me that Rabbi Daniel had died and that she was going to the funeral to pay her respects to the man who saved her and her family. As we spoke on the phone, she reminded me that the rabbi used to lay hands on me and pray and bless me. I was sad to hear that this extraordinary man had died, but I didn't really understand all that she was talking about, though I knew he was special to our family and we were extremely grateful.

The next morning, November 14, 1979, my parents took a bus from Zichron Yaakov to Jaffa.[23] My father later told me that on the way to the funeral that day, he had reflected on how this rabbi had acted to save his Jewish community from destruction.

When they arrived at the funeral, they were both surprised and touched to see that so many people had come to honor this remarkable rabbi. Daniel Zion's body was laid out at 2:00 P.M. in Jaffa's central square with a military guard. At 3:00 P.M., his body was carried on foot to the cemetery in Holon.[24] Although buses were provided, my parents and many others walked the seven-kilometer procession to accompany Daniel on his final journey. My mother was blessed to see that even though he had been persecuted and suffered much for his faith, at his funeral Rabbi Daniel Zion was given military and state honors. It made no difference whether people agreed with his beliefs and opinions; they could not ignore what he had done for them. He was finally recognized as a hero of Israel.

Rabbi Daniel was buried in the Jewish cemetery in Holon, and his tombstone bears the words, "Rabbi Daniel Zion, Chief Rabbi of the

22 | The Central Archives for the History of the Jewish People (CAHJP), file BU-456 at the Hebrew University of Jerusalem. The Edmond J. Safra Campus Givat Ram.

23 | Israelis gathered at the Fountain Square in Jaffa for the funeral.

24 | Shulam, "Remembering Rabbi Daniel..." https://ffoz.org/discover/yahrzeit/yahrzeit-of-rabbi-daniel-zion.html (accessed: 24.05.2018).

Bulgarian Jewry." After his body was buried, my mother picked up a stone and put it next to his grave, according to Jewish tradition. Then she looked at the grave and, with a sob, whispered, "*Toda*" ("Thank You").

Looking back, I wish I had taken the time and asked my parents more questions about this extraordinary rabbi. When he died, I was distracted with my army service, and I didn't take the time to learn the whole story. I didn't realize the significance of what this man had done. I knew some stories that they told me while I was growing up, but I missed others. Only years later would I fully understand what this man had done for my family. One of my significant memories while writing this book was of when I was able to go to the cemetery with Shlomo Zion, the grandson of Rabbi Daniel, and together go to the Rabbi's grave (see photos #40 - #41). I was then able to take a stone and put it on his grave as my mother did over forty years ago.

Ending this chapter, I would encourage the younger generation to study and learn more from the different pioneers that plowed the path before you. Learn and study their stories so that future generations will not forget their sacrifice and work.

PART IV

The Mizrachi Legacy

CHAPTER 16

Messiah and Me

"They will live in the land that I gave to My servant Jacob, where your ancestors lived … their children and their children's children, forever, and My servant David will be their prince forever…" (Ezekiel 37:25, TLV).

As this book draws to a close, I walk in silent awe while tending the plants growing in my beautiful backyard garden. My grandchildren play in the background, running and chasing each other or whatever little leaf or butterfly movement catches their attention. So much joy and love emanates from them, so much exuberance, I can't help but smile as I realize it is love and love alone that brought us all to this very moment.

I stop and feel the warmth of the sun on my shoulders, as I think of how my parents endured so much, always praying that I, my children, and generations to come would grow up in a free Jewish state. My parents loved this Land even before they set eyes on it; before their feet touched the ground, they treasured it in their hearts. They passed on this love to me, and now I pass that same love to my children and grandchildren. However, it is not only the love for the Land or Zionism that brought us here, though both were strong motivators. I believe there was a deeper, far-reaching love that brought us to this point in history.

As I again gaze upon my Jewish grandchildren, playing freely and full of love in the Jewish state of Israel, I am deeply moved. I remember the courageous people, families, and generations God used to save an entire people group—50,000 Bulgarian Jews, including my parents. However, I understand—more now than ever—that for every Jewish person saved at such a dark time in history, there follows a continuing story that impacts the generations yet to come.

In the following paragraphs, I will humbly try to pen the incredible impact in my personal life from each of these stories and people as they are closely woven into everything I am today. I write this chapter, not to boast of what I have done or become, but rather to show from a personal viewpoint the continuing, saving love of God and what He did for the Jewish people of Bulgaria. In short, I love my people, my country, and my heritage, but above all, I love my God, the God of Israel.

Serving My Country

It was the height of the summer of 1979, as sweat rolled down my sun-beaten face and all I could think about was, when will this all be over?

"Again!" shouted the drill sergeant. "Again! Left, right, left!"

My comrades and I were completing basic training by preparing for the most significant ceremony of our military careers, the swearing-in to the Israeli Defense Forces. At the age of eighteen, I, like most Israeli men and women at the time, was drafted into the Israeli military for a four-year service in the Israeli air force. I was trained as a technician of Electronic Warfare (EW), specializing in various helicopters (see photo #42). My basic training, like most basic trainings at the time, amounted to days filled with physical training, military lectures, and weapon training. Early-morning wakeups, runs, drills, and latrine duty, followed by late-night marches, became a staple of my military life as a private. After basic military training for one month, I did a six-month course of technical training in the air force before receiving my final post at the Israeli air force base.

My mind was suddenly jolted back from the memories of the past months of basic training when the drill sergeant yelled, "At ease!" Then the sergeant shouted specific instructions for the swearing-in ceremony, which was to be held later that evening.

"Shoes shined till I can see my face in them! Don't forget to wear your dress class-A uniform tonight! Dismissed!"

The second I heard these commands, I raced to my bunker to take full advantage of the couple hours of leisure time we'd been afforded before the ceremony. I changed into my running shorts and hurried outside to join a game of football (soccer). I was free! Well, at least for the next couple of hours.

I was happy to be able to play football with friends I had come to respect and love, and not worry about military protocols and rules. A short time later, while I was getting dressed in my class-A uniform and shining my shoes, I thought of my father. This was the first time I realized how it must have been for him to put on an Israeli military uniform. I was deeply impacted to think he grew up in a time when there was no army to protect him or his family from the Holocaust or from attacks solely for being Jewish. Immediately following the war, at the age of twenty-one, he had become a soldier for the state of Israel, despite not knowing the language fluently or having any friends or close family to support him. I concluded that for my father to put on the uniform of the Israeli military was more than meaningful for him; it represented the hope and resolution that *never again* would such a horrific tragedy befall the people of Israel.

Thinking of all this put things in perspective for me. Even though being in the military was no picnic and at times extremely challenging, I too felt the same love for this country as my father, who had so diligently passed it on to me. While I was growing up, my parents didn't often show love in a physically affectionate way, by means of hugs and kisses, but one thing they did fervently instill in us was a love of the Land and the people of Israel. They stressed the need to fight to protect our divine heritage and to guard it with our lives. Because my siblings and I were the generation born after the Holocaust, the memories of the atrocities that occurred in WWII were still fresh. The combination of all these factors was the strong motivator for us to be the best at whatever we did in order to guard and protect our people, together with our comrades, from future annihilation.

The swearing-in ceremony was regal, opened by the parade of flags from all the various air force units leading the way. We were each handed a Tanach, which we held together with our gun in one hand and raised the other hand as we swore in one voice to guard and defend with our lives the Land of Israel. The ceremony concluded with all of us soldiers and commanders singing our national anthem, "Hatikva" (The Hope).

At this moment, I remember feeling such overwhelming joy and sense of accomplishment that I was officially an Israeli soldier in the great Israeli air force.

Most of my military service as an EW (Electronic Warfare) air force serviceman was like most servicemen at the time. We spent our time in the hangars or repair depot rooms, working on or replacing parts for the various aircraft we were assigned. Many details of my service are still classified due to security; however, I can say that in addition to my incredible responsibilities as an EW serviceman on aircraft, my early military days were also filled with menial tasks such as guard duty, latrine duty, mess-hall duty, base-maintenance duty, and such things that had to be done but were not always interesting or enjoyable.

At the age of twenty-two, my unit and I were an integral part of Operation Peace for the Galilee (1982). This little-known yet crucial war broke out after years of provocation and skirmishes on the Israeli Northern border. The purpose of Operation Peace for the Galilee was to bring an end to the daily terror attacks and threats from the PLO (Palestinian Liberation Organization).[1] The PLO at the time was controlling the Southern Lebanese area, which entirely bordered with Northern Israel. They regularly fired Katusha rockets on the Jewish towns and villages in the Northern Galilee area of Israel. This operation would very soon come to be known in Israel and around the world as the first Lebanese War with Israel, though the conflict itself never was between Lebanon and Israel but rather between the PLO and Israel.

I can distinctly remember hearing the bomb sirens going off almost non-stop as my unit and I participated in covert missions, hoping to bring us closer to the end of the war. Little did we know that the end of the war was not near, not even close. In the summer of 1983, I was honorably discharged at the completion of my military service and placed in a reserve unit (see photos #43-46) while the war with the PLO and eventually with Hezbollah raged on for another eighteen years and even beyond that.

---

1 | Wolff, *Israel*, pp.459-463.

Visiting the United States

In December 1983, following my military service, I flew to the United States for the first time. I wanted to relax, have fun, see the cities I saw from American TV shows, like Dallas with J.R., and maybe even find love. I just wanted to "break loose" and have a good time. In the end, I decided to fly to Las Vegas. My plan was that once I arrived in Las Vegas, I would go to every bar, disco club, pub, and casino to make a fortune gambling and "to let off some steam." This, I foolishly thought, would fill the ever-growing emptiness I felt in my heart.

As I boarded the plane to the United States, I was determined, excited, and even thrilled by the thought of the experiences and adventures that lay before me. When the captain of the flight announced that we had landed, I felt my heart rate increase. *Finally*, I thought. *I'm going to experience life like never before.*

I had just one quick stop to make on the way to Las Vegas. Simcha, who at the time lived in Florida with her husband, Erwin, had invited me for a visit. I hadn't seen them since their wedding day a few years prior, so I thought it would be good to stop for a few days before continuing my travels to my ultimate destination, Las Vegas.

I landed in Florida on Friday morning and was immediately overwhelmed by the extreme humidity as I exited the airport into my sister's heartwarming embrace. "It's hot and humid here," I said, as I quickly took a step back.

Simcha laughed. "Welcome to Florida, brother. Let's go get you something to eat. You must be starving."

During dinner, Simcha and Erwin told me about all that had transpired in their lives over the past few years since we last saw each other. As dinner came to a close, Simcha asked me what, at the time, seemed a peculiar question: "Avi, dear, it would be nice to have you accompany us to church on Sunday. We will leave around nine in the morning. Could you be ready then?"

Stunned and slightly confused, I blurted, "What? Excuse me? A church? I am a Jew! You are a Jew! Jews do not go to church. Why would we go to a church? What is this nonsense?"

In my shock, a memory was triggered from growing up in Yafo, Tel Aviv. Most late Saturday afternoons, both my mother and sister would leave the house together to go to the synagogue for a group study of the Hebrew Scriptures. Occasionally, I accompanied them, though I didn't actively participate. The study was led by a rabbi I had seen a few times but hadn't made an effort to get to know. During these studies, the attendees would read in Hebrew from the Scriptures and also sing songs and psalms of praise. I knew then there was something different about those people and the rabbi, but I had dismissed the memory as time went on. But now? Attending church? This was going too far!

Simcha, her heart obviously overflowing with compassion and great love, responded, "It's not what you think. There are nice people there, people who love God and love the Messiah." She smiled and patted my hand. "Take your time to think about it, and I hope to see you ready to come with us on Sunday."

On Sunday morning, if for no other reason than curiosity, I decided to accompany Simcha and Erwin to the church, though I strutted in carrying my Hebrew Bible. I must now admit that I went to the church service filled with pride. I thought I knew better than they did in their faulty beliefs, and I intended to show them how wrong and pagan they were in their ways.

However, once we arrived, I was stunned to find a loving, joyful, and accepting group of people who, to my surprise, claimed to love the God of Avraham, Yitzhak, and Yaakov—and also the Messiah Yeshua. I didn't know it then, but I was being provoked to jealousy, as is written in Romans 11:11: "I say then, they did not stumble so as to fall, did they? May it never be! But by their false step salvation has come to the Gentiles, to provoke Israel to jealousy" (TLV).

As the congregation sang and praised God, I sensed something beginning to change deep in my heart, in a place I had recently been feeling such emptiness. Later, a speaker presented a lesson or talk in which he spoke of a loving God who was also a loving heavenly Father. When I heard those words, I turned to my sister and asked, "What in the world is this guy talking about?"

She shushed me and told me to listen. With seemingly no other options, I temporarily squelched my questions and continued listening. The more I listened, the more I felt something happening deep in my heart, which I could not understand or put into words. As a Jew, I knew *of* God and *about* God. I knew many of the stories from the Bible about Moshe (Moses), Avraham, Yitzhak, and Yaakov, as well as the prophets. But I had no personal relationship with God, and I certainly did not know the Messiah as Yeshua.

Growing up in Israel, I was not interested in hearing about Yeshua. I was not interested in the beliefs of my mother, sister, or the strange rabbi I recalled leading the synagogue in Yafo. However, though not personally interested, I did accept them for their beliefs and did not shun my mother or sister. I never dreamed those beliefs would one day become my own. I was perfectly content to go to synagogue with my father and keep the Jewish traditions as I had been raised. I was, as most Jewish people, still waiting for the Messiah to come. As far as I was concerned, *Mashiach Ben David* (Messiah, son of David) had not yet come or revealed himself to the people of Israel. Yeshua was only for the Gentiles. I could not conceive of God as a loving Father or a Messiah who saved. In fact, I often imagined God lurking around the corner with a big whip, waiting for me to make a mistake so He could punish me. I certainly never imagined a God so loving that He would freely give of Himself for my sake, or that Yeshua was indeed the long-awaited Jewish Messiah.

Meeting the Messiah

As I sat there in the congregation that Sunday morning, I felt this strange and previously unknown emotion start to well up in my heart. Tears formed in my eyes, and I wanted to cry for no apparent reason. I fought this feeling, not willing to show any emotion, particularly not one I couldn't understand myself. As soon as the meeting was over, I raced out of the church, refusing to discuss my experience with Simcha or anyone else.

A few days later, I received an invitation to attend a church camp for young adults. My first reaction was to turn down the invitation, but my curiosity won out and I went to see what this camp was all about. I was pleasantly surprised to find people close to my own age playing sports, such as basketball and baseball, but I was slightly disappointed that they weren't playing football (soccer) as we did in Israel.

After eating dinner, we were divided into small groups for Bible lessons. I was only slightly comfortable with this setting since I recognized the concept from my days growing up in Yafo with my mother, sister, and the rabbi who held similar lessons. Still, I had willingly come to the meeting, so I went along with the planned schedule.

The leader of my group was an older lady, who told us to open the Bible to the Book of John. I was puzzled and also somewhat embarrassed. *Who is this John?* I wondered. *Why isn't that book in my Bible?* Finally, because the Book of John was not included in my Hebrew Bible, I decided to simply listen to the message.

The more the woman read from the Book of John, the more stunned I became at how much was written of God being a loving Father. Then she read from John 3:16: "For God so *loved* the world that He gave His one and only Son, that whoever believes in Him shall not perish but have eternal life" (TLV, emphasis mine). As she read, I suddenly understood that the book was talking about the Messiah and the evidence that God is love. It explained that our God gave His only Son, the Messiah—His name being Yeshua—to be a perfect sacrifice for our sins. The more I listened, the more it began to make sense to me in my Jewish-Israeli mind. Again, I was struck with memories of my mother and sister—and their strange rabbi. And there I was, hearing and actually listening to the same beliefs written out, thoughts I knew about but never wanted to pursue. Could it truly be that Yeshua was the Jewish Messiah, *Meshiach Ben David*?

At that moment, I felt something in my heart, the same feeling I had when I attended the church service earlier that week. Though I didn't know it at the time, I now know that I was sensing the presence of *Ruach HaKodosh*, the Holy Spirit. As I had done the previous Sunday, I fought against the emotions and the urge to cry. I told myself I was a tough Israeli, ex-air force serviceman, raised without emotions, and I could fight these emotions. In fact, the moment the lesson was over, I ran to my room, telling myself again and again, "Forget about the love of God!" I shut the door behind me, thinking I could somehow run away from God and escape this strange feeling inside me.

There, alone in my room, I thought of what I had heard, and I began to understand that Yeshua was indeed the truth, the way, and the life (see John 14:6). I realized what I stated previously, that I knew *about* God but did not have a personal relationship *with* Him. I had gone to synagogue and read the Tanach. I knew the prophecies, as well as the history of the Jewish people and the temple. I understood that my sins separated me from the Holy One of Israel. I believed all my life that if I prayed, beat my chest for every sin I could think of, and fasted on Yom Kippur, I might be made righteous for the coming year. However, I was never 100 percent sure that my *mitzvot* (good deeds) and prayers would be enough to earn atonement for my sins.

I wanted to see for myself the laws concerning the atonement for sin and the sacrifices required in the Torah. In school in Israel, we had been taught that the Book of Leviticus spoke of these things, so I began reading from Leviticus. As I did so, everything I was feeling started to make sense.

When I came to Leviticus 17:11—"For the life of the creature is in the blood, and I have given it to you on the altar to make atonement for your lives—for it is the blood that makes atonement because of the life" (TLV)—I was astounded. In that moment, the veil fell from my spiritual eyes, as I realized only Yeshua could be the perfect Lamb that atoned for all the present and future sins of the world. I suddenly understood that a temple to offer sacrifices to atone for sin was no longer needed because the Messiah (Yeshua) had already come before the destruction of the second temple.

And then I remembered my mother telling me about a chapter in Isaiah that talked about the Messiah. I quickly took my Jewish Bible and started reading that book. When I got to chapter 53, my eyes were opened to the truth, and I understood that Yeshua had to be the Lamb of God, fulfilling all the prophecies written about the coming Messiah in that chapter:

> But He was pierced because of our transgressions,
> crushed because of our iniquities.
> The chastisement for our *shalom* was upon Him,
> and by His stripes we are healed.
> We all like sheep have gone astray.
> Each of us turned to his own way.
> So *Adonai* has laid on Him the iniquity of us all.
> He was oppressed and He was afflicted
> yet He did not open His mouth.
> Like a lamb led to the slaughter,
> like a sheep before its shearers is silent,
> so He did not open His mouth (vv. 5-7, TLV).

I was so touched by this that I turned to the Book of Jeramiah. At that point, there in that camp room by myself, I saw this verse: "I will make a new covenant with the house of Israel" (31:30, TLV). I was surprised to find the words *"Brit Chadasha"* (New Covenant or New Testament) within that verse. With all my time in synagogue and Hebrew studies, I had never noticed that before.

Now, realizing the reference to a new covenant/testament was in my Hebrew Bible, I decided to read from the New Covenant for the first time. I left my room and borrowed a Bible, as I knew it would contain the New Covenant.

Opening the book, I read the first verse of the New Covenant and was speechless: "The book of the genealogy of Yeshua ha-Mashiach, Ben-David [Son of David], Ben-Avraham..." (Matthew 1:1, TLV). I couldn't stop reading and continued on to the book of Luke. I was moved with even more emotion as I read: "He will be great and will be called *Ben-Elyon*. *Adonai Elohim* will give Him the throne of David, His father. He shall reign over the house of Jacob for all eternity, and His kingdom will be without end..."

(Luke 1:32-33, TLV). After reading these Scriptures, I understood that Yeshua was the *Mashiach Ben David* (Messiah, son of David), whom I had been waiting for my whole life.

This revelation and understanding were followed by the Spirit of God falling upon me. I can't completely explain in words everything that happened and all the emotion I felt at the time, but I remember clearly knowing in my heart that I needed to turn to God and repent. I didn't know exactly how to pray, but I started to speak to God, and the words just flowed. I prayed to Him to forgive me for all my sins. I appealed to God for atonement, and I asked that Yeshua come into my life and be Lord of my life. The moment I ended my prayer, I felt as if a great weight had been lifted from me. I knew that God in His infinite love had given me a new heart and a new spirit, as is written in Ezekiel 36:26-27: "Moreover I will give you a new heart. I will put a new spirit within you. I will remove the stony heart from your flesh and give you a heart of flesh. I will put My *Ruach* [Spirit] within you. Then I will cause you to walk in My laws, so you will keep My rulings and do them" (TLV).

God led me to recognize and receive the Jewish Messiah, Yeshua. I now felt the love of God the Father for the first time in my life. He took away the heart of stone and gave me a heart that feels and knows what true love is.

I knew I needed to come back home to the land of Israel. Needless to say, I never made it to the city of Las Vegas.

From Generation to Generation

This story is one about generations being saved. Because of this, I feel I must fill in some of the recent gaps in my father's story.

My father, Nissim Mizrachi,[2] did not have an easy life. As written about in the first part of this book, Nissim was a Holocaust survivor from Bulgaria (see photo #47) who remembered the tragedies that occurred during those years. He lived through the anti-Semitic legislation

2 | My father passed away in 2018.

in Bulgaria, the Nazis in the streets of Sofia, and even the attempts to deport the Jewish community to their deaths (see Chapter 5 "Plans for Deportation"). He spent his teenage years in the forests hiding out with the partisans, fighting the Nazis until the end of World War II. He endured the difficult journey to Israel, the harsh conditions at the detention camp on Cyprus, and fighting again for survival of the Jewish homeland, Israel, for five more wars. From the War of Independence to the Yom Kippur War, he served loyally side by side with other Holocaust survivors because of their shared love and belief in the Jewish State of Israel. It was their way of proclaiming that *never again* would the Jewish people be annihilated without a military to protect them. Even after many years had passed, he was still unable to overcome the pain and trauma the German Nazis had caused him and his family. However, all this time, the Lord was preparing his heart.

Several years before I came to faith, my father met some people on the street in Israel. They were speaking German, and it deeply disturbed him, as hearing the language revived his intense feelings of pain, loss, anger, and misery. Indignantly he thought, *What are they doing in Israel?*

Unable to ignore or put aside his painful memories, he decided to confront the Germans and demand an explanation for their presence in the Land. After speaking, albeit almost yelling, at them for a few minutes, he learned they were actually Christians who loved Israel and the Jewish people. At first, it was hard for him to accept this fact about them. However, these German Christians continued to speak in love to my father, telling him over and over that they loved the Jewish people. He finally calmed down enough to tell them he was from Bulgaria and had lived through WWII. Immediately these German believers looked at him and did something totally unexpected. In a soft, kind voice, one of them said, "In the name of the German people, we are sorry for what our people did to you and the Jewish people."

My father could hardly contain the tears welling up in his eyes. He was so touched by their words that he felt his heart begin to soften. Almost immediately, he felt his angry heart being healed and filled with love.

Following this encounter, he began to accompany Rivka, my mother, to meetings with other believers in Yeshua.

Some time passed, and my father came to understand that in order to have true love and peace in his life, he had to place his full faith in Yeshua as his Messiah. He knew it in his heart, but he resisted until I came to faith a few years later.

At first, when my father heard that I, his eldest son, had become a believer in Yeshua, he had a hard time accepting it. It was difficult for him to reconcile the fact that not only his wife and daughter believed in Yeshua, but now his eldest son did as well.

When I married Chaya, we lived with my parents for some months in Zichron Yaakov (see photo #48). It was here that my father began to see for himself the changes in my life and character. He began to remember other miracles and stories he had heard or even seen for himself (as recounted in this book) of others following this Jewish Messiah. As my father's heart continued to soften, he started asking me questions about this Yeshua and the love of the Father. Soon, I was overcome with joy when my father asked to receive Yeshua as his Messiah and Lord of his life. From that point onward, my father walked closely with his loving Messiah Yeshua.

This is the complete story of my family as they experienced the everlasting love of God and embraced that eternal love, never again to be the same. I see now, more than ever, that God, my loving heavenly Father, regardless of the circumstances, was beside my family during every moment of their lives and throughout every generation that passed. He is a good God, He is a loving Father, He is my God and Father (see Exodus 15:2).

If you allow Him, He will completely change your life as well, giving you a loving heart, a soft heart, a heart full of His love.

"...for God is love" (1 John 4:8, TLV).

Afterword

Coming Full Circle

"And whoever saves a life, it is considered as
if he saved the entire world..."[1]

Throughout the entirety of this book, the distinguished personality that connects all parts so intricately woven together is the Rabbi Daniel Zion. As I wrote earlier, I believe the Lord used Rabbi Zion to save my family and the thousands of Bulgarian Jews from the gas chambers in WWII. And as I also noted earlier, Rabbi Zion was used by God to persuade my mother not to commit suicide, thus saving her, me, and my brother who had not yet been born. Because of this rabbi, my mother and years later my sister also came to faith in Yeshua as the Messiah. Fast-forward a few years later, I came to faith in Yeshua when my sister took me to her church that day. As a result, my life and heart were changed completely. In the end, as I wrote previously, my father, a Holocaust survivor, seeing the true love of his family for one another and for God, also came to faith in Yeshua as his Messiah.

Without the direct influence and even the existence of Rabbi Daniel Zion, my family's story would have turned out completely different. It is quite possible in a different scenario that we as a family might not have existed at all. The Rabbi Zion had a great impact on all of us. He was used by God to both physically and spiritually save our family and the generations to follow.

Conclusion

The story of Rabbi Daniel Zion reveals in an absolute way how God will use one man to affect an entire family for generations to come. All that

1 | Mishnah Sanhedrin 4:9; *Yerushalmi Talmud*, Tractate Sanhedrin 37a.

is necessary is simply the desire and the courage to act. Because of Rabbi Daniel Zion, my family has continued to live on for the four generations following WWII.

In Dr. Stern's book *Messianic Jewish Manifesto,* written in 1988, he stated that "many autobiographies, testimonies, and testimony collections" have been written over the years, but strongly suggested that "a modern update including the lives of this century's [Jewish] believers would be necessary in order to preserve the legacy for future generations to come. We will otherwise forget them.... [Rabbi Daniel's] story is one of many that will be lost unless researchers and writers get busy!"[2] I praise God that David had the insight back in 1988 to realize this story was vital to the continuing generations. I am grateful to have had the privilege of researching and writing this monumental story of Rabbi Daniel as it beautifully interweaves together the struggles and joys from my own personal family story.

While researching this book, a significant question kept returning without a satisfactory answer. The question I asked myself continuously throughout the writing was, *Why did the government of Bulgaria, which was already aligned with Nazi Germany, decide in the very end not to give over the entire Jewish Bulgarian population to be annihilated by the Nazis?*

I know now, of course, that many factors played into that decision, including the ever-growing likelihood of the German defeat in WWII. However, I truly believe God's hand orchestrated the miraculous outcome that saved 48,000 Jewish lives. I also know God used two faithful and courageous leaders entrusted with the fate of their people. These great leaders paid a heavy price for the stand they took for righteousness. The Metropolitan Stefan, a Christian, was threatened during World War II for his actions and later suffered at the hand of the Communists for standing against their authority and rule. The Rabbi Daniel Zion, a Jew, was at times misunderstood and rejected by his own people. These men suffered loneliness and rejection as they resolutely walked the paths God had set

2 | David H. Stern, *Messianic Jewish Manifesto* (Clarksville: Jewish New Testament Publications, INC, 1988), pp. 213-214.

before them. They are my heroes, people who were willing to do what was right, no matter the price and without any required recognition whatsoever.

Only after each had passed away were these courageous men honored. The Rabbi Daniel was given a state funeral by Israel with a processional of state officials and dignitaries originating in the city of Jaffa leading all the way to the city of Holon. The Metropolitan Stephen was also honored after his death as he came to be recognized as "Righteous among the Nations" by thousands of grateful Israeli Jews.[3] These men, along with many others mentioned in this book, are unsung but true heroes who were willing to fight for the Jewish people and to fight for what is right, true, and loving, no matter the outcome. Sadly, in the end, most of these bold men and women would not live long enough to see the full impact and extent of their consistent daily righteous actions on the generations to follow.

Among some of these unsung heroes in this book are my parents. I honor them as heroes because of the legacy they left for me and my children. They came to the Land of Israel as young people with nothing but hope and a dream that this would be their home. My mother was only a teenager when she arrived alone from Turkey and fought in the Israeli Independence War. My father, a young man when he left Bulgaria, came to Israel and served valiantly in the newly formed IDF throughout most of Israel's wars. My parents both knew and believed the prophecies written of the return to the Land of Israel. They truly believed in their hearts that God was calling them back to their homeland to rebuild the nation of Israel after 2,000 years of exile. My parents learned the Hebrew language, fought in wars, adapted to a new culture, and did whatever it took to build a home and a future in a country that was struggling to survive. They raised a family here with the belief that with God's help they would get through any trials that might come their way. They witnessed the prophecies coming true before their own eyes in their lives—from exile in the Diaspora, to the return and rebuilding of Israel, to finding Yeshua as their Messiah and Lord, the ultimate fulfillment of prophecy. Their love for this nation and

3 | "Two Bulgarian Clergymen Honored as Righteous Among the Nations", *Yad Vashem*, http://www.yadvashem.org/events/12-march-2002 (Accessed: 29.12.2016).

the staunch belief that Israel was the homeland for the Jewish people made it possible for future generations to be born and live in Israel (see photos #49 - #53).

It has been said many times that heroes are ordinary people who do extraordinary things. I agree, knowing these heroes were people who never gave up and continued consistently on the path God put before them. In dark and uncertain times, this required great sacrifice. However, because of those great sacrifices, thousands of people who would not otherwise live in Israel, including my own family, now do so. I see so clearly the story of my family in reading Ezekiel 36:24-28: "For I will take you from the nations, gather you out of all the countries and bring you back to your own land. Then I will sprinkle clean water on you and you will be clean from all your uncleanness and from all your idols. Moreover I will give you a new heart. I will put a new spirit within you. I will remove the stony heart from your flesh and give you a heart of flesh. I will put My *Ruach* within you. Then I will cause you to walk in My laws, so you will keep My rulings and do them. Then you will live in the land that I gave to your fathers. You will be My people and I will be your God'" (TLV).

When I contemplate the incredible legacy I received from my parents, I wonder, *How will I be able to communicate this paramount legacy in such a way that it will effect for good and greatness in the coming generations while giving honor to those who shaped this legacy?*

As a Tsabar, a native-born Jewish Israeli, I believe this legacy of those who came before us ultimately shaped the nation of Israel into what it is today. This legacy helped the Zionistic movement with mass Jewish immigration to the homeland of Israel, and sequentially today is continuing to mold the faith of Jewish believers in Yeshua as the Messiah of Israel. Inevitably, this legacy of hope is an integral part of the nation of Israel and its future. I believe that we, the Jewish believers in Yeshua as the Messiah, have a duty and calling to pass on this legacy. However, I ask myself, *How and in what manner should we pass on the legacy to the next generation and generations to follow?* The answer I unfailingly come back to time and time again is to convey the great legacy in *love*.

When I think of all the Jewish people have been through and experienced over the centuries, I am pained in my heart of hearts, yet inspired. I am pained because for years we as a people have been persecuted, tortured, killed, and even exiled from our land and other lands around the world. This, coupled with our stubborn heart and stiff neck, has led to the formation of a spiritual veil over our spiritual eyesight.

However, as I said, I am also inspired because I see seemingly impossible prophecy being fulfilled in our day and the spiritual veil slowly being removed from the Jewish people's eyes (see 2 Corinthians 3).

My prayer, therefore, is that we, in the love of our Father in heaven, would be able to convey the greatest legacy of love to the next generations, the legacy of Yeshua the Messiah.

Yeshua, in all His love, was heartbroken, and it pained Him to see that His people in His day would not accept the message of true salvation. With tears of love pouring down His face, Yeshua said these words in the great city of Jerusalem: "For I tell you, you will never see Me again until you say, '*Baruch ha-ba b'shem ADONAI.* Blessed is He who comes in the name of the Lord" (Matthew 23:39, TLV). When Yeshua said these words, He was speaking to my own people, the Jewish people. My hope is in one of the final prophecies taking place because of God's great love for His people, as it is written, "… all Israel will be saved…" (Romans 11:26, TLV).

I believe it is important to understand that Jewish people who come to faith (believe) in Yeshua as the Messiah still fully retain their Jewish identity, as the many different tribes and nations who come to faith in the Jewish Messiah retain their cultural identity. This was debated and decided by the first Jerusalem Council (see Acts 15). Yeshua remained a Jew throughout His life on this earth and continues to retain His Jewish identity into the age to come (see Rev. 5:5).

Rabbi Daniel Zion believed this with all his heart and strongly kept his Jewish identity in full while believing in Yeshua. His faith and boldness were an inspiration for me. Like Rabbi Daniel, I was born a Jew, I live as a Jew, and I will die a Jew, even as I follow our Jewish Messiah Yeshua.

I am filled with great joy as this legacy of God's unfailing love inspired faith in Yeshua for Rabbi Daniel, for my family, and for myself. This faith continues to spread and grow more now than ever before, with both Jews and Arabs in Israel and the surrounding nations coming to know Yeshua as their Messiah and Redeemer. Hallelujah!

I am privileged and yet honored to live in the Land of Israel together with my wife, Chaya. We have raised our four beautiful daughters with the deep values formed at the core of the legacy passed on to me, which were: love the God of Israel, love our people, love our Land, love our heritage, and most of all love our Messiah Yeshua. I am proud to say these values have continued on as my daughters served in the Israeli Military (IDF), continued to give of themselves in love to the nation of Israel, and today are passing on the greatest legacy of love to the next generation.

The fact that my family and I are alive today gives a glimpse of the big picture of the rebirth of Israel as a nation and a glimpse of rebirth of the Messianic community in Israel. These glimpses simply show us time and time again the awesome faithfulness and great love of our God.

Despite how impossible the situation may have seemed at many junctures in times past, our great and loving God raised for His glory a faithful and courageous people to stand against evil. Therefore, this story is truly a courageous legacy, a legacy of hope. It is also a legacy about the faithfulness and love of God to His people, the Jewish people. He is our God, our good Father, who will always keep His promises to us. I am grateful and indebted to those who have come before me to have had the opportunity to write this book and tell of His faithfulness. *Am Yisrael Chai!* (May the People of Israel live!)

Tell your children about it—
your children to their children,
their children to another generation.
(Joel 1:3, TLV)

Appendix A

Five Songs by Rabbi Daniel Zion

I Am Poor

I am poor, frail, and destitute—despised, broken, and weak.
Yeshua has conquered me, made me into a new man!
The Messiah has freed me from the old and from my ego,
And honored me with the new; He has loved me with great love.
Without Him I am alone; my heart trembles in terror
Lest the adversary—the despoiler—rob me of good courage!
I shall be released and freed from the deception
of a dominating adversary!
I shall overcome all if I am joined with the Messiah.
The whole world is against me; in my faith I stand alone!
I relinquish my honor for the sake of the Messiah—my friend!

אני עני, דל ורש, נבזה, נדכה וחלש,
ישוע אותי כבש, עשה אותי אדם חדש!
המשיח שחררני מהישן וה"אני"
ובחדש כבדני; אהבה רבה אהבני.
בלעדיו אני בודד, וממורא – ליבי רועד,
פן השטן השודד יגזול ממני מעודד!
אחלץ ואשתחרר מעצת שטן שורר.
על הכל אתגבר אם המשיח אתחבר.
כל העולם כולו נגדי; באמונתי – לבדי!
אני מוחל על כבודי למען המשיח, ידידי!

* * *

Not I

Not I, not I—only You, Yeshua, in me;
Only You bring me before my God, my Father.
Only You heal me from all my affliction.
Not I, not I—only You, Yeshua, in me;
Only You teach me to love the Rock of my salvation.
Only You teach me to love all creatures.
Not I, not I—only You, Yeshua, in me;
Only You teach me to love even enemies.
Thus shall I cleave in love and be with You forever;
Not I, not I—only You, Yeshua, in me!

לא אני, לא אני, רק אתה ישוע, בי;
רק אתה מביא אותי לפני אלוהי-אבי.
רק אתה מרפא אותי מכל מחלתי.
לא אני, לא אני, רק אתה, ישוע, בי;
רק אתה מלמד אותי לאהוב צור ישועתי.
רק אתה מלמד אותי לאהוב כל הברואים.
לא אני, לא אני, רק אתה, ישוע, בי;
רק אתה מלמד אותי לאהוב אף את האויבים.
לכן באהבה אדבק, עמך אהיה לעד;
לא אני, לא אני, רק אתה, ישוע, בי!

* * *

Awake, O Shine!

Awake, O shine, for your light has come—shake the yoke off your neck!
Raise your voice forcefully in a shout together
with the holy ones and all of creation!
Sing, sing a song of freedom, for God has given us freedom!
Sing, sing a new song—let the name of the God of hosts be sanctified!
There is no breach, no screaming in our squares—
only peace, quietude, and love.
Redemption will come; it is even nigh. The Messiah
will return—blessed is he who comes!
The Anointed of the LORD will reign forever,
together with His holy ones!
There is no more adversary, no evil disaster; Yeshua
the Messiah has paid off our debts!

עורי אורי, כי בא אורך – פרקי העול מעל צווארך!
הרימי בכוח קולך בתרועה, יחד עם הקדושים וכל הבריאה!
שירו, שירו, שיר חופש – אלוהים נתן לנו נופש!
שירו, שירו, שיר חדש; שם אלוהי צבאות יתקדש!
אין פרץ ואין צווחה ברחובותינו – רק שלום, שלווה ואהבה;
הגאולה תבוא, היא קרובה; המשיח ישוב – ברוך הבא!
משיח יהוה ימלוך לעד עם קדושיו יחד!
אין שטן, אין פגע רע, ישוע המשיח חובותינו פרע!

* * *

All of Us, As One

All of us, as one, shall live together in peace.
We will serve the one God, the unique and distinctive God!
All of us, as brothers, shall be joined together.
Yes, we shall be blessed, sent out by the Lord!
To love our God with all our heart and mind, with
our spirit and breath, with all our strength.
To love our Lord, Yeshua our Messiah, who was
crucified on our behalf to atone our iniquities.
To reveal our love, in our passing thoughts, our feelings, our
speech, our deeds—toward every person according to our image.
We shall serve Adonai of Hosts every day. That will be
our identity, as well as the purpose of our life.

כולנו כאיש אחד נחיה בשלום יחד, נעבוד לאל אחד, לאל יחיד ומיוחד!
כולנו כאחים נהיה מסופחים. כן נהיה ברוכים מאדוני שלוחים.
לאהוב את אלוהינו בכל ליבנו ושכלנו, ברוחנו, בנשמתנו ובכל מאודנו.
לאהוב את אדוננו, ישוע משיחנו, הוא נצלב בעדנו, לכפר חטאותינו.
לגלות אהבתנו, בהרהורינו ורגשותינו, בדיבורנו ובמעשינו לכל אדם כדמותנו.
בכל יום נעבוד את יהוה צבאות, זאת תהיה תעודתנו וגם מטרת חיינו.

* * *

My Purpose

The word of the LORD is my guide.
The lamp of the LORD is a light unto my path.
The fear of the LORD is the beginning of my wisdom.
The love of the LORD is the life of my being.
To do His will is my purpose.
Justice and justness are my desire;
Torments of sacrifice are my sin offering.
And by the blood of Messiah have I been purified.
Cleansing and purity are my purpose.
A servant to the Rock of my salvation,
A faithful son I have tried to be.
The ways of the LORD are my holiness.
Save me, LORD, from my distress!
Raise me up when I fall.
Then shall I praise you with all my breath.
Hallelujah, hallelujah, hallelujah!
To do His will is my purpose!

דבר יהוה – הדרכתי.
נר יהוה – אות לנתיבתי.
יראת יהוה – ראשית חכמתי.
אהבת יהוה – חיים חייתי.
לעשות רצונו – מטרתי.

צדק ומשפט – שאיפתי.
יסורי קרבן – חטאתי.
ומשיח – בדמו טהרתי.
ניקיון וטהרה – מטרתי.

עבד לצור ישועתי.
בן נאמן – השתדלותי.
דרכי יהוה – קדושתי.

יה הושיעני מצרתי.
הקימני מנפילתי.
ואודה בכל נשמתי.
הללויה, הללויה, הללויה!

לעשות רצונו – מטרתי!

YIZKOR - IN MEMORIAM

The War of Iron Swords

> "No one will ever forget the heart-rending scenes in the Jewish streets and neighborhoods in those hellish days, during which our brothers and sisters were parting with friends and family with tears soaked with blood."
>
> — *Rabbi Daniel Zion on the dark days experienced by the Jews of Sofia in 1943*

These words of Rabbi Daniel Zion are applicable to what is happening here and now in Israel. They show how very relevant his story is for us today.

The struggles to survive through World War II, and then to immigrate to the land of our forefathers, were far from the only difficulties faced by the people of our nation. In many ways they were a sign of more trials to come. From the War of Independence until the War of Iron Swords today, we, Israelis, have had to defend our land in order to ensure our survival.

The horrific events of October 7, 2023, on the holiday of Simchat Torah 5784, changed the face of the State of Israel. In Israeli society this date will forever be remembered and engraved in infamy.

On that date the Hamas organization launched a vicious and cruel surprise attack on the State of Israel and its residents. It was the most murderous terror incident driven by antisemitism and hatred of Jews since the Holocaust. With unfathomable cruelty and in cold blood, the terrorists of Hamas murdered, maimed, and kidnapped the elderly, children, babies, young girls and boys, men and women.

What is happening in the here and now connects to what befell the Jewish people some eighty years ago. Therefore, it is the moral obligation of all citizens of Israel and, indeed, of the whole world, to commemorate the heroes and saints who sacrificed themselves for the sake of the people of Israel.

May their memory be blessed forever.

ABOUT THE AUTHOR

Avi Mizrachi was born and raised in a Jewish family in Israel. He served in the Israeli Air Force and did his reserve duties in the Israeli Defense Force. Avi is the founder and leader of Dugit Outreach Ministries. He still resides in Israel today with his wife, Chaya, his daughters and grandchildren.

Made in United States
Troutdale, OR
01/27/2026

46217536R00173